Triadosis

Triadosis
Union with the Triune God

Eduard Borysov

James Clarke & Co

*To my faithful friends and supporters
Dennis and Susan Nystrom*

JAMES CLARKE & CO
P.O. Box 60
Cambridge
CB1 2NT
United Kingdom

www.jamesclarke.co
publishing@jamesclarke.co

Paperback ISBN: 9780227177495
PDF ISBN: 9780227907481

British Library Cataloguing in Publication Data
A record is available from the British Library

First published by Pickwick Publications, 2019

This edition published by James Clarke & Co, 2021,
by arrangement with Wipf and Stock Publishers

Copyright © Eduard Borysov, 2019

All rights reserved. No part of this edition may be reproduced, stored electronically or in any retrieval system, or transmitted in any form or by any means, electronic, mechanical, photocopying, recording, or otherwise, without prior written permission from the Publisher (permissions@jamesclarke.co).

Contents

Preface | vii
Abbreviations | ix

Chapter 1: Introduction | 1
   Outline and Sources | 3
   Methodology | 4
   Potential Hermeneutical Objections | 6
   Limitations of This Project | 11
   Recent Scholarship on Theosis in Paul | 13

Chapter 2: Early Approaches to Theosis | 18
   Introduction | 18
   Apotheosis | 19
   Christosis | 39
   Triadosis | 55
   Energeosis | 71
   Conclusion | 81

Chapter 3: Reformers and Triadosis | 84
   Introduction | 84
   Traditional Lutheran and Calvinist Interpretations | 85
   Luther and Deification | 88
   Calvin and Deification | 102
   Conclusion | 119

Chapter 4: Contemporary Eastern Orthodox Retrieval of Triadosis | 123

Introduction | 123

Zizioulas's Critiques of *Apotheosis* and *Energeosis* | 123

Zizioulas's View of Personhood | 125

Conclusion | 147

Chapter 5: Recent Retrievals of *Theosis* in Paul | 149

Introduction | 149

M. David Litwa | 149

Ben C. Blackwell | 176

Michael J. Gorman | 188

Conclusion | 193

Chapter 6: Conclusion | 195

Summary of Argument | 195

Original Contribution | 196

Further Implications | 197

Bibliography | 199

Subject and Author Index | 217

Scripture Index | 225

Preface

IN RECENT YEARS, AS supposedly "Lutheran" readings of Paul's doctrine of "justification by faith" have increasingly come under attack, and as the weaknesses of the New Perspective on Paul have been identified, there has been a growing interest in reading the apostle as teaching something best understood in participationist terms. Particularly, there have been multiple attempts to retrieve the patristic concept of "theosis" as a counterpart of union with Christ. This move is particularly associated with the work of Michael J. Gorman, Stephen Finlan, M. David Litwa, and Ben C. Blackwell and is connected to the recent interest in deification as a widespread concept in Christian theology, one with significant ecumenical potential (as attested by the Finnish Lutheran School).

To date, however, inadequate attention has been paid to the complex character and history of *theosis* in the theological tradition, meaning that the word is used in biblical studies in a way that is over-simplistic. All of the studies to read Paul in terms of *theosis* have been too over-imposing (Litwa), too narrow (Blackwell), or too general (Gorman, Finlan) in their comparison of Paul with the Jewish, Greco-Roman, and Orthodox traditions to adequately address the validity of the category of *theosis* for the analysis of Paul. This study will deal with this deficiency by tracing the four trajectories of *theosis* in the patristic era and beyond. This monograph proffers a concept, tentatively labeled *triadosis*, which intends to present the whole complex that is treated elementally in the various trajectories. Further exploring what we have labeled *triadosis* in the later theological traditions, the study rereads Luther and Calvin with the help of the Finnish Lutheran School and J. Todd Billings. These scholars argue that the idea of union with Christ is central for both Luther and Calvin and always includes the Father and the Spirit, hence presuming a Trinitarian dimension.

The final chapter addresses the deficiencies of three significant *theosis* proponents as an appropriate category to describe Paul's soteriology. This analysis stresses that the historical rediscovery of deification in surrounding culture should not minimize the apostle's distinction from his polytheistic contemporaries (Litwa). Equally, the Christocentric soteriology misplaces the appropriate emphasis on the Father and the Spirit (Blackwell). Finally, the use of essentialist terminology should be grounded in patristic and contemporary theological discussions (Gorman). Thus, the theme of *triadosis* helps the reader to view Paul's soteriology as the Father's endeavor to bring redeemed humanity in union with himself in Christ through the power of the Holy Spirit.

Abbreviations

I HAVE PREFERRED ABBREVIATIONS for ancient sources, modern series, and journals from *The SBL Handbook of Style: For Biblical Studies and Related Disciplines*. 2nd ed. Atlanta: Society of Biblical Literature, 2014.

ACO   Cyril of Alexandria. *Acta conciliorum oecumenicorum*. Edited by Eduard Schwartz. 2 vols. Berlin: de Gruyter, 1924.

Comm.   Calvin, Jean. *Calvin's Commentaries*. 22 vols. Calvin Translation Society. Grand Rapids: Baker Books, 1996.

CR   Calvin John. *Johannis Calvini opera quae supersunt omnia, Corpus Reformatorum*. 59 vols. Brunsvigae: C. A. Schwetschke et filium, 1863.

Inst.   Calvin, John. *Calvin: Institutes of the Christian Religion*. Edited by John T. McNeill. Translated by Ford Lewis Battles. 2 vols. LCC. Louisville: Westminster John Knox, 2006.

LW   Luther Martin. *Luther's Works*. Edited by Jaroslav Pelikan and Helmut T. Lehmann. 55 vols. St. Louis; Philadelphia: Concordia; Fortress, 1955.

PG   Migne, J.-P., ed. *Patrologia Graeca*. 162 vols. Turnhout: Brepols, 1857.

TT   Calvin John. *Tracts and Treatises on the Reformation of the Church*. Edited by Thomas F. Torrance. Translated by Henry Beveridge. 3 vols. Grand Rapids: Eerdmans, 1958.

WA   Luther, Martin. *D. Martin Luthers Werke: Kritische Gesamtausgabe (Weimarer Ausgabe)*. 65 vols. Weimar: Hermann Böhlau, 1883.

Chapter 1

Introduction

THERE HAVE BEEN MULTIPLE attempts to retrieve the patristic concept of "theosis" as a means of explicating Paul's concept of "union with Christ." This move is mainly associated with the work of Michael J. Gorman, Stephen Finlan, and Ben C. Blackwell. These recent works demonstrate the interest in deification as a widespread concept in Christian theology, one with significant ecumenical potential (as attested by the Finnish Lutheran School). It is argued that this concept allows bridging the gap between the historical reconstructions of Paul's teaching on salvation by participation in Christ and the church's doctrinal appropriation of it. M. David Litwa also employs this concept for understanding Paul in his historical and religious context. Unlike the scholars mentioned above, Litwa reduces his research to the antecedent material and considers subsequent Christian developments of *theosis* anachronistic.

To date, however, inadequate attention has been paid to the complex character and history of *theosis* in the theological tradition. This word has created much confusion in biblical studies.[1] For some theologians, the word points to widespread ancient beliefs about the transformation of worshippers into the likeness of a deity that influenced Paul's thinking; for others, it points to a distinctive element in early Christian theology radically different from other ancient thought. For some, the word points to a single neglected strand of Paul's soteriology; for others, it serves to bring all of the strands together. For some, the significance of the concept is purely historical; for others, the significance is theological or ecumenical. If the range of meanings

---

1. Wisse rightly points out how *theosis* may mean different things for thinkers. He distinguishes three boundary markers of deification: ontological (the realization of innate capacity), christological (participation in Christ), and soteriological (grace or synergy). In my view, any account of deification involves a combination of these types. Wisse, *Trinitarian Theology*, 304–9.

is not to confuse, there needs to be a study that examines its complexity, offering some criticism of the various approaches and their inadequacies.

This study is intended to probe the complexity of the term "theosis" particularly in Pauline studies, recognizing the ecumenical significance that the concept has.[2] As well known, *theosis* has become a point of contact between Protestant and Eastern Orthodox theologians in the discussion of soteriology in a broader sense than mere justification by faith.[3] The exploration of patristic views on *theosis* will indicate that it is not exclusively a modern problem. Hence, this monograph will advocate for a nuanced definition of *theosis*, as a result of the Trinity's salvific activity. For lack of a precise term in patristic scholarship, I tentatively called it *triadosis*. The concept of *triadosis* can serve better for the appropriation of the church's doctrine in the quest for ecclesial unity.

The goal of this monograph is to assess how the concepts of *theosis* and the Trinity can inform and transform the traditional anthropocentric reading of Paul's soteriology into one that is theocentric or even trinitycentric. On the one hand, previous attempts to retrieve the doctrine of *theosis* are pervasively christological or anthropological in nature. This shift from the traditional trinitarian groundings to isolated christological or anthropological inquiries can lead to "binitarianism" or anthropocentric soteriology respectively. As Ingolf Dalferth notes in his recent book *Crucified and Resurrected*, modern biblical studies tend to prioritize Christology at the expense of trinitarian moorings.[4] Even when asserting and defending a high Christology, some scholars (most notably Larry Hurtado) present it in binitarian terms.[5] English theology has played a big part in this, in its response to German theology, which was heavily shaped by the dominance of certain Anglican theological paradigms in the nineteenth century. The value of Christology and anthropology notwithstanding, once dislocated from the traditional identification with the Spirit, they suffer a truncated biblical presentation. Consequently, biblical scholars often identify *theosis* with Paul's teaching on union with Christ and moral transformation of those, who are "in Christ." On the other hand, theological reflections on Paul's trinitarian theology are mostly perceived as foisted on the apostle and discussed (if at all) with some hesitation. In those rare occasions, when researchers acknowledge the full trinitarian account in Paul, they do not

2. As this was evident during a conference at the Catholic University of Leuven. "Theosis/Deification."

3. This is true for Roman Catholics as well, although I will not engage with this group here.

4. Dalferth, *Crucified and Resurrected*.

5. Hurtado, *Lord Jesus Christ*.

explore the soteriological implication of such an account.⁶ By asserting the connections between *theosis* and the Trinity, this book will seek to redefine the former notion as an essentially trinitarian project, whereby believers experience transformation into the image of the triune God, not merely Christ or a new humanity. Also, it will have insightful bearings on Paul's soteriology and theology proper.

A potential contribution of this project is a re-appropriation of Paul in light of subsequent theological tradition. In particular, this book will seek to apply the relational model of the Trinity to Paul's teaching to see whether a trinitarian soteriology can make a coherent sense of the Paul of history and the apostle of the church. I intend to explore how a trinitarian dimension of *theosis* helps to unfold Paul's soteriology-talk. To do that one needs to take into account a patristic treatment of *theosis*.

Outline and Sources

Chapter 2 will deal with the question: How did the church fathers express the doctrine of participation in Christ? This study will focus on four main emphases or trajectories, how these early theologians understood human and divine union in Christ and humans with God, traditionally called deification or *theosis*. The degree of human transformation in the likeness of God varied from a mere moral imitation to a mystical union with the divine by the loss of human corporeality. The goal is to understand whether these fathers contended for a specific form of personal, natural or energistic union with God. Does the union of humanity with God occur on the level of natures, energies or persons? Is it fair to state that *theosis* is a process, which involves participation in the persons of the Trinity with the aim to become Trinity-like?

Is the concept of *theosis* crucial only for the Eastern fathers or can its theme be found in the Protestant Reformers? Chapter 3 will continue the historical analysis of *theosis* in the Reformation period. Notably, it will focus on a recent rereading of Luther and Calvin, both of whom, it is claimed, advocated for a participationist understanding of salvation. Christ is the gift and the giver of divine righteousness and holiness. Thus, the Finnish Lutheran School and J. Todd Billings, in particular, contend for the appropriateness of the term *theosis* to Luther and Calvin studies.

With the recent reformulations of personhood as a relational being by such theologians as John Zizioulas, the idea of personhood became a

---

6. For instance, Hill, *Paul and the Trinity*.

valuable aid not only in trinitarian but also in soteriological discussions.[7] Hence, chapter 4 will critically assess the trinitarian relational model in the context of *theosis* to see whether this ecumenical concept should be nuanced before its application to Pauline studies.

Chapter 5 will engage in the evaluation of three recent Paul interpreters. Firstly, I will assess Litwa's historical approach from four angles: 1) the adequacy of purely historical background; 2) the legitimacy of posterior theology; 3) the use of later "essentialist" terminology for understanding Paul; and 4) the adequacy of Litwa's account of Paul's Christology, taking into account the discussion of "monotheism." Secondly, I will probe Blackwell's concept of *christosis* from the standpoint of theology proper, pneumatology and eschatology. Thirdly, Gorman's application of *theosis* as a hermeneutical lens for reading Paul will be examined on theological and patristic grounds.

It is evident that the patristic doctrine of *theosis* originated from the whole of Scripture, not only from Paul. This fact leaves no reasonable ground to claim whether Paul would definitely espouse this later development. Nevertheless, chapter 5 aims to engage critically recent publications that propose reading the apostle's soteriology in light of deification in Greco-Roman, patristic and exegetical studies. In my view, Wesley Hill and Chris Tilling are correct in advocating that Paul defined the identity of God by the mutual relationships of Father, Son, and Spirit.[8] Therefore, Paul's soteriology is fundamentally trinitarian teaching. In the end, this book hopes to prove that a fresh reading of Paul's soteriology with the help of the historical-theological development of *triadosis* can become a helpful instrument to overcome old soteriological dichotomies and become a ground for further ecumenical appropriation and appreciation of Paul's multifaceted teaching.

Methodology

The approach undertaken in this book is complex. This is due to the fact that the retrieval of *theosis* in Pauline scholarship has itself been complex. The variety of approaches undertaken requires a variegated methodology. One strand will involve simple historical criticism, applied in response to the historical-critical (*religionsgeschichtliche*) work of Litwa. Importantly,

---

7. Vanhoozer develops a similar approach to the Trinity as being in communion, but more from a philosophical and apologetic angle. For him, the concept of the Trinity revealed in history allows upholding both oneness and plurality. The Trinity invites creation in a noncoercive communion of love between God and people that preserves the diversity of participants. Vanhoozer, *First Theology*, chap. 2.

8. Hill, *Paul and the Trinity*; Tilling, *Paul's Divine Christology*.

however, Litwa does not limit his research to pre-Pauline texts but looks at post-biblical/patristic literature as part of his historical research. Moreover, Litwa's historical investigation leads him to exegetical and theological claims about the identity of Jesus and the nature of salvation in Paul, which proves that historical criticism is unavoidably theological in nature. An adequate response to Litwa's project will include multiple layers of research: 1) a patristic account of *theosis*, to assess the fairness of his historical arguments, 2) an exegetical analysis of relevant Pauline material, and 3) a theological evaluation of his doctrinal conclusions.[9]

A second strand will involve looking at reception history, applied in dialogue with Blackwell. His approach corresponds to what is known as "effective history" (*Wirkungsgeschichte*), which he discusses in the section on methodology.[10] That section aims at developing further Blackwell's critical reflection on effective history. He ascribes a specific efficacy to the text that can be considered philosophically in terms of *Wirkungsgeschichte*, or theologically in terms of Scripture's efficacy, and can be investigated only through looking at the traditions shaped by the Word, i.e., by looking at its reception more broadly. This process involves more than just the tracing of the reception of particular verses, but rather the way in which the whole Scripture has been received. Blackwell's retrospective reading of Paul through Irenaeus and Cyril will be expanded to include a broader range of church fathers as well as Reformers and a contemporary Eastern Orthodox view. The inclusion of Luther, Calvin, and Zizioulas into the discussion is called to show a degree of similarity and continuity between different Christian traditions on the topic of deification. In contrast to Blackwell, this expansion will also include a robust theological account: this approach recognizes the place of the church's theological tradition within the rule of faith and the superintendence of the Spirit. A genuinely theological account of patristic (and arguably Pauline) view of *theosis* is characteristically trinitarian. By being sensitive to theological interpretations of Paul, New Testament scholars can gain not only the historical data and authorial intent but also the theological underpinning behind the apostle's writings. The theological interpretation of this monograph aims to contribute to a holistic understanding of Paul's big ideas about God and salvation through such concepts as *theosis* and the

---

9. Macaskill correctly reminds that background study, the value of it notwithstanding, should not overshadow the biblical context (of Paul, in this context) and the theological bearing of Scripture. Macaskill, *Union with Christ*, 2. Two pages later, Macaskill cautions against uncritical application of *theosis* to Pauline soteriology. This book attempts to avoid just that.

10. Blackwell, *Christosis*, 15–25.

Trinity. The adequacy of and objections to theological interpretation for Pauline studies will come to focus in the next section below.

A third strand proceeds from the one just outlined and involves an awareness of the fact that the theological traditions use the concepts of *theosis* and deification in ways that are more complicated and nuanced than some New Testament scholars recognize. These scholars use the word uncritically, naïve to the range of meanings and associations that it carries. In the case of Gorman, he recognizes the value of the tradition's reading of Paul for a theological hermeneutic. The critical task, however, will be to evaluate whether Gorman uncritically collapses tradition back onto Paul, neglecting the logic of *theosis* within diverse theological traditions. A more sensitive approach to *theosis* utilizes a synthesis of complex themes in Paul, without bringing unwarranted categories foreign to both Paul and tradition.

The second and third strand will operate distinctly from the first, but all are necessary to this project due to the diverse nature of Pauline scholarship on the topic. To be sure, these strands overlap in the areas of patristic accounts and anthropological soteriology. They naturally diverge, dealing with openly anti-theological and anti-traditional approach (Litwa) and openly theological and traditional (Blackwell and Gorman).

Potential Hermeneutical Objections

Most of the contemporary biblical studies employ different historical, linguistic, social, and other approaches to the biblical text (like to any ancient text), which often (intentionally) lack any theological implications. Biblical studies predominantly have become a study of the Bible as a human product and presumed a naturalistic account of religious history. The nature of this study is an attempt of a theologically informed interpretation of Paul that understandably is objectionable to those practicing the historical-critical approach. I want to address these objections before proceeding to the analysis of *theosis* in patristic and medieval writers.

The first hermeneutical objection relates to the legitimacy of theological interpretation in general. Is a theological approach to the Scriptures as treacherous as the proponents of the historical-critical method argue? On the one hand, scholars like Heikki Räisänen and Michael Fox, following Wrede, envision no place for "faith- or theology-based" academic biblical scholarship.[11] They bemoan the fact that for a long time the unadulterated historical study of the biblical text was hampered by theologies and traditions of the church. On the other hand, Richard B. Hays questions the

---

11. Räisänen, *Beyond New Testament*, 8; Fox, "Bible Scholarship."

relevance of critical biblical scholarship advocated above for non-Christian and Christian audiences. For a secular audience, any biblical studies are superfluous, unimportant, and, therefore, leading biblical scholars to the dead-end. For a Christian audience, i.e., faith communities, a "secularist study" of the Bible is pointless and, therefore, leads Christian scholars to recover theological exegesis for the church.[12] Hence, Angus Paddison rightly contends that the reading of Scripture has its real meaning only in the church's life and practice, "The church's liturgical repetition of Scripture is not a returning again and again to the same 'meaning' but rather a deepening or a chastening encounter with the triune God who providentially orders the texts of Scripture."[13]

During the past two decades, a movement that can be labeled "theological interpretation" has attracted a number of scholars from different Christian traditions. In the *Dictionary for Theological Interpretation of the Bible*, Kevin J. Vanhoozer defines theological interpretation as an escape from the dichotomy between dogma and natural historicism.[14] In my view, a problem of New Testament scholarship in some circles, in the past several decades, has been mainly to provide an a-theological reading of the Bible using historical criticism in a supposedly objective way.[15] Particularly, in the

12. Hays, "Reading the Bible," 10.

13. Paddison, *Scripture*, 26. I concur with Paddison's assertion that the readers of ancient texts always start "in the middle," rather than pretending to commence from the beginning. Paddison, *Scripture*, 7–8, 30. Paddison, I think, overemphasizes the eschatologically oriented reading of Scripture in the church, diminishing a proper value of the "archaeological" reading. There is no faithful eschatological reading without its roots in historical text and context.

14. Theological interpretation is not "*an imposition of a theological system or confessional grid onto the biblical text,*" whereby the Scripture is mainly used as a proof-text for a theological system. It is not "*an imposition of general hermeneutic or theory of interpretation,*" because the Scripture is a sacred text that poses theological questions. It is not "*a form of merely historical, literary, or sociological criticism,*" but presupposes an active divine agency in the production and interpretation of the Bible. Vanhoozer, "Introduction," 19–20 (emphasis original). The editors of *DTIB* define "the ultimate aim of theological interpretation of the Bible: to know the triune God by participating in the triune life, in the triune mission to creation." Vanhoozer, "Introduction," 24. In addition, Gorman, in his review of the dictionary, calls such theological interpretation of Scripture "an inherently ecumenical and multicultural practice" and invites paying more attention to the Orthodox hermeneutics. Gorman, "'Seamless Garment' Approach," 118.

15. Davies advocates for the separation of a "confessional" or ecclesial discourse on the biblical texts from a "non-confessional" discourse "outside" the canon and receptive community. Davies, *Whose Bible Is It Anyway?*, 13–14. In this call, it seems, Davies echoes Johann S. Semler's (1725–91) and Johann P. Gabler's (1753–1826) separation of the dogmatic reading of Scripture from academic biblical theology. An exception to this trend of a non-theological reading of the Bible is a theological interpretation

discussions of Paul's soteriological views, it is usually regarded anachronistic to use later theological concepts and developments. Hence, in the historical reconstructions of the Christ-event and salvation, some New Testament scholars present Christologies and soteriologies that are pneumatology-less, because the Holy Spirit is not a history-bound figure that can be studied using historical research. Since Jesus is the only "historically palpable" person of the Godhead, the historical studies of Paul are predominantly christological, rather than trinitarian. When someone presents Paul's theology based on the existent textual evidence and historical studies of the Jewish and Greco-Roman theologies and ideologies of his time alone, she can well depict Paul's God in binitarian categories[16] or as the Metropolitan Zizioulas calls it "the 'christo-monism' of Western ecclesiology."[17]

The second hermeneutical objection relates to the use of later theological interpretations for Pauline theology. For a Western reader, the patristic formulation of deification might present a challenge and an opportunity to read Paul anew. It is evident that each Christian tradition brings its concerns and methodologies to the study of Pauline soteriology. The question is whether a historical and theological reading of ancient texts can be a legitimate and helpful methodology for the study of the apostle to nations. Scholars like Wright contend for studying the "Apostle of Faith" in light of the "Paul of History."[18] Is not the former impeding the latter or the other way around? Can they be reconciled and mutually informative? Can the later dogma inform our understanding of Paul's soteriology? This study assumes that it can.

First, however, one needs to ask whether a non-contingent study of Paul is possible. As postmodern critics remind us, there is no such thing as an unbiased or unconditional reading of ancient texts by subsequent generations of readers. Deconstructionists particularly emphasize that there is no "single plain meaning" of a text contained in semantic boundaries. By acknowledging an "underdetermined" meaning of a text, however, this monograph seeks not to erase all hermeneutical boundaries or to violate the integrity of the text.[19] The advocates of theological interpretation allow

---

approach advocated since the 1990s by such authors as Watson, *Text, Church, and World*; Fowl, *Engaging Scripture*. Even prior to that, Childs's work on canonical reading stood out in contrast to historical-critical approach, see e.g., Childs, *Introduction to Old Testament*.

16. For example, Hurtado, *One God, One Lord*, 127–28; Hurtado, *At the Origins*, chap. 3.

17. Zizioulas, *Lectures in Christian Dogmatics*, 149.

18. Wright, *Paul and Faithfulness*, 69.

19. Rae, "Texts in Context," 25. Using Isa 53, Rae argues that "determinate"

for the "hermeneutical plurality" of meaning, which, according to Murray A. Rae, can be appropriated differently by subsequent generations of readers.[20] Although the historical-critical method proponents consider alternative approaches, such as theological interpretation informed by historical theology, anachronistic, they cannot avoid a fragmentary and disinterested reading of Paul.[21]

To demonstrate this, one can turn to the work of David C. Steinmetz, who notes the following points. He points that historians, who live after some events in question, cannot check their memory at the door. In like manner, biblical interpreters, who live after a long tradition of interpretation, cannot—and should not—ignore this tradition or not be influenced by the aftermath of the theological investigations of the past. Hence, Steinmetz concludes, "It is not anachronistic to believe such added dimensions of meaning exist. It is only good exegesis."[22] It is hopelessly idealistic to think that one can attain the single true inherent meaning of the ancient text by applying one method of interpretation. Even the first readers of Paul were not immune from misunderstanding him at first, as is evident in the Corinthian correspondence. Does this assessment discard any historical inquiry of Paul's context?

Quite the contrary. A theological interpretation, according to Konrad Schmid, helps the historical-critical interpretation be historically faithful to the text because some texts could be rendered superfluous without an appropriate theological context.[23] Blackwell, following Gadamer's incentive, remarks that the history of interpretation helps us to understand our own reading of ancient texts, why we understand Paul's theology the way we understand it.[24] Since a reader cannot avoid coming to the text with personal presuppositions and theological context, she, at least, should be aware of

---

interpretation of a single meaning would have to read this passage either in its original Sitz im Leben or christologically, but never in a complimentary way.

20. Rae, "Texts in Context," 39. Rae thinks that presumptuous mastery of the text by historical-critical method is misleading. See also the fourth thesis of the Scripture Project that states, "Texts of Scripture do not have a single meaning limited to the intent of the original author. In accord with Jewish and Christian traditions, we affirm that Scripture has multiple complex senses given by God, the author of the whole drama." Davis and Hays, *Art of Reading Scripture*, 2–3.

21. Steinmetz, "Uncovering a Second Narrative," 54; Barton, "Historical-Critical Approaches," 11–13.

22. Steinmetz, "Uncovering a Second Narrative," 65. For a similar point see Hays, "Reading the Bible," 14–15.

23. Schmid, "Sind Die Historisch-Kritischen?"

24. Blackwell, *Christosis*, 12–14. Blackwell bases this argument on Gadamer, *Truth and Method*.

such conditionality and recognize that alternative traditions can be a fruitful ground in the mutual quest for the understanding of Paul's writings and theology.

In this regard, Hays incisively criticizes Wright for not recognizing that the latter's religious convictions influenced his historical reading of Jesus. Hays writes, "But if that is the case, why not acknowledge that the church's tradition might provide aid rather than a hindrance in seeking to understand the New Testament's witness to the identity of Jesus?"[25] Further, he states, "Precisely because the church's dogma names a truth the world does not or cannot know, it rightly describes the truth about history in a way that secularist history is bound to miss."[26] More strongly, Brian E. Daley censures the historical study of the biblical text that presumes exclusively natural cause-effect relationships and rejects any possibility of a supernatural cause as "methodologically atheistic."[27] It seems that some biblical scholars lose the particularities of the personal identity of Scripture's God. They reduce the Trinity to undifferentiated sameness like pluralist theologians.[28]

Another reason why subsequent interpretations can be useful for the interpretation of Paul is that a multilayered meaning of a text may not be fully comprehended and appropriated by the author and his or her contemporaries within their conceptual and linguistic framework. As the Russian literary theorist, Mikhail Bakhtin, suggested, the subsequent generations of interpreters can discover or expound additional meanings as their corresponding conceptual and linguistic worlds change.[29] Frances Young rightly asserts that authorial intent does not exhaust the meaning of a text.[30] In addition, Rae "defend[s] the legitimacy of *variant* readings *informed by* and

---

25. Hays, "Knowing Jesus," 56–57.

26. Hays, "Knowing Jesus," 61.

27. Daley, "Is Patristic Exegesis Still Usable?," 72. Daley argues not only for historical and theological interpretation but also for the theologically ecumenical reading of sacred text together with the previous generations of Christians. Daniel J. Treier considers typical scientific, historical reading "methodological naturalism" and advocates for reading that has "the trinitarian rule of faith" as its framework. Treier, "Biblical Theology?," 28–29. Kathryn Tanner echoes this assessment, calling historical criticism "methodological agnosticism (if not atheism)." Tanner, *Jesus, Humanity and Trinity*, 7.

28. Vanhoozer, *First Theology*, 52–54. It appears that, for some New Testament scholars, Paul's God is a rehashed version of the one God of Jews with unclear modifications in light of the Christ-event. In contrast, the church fathers spoke equally of the "oneness and threeness" of God against the subordinationism of the Son and the Holy Spirit.

29. Blackwell, *Christosis*, 16. This idea was developed in Bakhtin, "Response to a Question."

30. Young, *Art of Performance*, 12.

congruent with the original purpose to which the text was directed."³¹ He assumes that an ancient text can play a different role in diverse contexts and yet comply with the authorial intent. Thus, church fathers can become "a heuristic device" in conversation with Paul.³²

If doctrinal developments can inform our reading of Paul—and I contend they can—then how should they be used? Blackwell states that new approaches to classical texts allow us to re-appropriate them in a new light.³³ A student of an ancient text should hold it in esteem as her dialogue partner. Paul's patristic interpreters may challenge our traditional understanding of the apostle, uncovering our own biases and agendas. The later patristic concepts should not be above an uncritical appropriation, but always clearly defined and nuanced in their complexity.

The third hermeneutical objection relates to the employment of later concepts in biblical studies. It is often argued that ecclesiastical leaders coined these notions under philosophical influences unknown or even foreign to the biblical authors. However, the lack of later terminologies, such as *theosis*, in Paul does not mean necessarily the absence of the concept or, in David S. Yeago's terms, "equal judgment."³⁴ In the same regard, much of the theological vocabulary, with which scholars now operate, such as "Theology," "Judaism," "Christianity," "Trinity," "Christology" and so on, is not found in the Scriptures. Nonetheless, recognizing their limitations and anachronistic danger, these terms constitute much of contemporary theological jargon and can be used with appropriate definition and clarification. Whereas Hill uses the Trinity as a hermeneutical lens to read Paul's theology, I will suggest using the same lens to reread Paul's soteriology.

Limitations of This Project

One can reasonably suspect that the breadth of this study will not permit adequate treatment of such theologically loaded concepts as "theosis" and "Trinity" that deserve focused studies in their own right. However, this research aims to investigate the interrelation of the two doctrines and its implication for Paul's soteriology. This book assumes that the relational model of the Trinity will inform the understanding of *theosis* as

---

31. Rae, "Texts in Context," 25.

32. Blackwell, *Christosis*, 17.

33. Blackwell, *Christosis*, 15. On this point, Blackwell follows Jauss, "Literary History."

34. Yeago, "New Testament and Nicene Dogma," 159.

communion with and transformation in the likeness of the Trinity envisioned by Paul in his writings.

This study takes into consideration the Protestant and Eastern Orthodox understandings of deification and does not include the Roman Catholic treatment of the doctrine. One of the reasons for such a choice is the history of the Protestant-Orthodox dialogue in Finland and in the USA that raised interest in rereading the Reformed theologians in light of the Orthodox traditions of *theosis*.[35] The examples of Protestants engaged with the Eastern Orthodox ideas are present in the work of the Finnish Lutheran School (Tuomo Mannermaa, Carl E. Braaten, Simo Peura, and others) since the 1970s and those scholars, who interacted with their claims.[36] Some American Evangelical scholars advocate for the appropriate use of *theosis* in soteriological discussions,[37] but, as was indicated earlier, many of such studies lack either in historical grounding or a thoroughly trinitarian framework. It also bears a personal interest to me, who comes from a predominantly Eastern Orthodox culture. This research can be mutually beneficial for Eastern and Western thinkers.

The scope of the study does not permit engaging with many church fathers and Orthodox theologians, whose treatments of *theosis* were significant for Orthodox theology.[38] Admittedly, the Metropolitan John D. Zizioulas's view (b. 1931) did not constitute the consensus on the topic and was not met uncritically.[39] But even his critics recognize Zizioulas as one of

---

35. For *theosis* in Calvin see Mosser, "Greatest Possible Blessing"; Billings, "United to God"; Billings, *Calvin, Participation, and Gift*. On *theosis* in other Protestant traditions, Kärkkäinen, *One with God*.

36. See, for example, Braaten and Jenson, *Union with Christ*; Cavanaugh, "Joint Declaration?"; Metzger, "Luther and Finnish School"; Kärkkäinen, "Salvation as Justification and Theosis"; Jenson, "Response to Mark Seifrid"; Briskina, "Orthodox View."

37. Clendenin, "Partakers of Divinity"; Rakestraw, "Becoming Like God"; Wesche, "Eastern Orthodox Spirituality"; Clendenin, *Eastern Orthodox Christianity*; Mosser, "Earliest Patristic Interpretations"; Wesche, "Doctrine of Deification"; Christensen and Wittung, *Partakers of Divine Nature*; Finlan, "Can We Speak?"; Gorman, *Inhabiting Cruciform God*.

38. One could also discuss the views of Athanasius of Alexandria (296–373), Maximus the Confessor (580–662), Symeon the New Theologian (949–1022), and Seraphim of Sarov (1754–1833). Among prominent modern Orthodox thinkers, which could be included in this project, are Vladimir Lossky (1870–1965), George Florovsky (1893–1979), Dumitru Staniloae (1903–1993), John Meyendorff (1926–1992), Kallistos Ware (b. 1934), Christos Yannaras (b. 1935), and others.

39. A cluster of critical articles was published in *Heythrop Journal*. Ables, "On the Very Idea"; Loudovikos, "Person Instead of Grace"; Awad, "Personhood as Particularity"; Turcescu, "'Person' versus 'Individual.'" Other critical sources will be mentioned in the fourth chapter.

the most prolific, provocative and stimulating Orthodox theologians of the last decades. Similarly, the number of *theosis* advocates is not limited to the three proponents discussed in chapter 5.[40] Nonetheless, these theologians are original thinkers, who break the mold of traditional approaches to trinitarian theology and Paul's soteriology. A selective, but hopefully fair, engagement with their ideas is essential for a critical analysis of the trend. Obviously, such eclecticism can be a potential problem to any construal, but it also can lead to a broadening of a typically narrow-focused perspective.

Finally, the treatment of Paul's recent interpreters in chapter 5 is threatened potentially by the lack of in-depth study of Pauline texts. However, the goal of this chapter is not to provide an exegesis of selected passages, but to demonstrate the appropriateness of historically and theologically informed doctrine of *theosis* and trinitarian language in expositions in the Pauline corpus. Through apparent assumption or direct reference to the Father (God), Son (the Lord Jesus Christ), and Holy Spirit (the Spirit of God or the Spirit of Christ) Paul lays the ground for trinitarian soteriology or *triadosis*. Consequently, the chapter will focus only on Litwa's, Blackwell's, and Gorman's presentations of the idea primarily in the undisputed letters, but not to the exclusion of the so-called deutero-Pauline.

Recent Scholarship on *Theosis* in Paul

For Paul, the dictum "in Christ" presupposed divine-human relationships. The character of these relationships has been discussed in a number of publications, which suggest articulating the apostle's soteriology in terms of deification.[41] In the following paragraphs, I will discuss the contribution of several prominent scholars, which deal with the issue of *theosis* in Paul. As with many other concepts, there is a whole spectrum of positive and critical responses to *theosis* in Paul.[42]

In his influential study, first published in French in 1938, Jules Gross discussed identification with, and conformity to, Christ in his death and resurrection.[43] The author described the character of the mystical union in the following words, "[A]ccording to the apostle [Paul] the glorified Christ, who

40. See footnote 37 above.

41. E.g., Billings, "United to God"; Braaten and Jenson, *Union with Christ*; Cavanaugh, "Joint Declaration?"; Christensen and Wittung, *Partakers of Divine Nature*; Gavrilyuk, "Retrieval of Deification"; Litwa, *Becoming Divine*; Mannermaa, "Theosis as a Subject"; Marshall, "Justification as Declaration."

42. I will discuss the contribution of Michael J. Gorman, Ben C. Blackwell, and M. David Litwa in chapter 5.

43. Gross, *Divinization of Christian*.

has become a 'life-giving spirit,' is like an atmosphere in which the baptized ones are immersed; He co-penetrates them to the point of being 'one body' and 'one spirit,' and 'one new human being' with them."[44] The goal of spiritual transformation is the internalization and intensification of the status "in Christ," experienced psychologically and mystically, being "possessed by Christ," rather than a mere legal status (Phil 3:12; 2 Cor 5:14; 1 Cor 9:16–19; Gal 2:20). Following Wickenhauser, Gross clarified that a believer has indirect access to God, whereby the mediatory role of Christ is essential.[45] For Paul, deification was participation in a uniquely divine attribute, that is, immortality through "mystical assimilation" with Christ in baptism. The gentile converts who were familiar with pagan mystery religions were not surprised to hear that their destiny would coincide with that of Christ in his sufferings, death, resurrection, and incorruptibility. Unlike the members of a pagan cult, divinized Christians experienced no absorption of personality in Christ. Gross concludes, "In brief, it is in Christ that a person is assimilated to God, that is, divinized."[46] Gross thus finds it appropriate to use *theosis* to describe Paul's teaching on mystical union with Christ.

Norman Russell published an extensive treatment of deification in the Greek patristic tradition.[47] In the few pages that Russell dedicates to Paul, he argues that some themes in the apostle's theology were precursors to the second-century notion of *theosis*. Contrary to Gross, Russell agrees with Schweitzer that deification was a foreign idea to Paul because, though believers are made one with Christ, they are never one with God.[48] Russell indicates several other compelling reasons why deification was not part of Paul's world of thought: 1) the divinity of Christ was not clearly established until the second century; 2) a multiplicity of images for Christian relationships with Christ suggests that Paul did not have a specific technical phrase for this union; and 3) deification assumes a metaphysical framework and language used by later church fathers, which is anachronistic to Paul's metaphors of human filiation with God.[49] Therefore, *theosis* is a later development, and not of Paul's origin. It is evident that Russell lands on the critical side of the spectrum.

44. Gross, *Divinization of Christian*, 84.

45. "Since it is an assimilation to Christ which is the condition of our salvation according to Paul, Pauline mysticism is a union with Christ and not with God directly." Gross, *Divinization of Christian*, 85n56; Wikenhauser, *Die Christusmystik*, 104.

46. Gross, *Divinization of Christian*, 88.

47. Russell, *Doctrine of Deification*.

48. Schweitzer, *Mysticism of Paul*, 3, 26.

49. Russell, *Doctrine of Deification*, 85.

Albert Schweitzer, affirming the idea of believers's sonship in respect to God, was confident that Paul "does not conceive of sonship to God as an immediate mystical relation to God but as mediated and effected by means of the mystical union with Christ."[50] Following Schweitzer, Constantine R. Campbell concurs that the union of believers with God is not unmediated, but is an eschatological reality, possible only through the present union with Christ.[51] Campbell assures that, while Paul expressed union with Christ and the Spirit, there are no passages that indicate believers are "in God" or "one with God," though such an idea might be implied. On the one hand, Paul may have avoided the "in the Father" phrase because of the unique role of the Son and the Spirit in salvation. On the other hand, the intimate union of the Son with the Father makes relationships of believers with the Father in the Son through the Spirit unavoidable. Again, the church is the body and the bride of the Son, not of the Father. One should not forget, however, that in Paul's mind, the Father is always in view and carries out his will, with respect to humanity, through the Son and the Spirit. Hence, Campbell states, "In the life of the believer, the Spirit becomes the means through whom union with Christ is lived out."[52] The idea of union with Christ is not only crucial for divine-human relations, but also for relationship within the Trinity because Christ—and the Spirit— often plays an instrumental role in God's redemptive activity.[53] Therefore, union with Christ contains both the relationship between the Father and the Son, as well as the relationship between humanity and Christ. For Paul, to be in Christ is the same as to be in the Spirit.[54]

While open to the idea Christocentric trinitarianism, Campbell, nonetheless, expresses reservations about the propriety of the term *theosis* for a Christian's union with God because of the asymmetry of the two unions. Campbell states, "While [a] believer's union with Christ is patterned after the Father's union with him, it is not equal to it; our union does not entail that believers become members of the Godhead. Rather, a carefully qualified sense of *theosis* points to human transformation that we might become

---

50. Schweitzer, *Mysticism of Paul*, 3.

51. Campbell, *Paul and Union*, 358–59; Stewart, *Man in Christ*, 170.

52. Campbell, *Paul and Union*, 362.

53. "Christ is the instrumental mediator of the Father's will toward humanity." Campbell, *Paul and Union*, 360, 367.

54. Campbell, *Paul and Union*, 362. It is appropriate to distinguish that "in the Spirit" language is more pertinent to the instances where the ethical outworking of salvific union of believers with Christ is discussed.

like God."[55] Thus, for Campbell, *theosis* is a not an inappropriate term, but one that requires precise definition.

Grant Macaskill recently published an extensive study of union with Christ in the New Testament.[56] There he commends Campbell's linguistic sensitivity and nuanced presentation of "union with Christ" as a multifaceted binding ingredient in Paul's mysticism, derived from the Scriptures and the apostle's Damascus experience.[57] Macaskill appropriately warns that *theosis*, being a theological and philosophical development of a biblical concept by the church fathers in the polemical contexts of the Cappadocians, Gregory Palamas, and others, acquired an extra-biblical meaning. The tradition of *theosis*, nonetheless, is helpful in providing a warrant against the confusion of the created and divine, as well as possible ways to understand transformation and relationships with the divine persons.[58] He concludes, "Participation in God, then, is participation in the community of God. Union with Christ demands unity in Spirit."[59] This community of created persons with the divine persons is the idea behind *triadosis*, which will become the focus of later chapters in the present book.

In a recently published dissertation, Wesley Hill questions the traditional approaches of "low" and "high" Christologies that attempt to identify Christ on a "vertical axis," spanning from God to creation.[60] In Hill's view, a much more fruitful discussion of Pauline Christology would involve horizontal *relational* conceptuality between God, Christ, and the Spirit. In the second chapter, he argues that, for Paul, the identity of the God of Abraham was not expanded by the later Christ-event, but was defined from the beginning as the-God-who-raised-Jesus-from-the-dead. In fact, both God's and Christ's identities are mutual and asymmetrical, because they are known through their equality and are still distinct in their relationships or roles as the one who sends and the one who is sent. In a like manner, the Holy Spirit is essential in defining who the Father and the Son are, thus sharing in divine equality and distinct in divine relations.

Granted the absence of the term *theosis* in Paul and its philosophical and theological baggage acquired through time, one might look with suspicion to its appropriateness for the task of exploring Paul's theology. Nevertheless, the ideas connected to *theosis*, such as attaining likeness to

55. Campbell, *Paul and Union*, 368.
56. Macaskill, *Union with Christ*.
57. Macaskill, *Union with Christ*, 39–40.
58. Macaskill, *Union with Christ*, 306–7.
59. Macaskill, *Union with Christ*, 308.
60. Hill, *Paul and Trinity*, chap. 1.

God, participation in the life of God, transformation into the image of Christ through co-crucifixion and co-resurrection, adoption as the sons of God, exchange of mortal bodies into glorious Christ-like heavenly bodies, becoming temples indwelled by God and so forth, are not foreign to Paul. What is missing or undervalued by many biblical scholars is a thorough treatment of the trinitarian dimension of Paul's soteriology, which I chose to call *triadosis*.

In the next chapter, I will discuss how the church fathers attempted to respond to the issues above, utilizing *theosis* in general, not limited to the Pauline corpus. The rationale for this historical survey is to show the complexity of the term *theosis* and to present a nuanced understanding of the term (as Campbell suggests) before it can be used to the study of Pauline interpretations in the penultimate chapter.

Chapter 2

Early Approaches to *Theosis*

Introduction

ONE OF THE ISSUES that have occupied the minds of Christian thinkers from the inception of Christianity was the nature of soteriological communion with God. The answers span from a mere imitation of divine attributes to essential participation in the life of God. In this chapter, I will explore several Eastern church fathers and their understanding of the communion between human and divine. It was almost exclusively axiomatic for the Greek fathers viewing the nature of God is imparticipable (e.g., Origen, *Sel. Ps.* 135, PG 12:1656a; Athanasius, *Syn.* 51, PG 260:784bc; Basil, *Con. Eun.* 2.4; Cyril, *Comm. Jo.* 1.9). A creature is neither able to comprehend, nor participate in the very nature of its Creator. The call to share in God's life has its ontological limitations. Human beings, as the bearers of the *imago Dei*, according to Christian tradition, are not called to acquire the divine essence and create a pantheon of gods. God is one. However, Eastern theologians followed the lead of several scriptural texts, primarily Ps 82:6 and 2 Pet 1:4, wherein people are called "gods" and "partakers of the divine nature" (θείας κοινωνοί φύσεως). In the language of church fathers, human beings are called to be deified (*theosis*) in the likeness of God.

To explain the process of *theosis* Eastern fathers traditionally resorted to four approaches.[1] The first group of fathers, including Clement of Alexandria, Origen of Alexandria, and Evagrius Ponticus, emphasized contemplation of the divine *logoi* and deification through imitation and attaining God's attributes. The second group of church theologians, including Irenaeus of Lyons and Cyril of Alexandria, expressed deification in categories of union with the incarnated Son of God, who deified the whole of the human race

---

1. Fairbairn in a stimulating article suggested two main patristic soteriological approaches. I argue that one can trace four of such "trajectories." Fairbairn, "Patristic Soteriology."

18

in himself. The third group, i.e., the Cappadocians, concentrated on deification as an integration process into the life of trinitarian relationships. Finally, Gregory Palamas developed an approach to deification by participation in the divine energies. In the following, I will present these views in nuce.²

I have applied an arguably appropriate term to each category that best represents the main emphasis of the group. These groups are in no way monolithic as each theologian proposed a nuanced approach to the topic. Moreover, the view of a particular author, to some degree, may overlap with the views of different church fathers from other groups. Nevertheless, I contend that the general theological trajectory or emphasis of every ecclesiastical figure permits grouping him into a broadly defined category.

Apotheosis

Clement of Alexandria (ca. 150–215 CE)

Clement of Alexandria was the first Christian writer who employed deification terminology.³ A distinguished teacher at the Catechetical School in Alexandria, a former Neoplatonist, influenced by Philo's Jewish philosophy, Clement, with the aid of his previous education, presented a fundamentally Christian teaching on human destiny. He drew heavily on the tradition of Justin Martyr with respect to Old Testament exegesis and the use of Greek philosophy. Similarly, Irenaeus influenced Clement in understanding the significance of the incarnation, divine image and likeness, and the "soft" fall of Adam from immaturity to imperfection. Clement engaged with Christian gnostic writings of Basilidean and Valentinian sects, arguing that the true Christian *gnostic* is in full agreement with the Orthodox Church and employs philosophy in service of theology.

Among many terms used by Clement for the deification of Christians, θεοποιέω is the most common.⁴ Ἀποθέωσις and its cognate verb appear six times in his writings. Russell points out the innovative character of Clement's theological expositions, "Furthermore, he not only found new uses for the term θεοποιέω, but is also the first Greek writer to endow ἐκθεόω with the meaning 'to deify' and the first to make θεοποιός mean 'deifying.'"⁵

---

2. In this survey of patristic approaches to deification, I will follow closely two comprehensive works on the topic. Gross, *Divinization of Christian*; Russell, *Doctrine of Deification*.
3. Collins, *Partaking in Divine Nature*, 57.
4. Russell, *Doctrine of Deification*, 122.
5. Russell, *Doctrine of Deification*, 123.

Clement preserved apophatic theology, stressing that, although human beings are called gods, there is only one God in a genuine sense of the word (*Protr.* 4.63.3). According to Henny Fiskå Hägg, the father's claims that God's being is beyond all being and essence (*Strom.* 7.2.2; 1.177.1),[6] or that the One is "beyond the One and above the unity itself" (*Paed.* 1.71.1), are intentionally inconsistent due to God's ineffable nature.[7] The only connection that exists between God and creation is the Word, who is the divine medium in originating all existent things. The unknowable God becomes known through the person of the Son, "God, then, who is indemonstrable, is not the object of knowledge. But the Son is wisdom, knowledge, truth and all such things related to these, and in that way he can be demonstrated and described" (*Strom.* 4.156.1). Since God's nature exceeds any human perception, he has no name or description, while the Son became the Father's face, power, will, and name in accommodated manner for the sake of limited human perception (*Paed.* 1.57.2). In his essence, οὐσία, God is inaccessible, but in his power, δύναμις, who is the Son, he became revealed (*Strom.* 2.5.3-4; 6.166.1-2).[8] The Son has no beginning in time, which caused Clement to think about the eternal generation of the Logos before he assumed human flesh on earth (*Prot.* 7.3).[9] The appropriation of the human body by the Logos, nevertheless, did not change his consubstantiality and unity with the Father (*Exc.* 8.1; 17.1-2).[10] The Logos united the divine and human essences in his incarnation, perfecting the human part of the union.

Since God is transcendent, human creatures cannot be images of God as such, but of the divine Image, i.e., they are *logoi* of the Logos. Clement utilized the Irenaean image-likeness distinction that is found in Gen 1:26. The divine εἰκών in people is contained in the mind (νοῦς) and is an innate possession.[11] On the contrary, the divine ὁμοίωσις is an actualization

---

6. Chadwick and Oulton, *Alexandrian Christianity*.

7. Hägg, *Clement of Alexandria*, 176-79. The issue of God's unknowability in Clement is extensively treated in chapter 5.

8. Hägg, *Clement of Alexandria*, chaps. 8-9. Hägg argued that Clement's distinction between God's essence and power, accidents, or energy is a significant precursor to the Cappadocian and later Eastern Orthodox essence-energy distinction in theology.

9. Hägg, *Clement of Alexandria*, 192-95.

10. Hägg considers *Excerpta ex Theodoto* "an indispensable source for our knowledge of Clement's concept of the divine, and especially, I think, it is important with regard to his doctrine of the Logos. It is interesting to witness the formative stages in the Christian tradition. In addition to passages that would affirm the Son's divinity as well as his consubstantiality with the Father, the book also contains arguments for the idea of a distinction in God between different persons." Hägg, *Clement of Alexandria*, 199.

11. Gross, *Divinization of Christian*, 132-33; Ashwin-Siejkowski, *Clement of Alexandria*, 149-50.

of the potential contained in the image and the attainment of perfection. Freedom from sinful passions and the unity of the soul are the two cardinal virtues that manifest the divine likeness. The first Adam lost his chance to mature in accordance with his divine potential while the second Adam prevailed. Although the Logos provided the means of salvific knowledge before his incarnation—law to the Jews and philosophy to the Greeks—after his incarnation, the full revelation of the truth became accessible to all people. Therefore, Christians are in the position to become like Christ and, consequently, godlike, because they can ultimately reflect the Logos (*Paed.* 7.101.4).[12] Believers exist not only as the image, like the rest of the human race (in a natural static way), but also are upgraded, so to speak, to the likeness of God (in a special dynamic way).

Clement's understanding of the incarnation was limited to the flesh only. Such Christology influenced the father's view of anthropology and soteriology. The human nature was not assumed fully. Therefore, Christ is only an example of incorruption and morality, rather than the Redeemer (*Paed.* 1.98.3). This realization led Clement to a conviction that the imitation of Christ and his qualities by saints, enabled by grace, is the primary way to godlikeness. On its initial stages, the process of spiritual perfection proceeds under the guidance of mature Christians, but then it is continued exclusively by the incarnated Logos, who alone knows and reveals the Father to people (*Strom.* 5.33.6–5.34.1). In imitating their Master, Christians will become deified like him, albeit remaining in the flesh (*Strom.* 7.101.4). Here is how the Alexandrian scholar defined Christ's revelatory role in the deification of humanity, "the Word of God speaks, having become man, in order that such as you may learn from man how it is even possible for man to become a god" (*Prot.* 1). In the *Paedagogus*, he expressed a similar thought, "By His heavenly doctrine He deifies humankind" (οὐρανίῳ διδασκαλίᾳ θεοποιῶν ἄνθρωπον) (*Paed.* 1.12). For Clement, unlike for Irenaeus, deification is an intellectual learning process how to become a god, not so much participation in the divine life. By imitating the Logos, Christians acquire beauty, beneficence, and immortality, i.e., become gods, according to God's desire. According to Clement, the spiritual progress of Christians is similar to Christ's, the archetype of *theosis*, "The same also takes place in our case, whose exemplar Christ became. Being baptized, we are illuminated; illuminated, we become sons; being made sons, we become perfect; being made perfect, we become immortal. 'I said,' says Scripture, 'you are gods and all of you sons of the Most High'" (*Paed.* 1.26.1; Ps. 82:6). Clement's statement that "God is in man, and man is a god" (*Paed.* 3.2.1), in Russell's view, probably echoes Justin's

12. Osborn, *Clement of Alexandria*, 233–35.

understanding of transcendent and immanent Logos.[13] The indwelling of the Logos allows a person to receive a title "god." As Itter indicates, the imitation of Christ by believers and union with him result in attaining the state of "unmixed oneness" (ἀχράντως μοναδικός), whereby saints become a monad like Christ (*Strom*. 4.157.1–3).[14] Moreover, Clement claimed that the deified souls come into such an intimate closeness in union with Christ that they become one with him and can participate in the event of creation and even self-creation. Believers become "causes of their own salvation" (*Strom*. 6.122.3) to the degree that "the gnostic even makes and creates himself" (ναὶ μὴν ἑαυτὸν κτίζει καὶ δημιουργεῖ) (*Strom*. 7.3.13).[15]

Transforming imitation process includes a contemplative, ecclesiastical, and virtuous life. According to Clement, the deified acquire divine knowledge through the contemplation (θεωρία) of invisible spiritual reality in line with the church's *rule of faith* and practical wisdom (*Strom*. 6.125.4). An intellectual ascent in the contemplation of God, whereby reason transcends everything corporeal and sensible, is a deifying activity that transforms a human being and prepares for immortal life. Clement stated that "the gnostic therefore is already holy and divine, carrying God within him and being carried by God" (*Strom*. 7.82.2). The mind's mystical ascent, nevertheless, is limited by human reason unable to comprehend the incomprehensible nature of God. The human observer remains in darkness—a state Moses experienced on Mount Sinai (*Strom*. 2.6.1; 5.78.1–3). Therefore, the Alexandrian Christian philosopher often talked about God in apophatic terms or resorted to silent adoration (*Strom*. 6.39.1–3; 7.2.2–3). Alternatively, Clement employed "kataphatic" language, i.e., revelation through the descent of the Logos.[16] Mystical learning comes from the Logos, who is both a philosophical principle, disseminated in all human wisdom, and a historical figure Jesus, who taught the secret wisdom to his disciples (*Hyp*. fr. 13, 3.199.21). Only through the mediator, God's Logos, who came into the world of senses and language, are we able to gain some knowledge and talk about God indirectly. This indirect knowledge of God is only possible through the Logos, who is the spiritual gnosis, and through sound knowledge. Both types of knowledge operate in the context of faith, without which there is no understanding (*Strom*. 6.2.4; 4.54.1; 1.8.2; 2.16.2).

---

13. Russell, *Doctrine of Deification*, 128.

14. Itter, *Esoteric Teaching*, 205–6.

15. Bucur, *Angelomorphic Pneumatology*, 45.

16. On the apophatic and kataphatic ways in Clement see Hägg, *Clement of Alexandria*, chap. 7.

For Clement, the Scriptures bear a deifying role because through them believers are conformed to the likeness of God (*Prot.* 9.87.1). The Christian philosopher distinguishes a majority of ordinary Christians of simple faith and a minority of Christian elites, which can distill deifying knowledge through the allegorical interpretation of Scripture.[17] These Christian gnostics, male and female, are true philosophers, who gain the real knowledge of the invisible God and complete divinization. This gnosis is a God-given capability and grace to contemplate things as they are in reality. As Ashwin-Siejkowski noted, this intellectual ascent toward an immaterial sphere of God's existence is, at the same time, an internal descent into one's self because God indwells believers.[18] The deified experience purification through the contemplation of heavenly reality, accessible only by intellect and through acts of love and virtues.[19] In distinction to Paul, who stressed the supremacy of love over knowledge in the Christian's spiritual experience (1 Cor 13), Clement perceived both virtues equally progressing in communion with God.

In practice, the Spirit, who indwells believers and leads them to immortality, performs deification, initiated in baptism. Baptismal regeneration is an essential starting point for believers on their way to spiritual perfection. Participation in Christ's incorruption depends on one's baptismal illumination and then in partaking in the Eucharist, a divine spiritual medicine (*Paed.* 1.6; 1.26.1; 2.19.4). Through these sacraments, the deified comingle and participate in the immortal divinity of Christ (*Paed.* 2.2.19–20). This sacramental aspect of Christian perfection underlies Clement's idea of an ecclesiastical framework for deification.[20] The church is "the Mother," who feeds not the children of her own and not with her own milk because she is a virgin. Instead, she nurses Christians with the spiritual milk, which is the Logos (*Paed.* 1.42.1–2).

The intellectual perfection coincides with a stripping of emotions, which distract a person from focusing on divine things. Ashwin-Siejkowski identified Clement's view of deification as a reasonable, rather than an ecstatic endeavor, "Assimilation to God, with the central role of the divine Logos as the 'mystagogos' (μυσταγωγός), is more of an intellectual encounter, a spiritual communion, than an uncontrolled emotional outburst."[21] Passions

---

17. Lilla, *Clement of Alexandria*, chap. 3. Lilla claims that Platonic, Philonic, and Gnostic roots are evident in these ideas.
18. Ashwin-Siejkowski, *Clement of Alexandria*, 158.
19. Gross, *Divinization of Christian*, 135–38; Lilla, *Clement of Alexandria*, 163–73.
20. Ashwin-Siejkowski, *Clement of Alexandria*, chap. 6.
21. Ashwin-Siejkowski, *Clement of Alexandria*, 181.

drive human nature. However, through his sufferings, the Son attained a passionless state in the flesh and became an example to his followers (*Paed.* 7.7.5). Ἀπάθεια as a divine quality and gift is one of the primary virtues, to which a human god is striving. The Christian gnostic possesses "apathy" not in terms of Stoic indifference, but in terms of assimilation to God's independence and impassibility gained through asceticism.[22] Thus, starting with faith and a reverent adoration of one true and invisible God, Christian sages constantly seek to master their passions. Unlike pagan temples that cannot accommodate the uncontained God, the Christian gnostics could become a place for God's habitation (*Paed.* 2.101.1; 2.100.4). In his treatment of Psalm 82, Clement gave this definition of biblical "gods,"

> "God stood in the congregation of the gods; in their midst he judges gods" [Ps. 82:1]. Who are the gods? They are those who mastered pleasure, who rise above the passions, those who know their actions, who are the Gnostics, who are superior to the world. Then [the] Lord says: "I said you are gods and all of you sons of the Most High" [Ps. 82:6]. To whom is the Lord speaking? To those who have detached themselves as far as possible from everything that is human (*Strom.* 2.125.4–5).[23]

Russell correctly thinks that the point here is control over passions in resemblance to a dispassionate God.[24] Clement, nonetheless, presented a uniquely Christian form of *apatheia* because divine perfection presupposes an individual devoid of evil emotions while growing in good and stable virtues, such as love and compassion (*Strom.* 2.87.2). Love that takes hold of its object, God, is a mystical union with God, which is manifested in good deeds. Love and reverence toward God assimilate true gnostics to angelic beings and become the way believers now "study to be a god" in eternity (*Strom.* 6.113.2–3). Training in knowledge restores one to the original state of humanity while untaught contemplative love restores humans to the likeness of God.

According to Russell, Clement espoused a sort of inaugurated eschatology, whereby deification is a present reality, but finalization of it still awaits future consummation.[25] In this respect, the church father echoed the Pauline soteriological twofold hope of "already" and "not yet" (Rom 8:24). The Alexandrian teacher perceived three grades of human achievement: sinners can become like beasts, merely saved, or glorious like gods. In the

22. Lilla, *Clement of Alexandria*, 109–11.
23. Cited in Ashwin-Siejkowski, *Clement of Alexandria*, 154–55.
24. Russell, *Doctrine of Deification*, 130.
25. Russell, *Doctrine of Deification*, 128.

often-cited passage from the *Stromateis*, Clement provided an extended treatment of spiritual progress from imperfection to perfection, from the human state to the angelic and even divine:

> And the name of gods is given to those that shall hereafter be enthroned with the other gods, who first had their station assigned to them beneath the Saviour. Knowledge therefore is swift to purify, and suitable for the welcome change to the higher state. Hence, too, it easily transplants a man to that divine and holy state [θεῖόν τε καὶ ἅγιον μετοικίζει] which is akin to the soul, and by a light of its own carries him through the mystic stages, till it restores him to the crowning abode of rest, having taught the pure in heart to look upon God face to face with understanding and absolute certainty (*Strom.* 7.56.3).

"To be enthroned with the other gods," in Russell's view, means to achieve the highest divine honor with twenty-four elders from Revelation, but still lower than Christ. Such interpretation finds support in the next sentence, wherein Clement stated, "For herein lies the perfection of the gnostic soul, that having transcended all purifications and modes of ritual, it should be with the Lord where he is, in immediate subordination to him." The perfect state of the gnostic soul that freed itself from sensual desires is equal to that of angels, ἰσάγγελος, who constantly worship in God's presence and serve people (*Strom.* 6.105.1).[26] Moreover, even this grand stage is not static, but advances into greater proximity toward God, or as Clement called it, "the endless end" (τέλος ἀτελεύτητον) (*Strom.* 7.56.3).[27] The pure heart advances into higher stages of perfection that allow her to have an unmediated contemplation of God as far as possible (*Strom.* 7.13.1). Russell points to Clement's optimistic view on the destiny of a deified person, "According to Clement, the Christian is deified by a heavenly teaching (*Prot.* 11.114.4); when fully perfected after the likeness of his teacher, he 'becomes a god while still moving about in the flesh' (ἐν σαρκὶ περιπολῶν θεός) (*Strom.* 7.101.4); and at the end of his life he is enthroned 'with the other gods' in the heavenly places."[28] The completion of deification is not attainable on earth, but only after the resurrection and reunion of the glorified body with a transformed gnostic soul. As Osborn notes, salvation is a progressive process with the

---

26. Ashwin-Siejkowski, *Clement of Alexandria*, 154–56.

27. Osborn, *Clement of Alexandria*, 231; Itter, *Esoteric Teaching*, 204–5. As Itter puts it, "An end where the soul learns of its ultimate relation to God as divine and immortal on the one hand, and created and mortal on the other; capable of intimacy with him, yet separated by an unbridgeable abyss."

28. Russell, *Doctrine of Deification*, 121.

aim of achieving a reciprocal relationship with God, rather than absorption into God.[29] The eternal destiny of the blessed soul is to live in a "face to face" contemplation of the Savior and eternal rest (*Strom.* 5.40.1; 7.57.1–6; 7.68.5). The true Christian gnostic, endeavoring in the earthly contemplation of the Logos, will reach "restoration to everlasting contemplation" (τῇ θεωρίᾳ τῇ ἀϊδίῳ ἀποκατάστασις) (*Strom.* 7.56.6). Unlike his philosophical teachers, Clement believed that Christ endows a believer with not only spiritual incorruption but also with incorruption of the flesh (*Paed.* 1.32.4; 1.84.3; 2.109.3). Russell adequately summarizes Clement's understanding of deification, "Deification is thus twofold: it has an ecclesiastical aspect in so far as it is brought about by Christ, and a philosophical aspect in so far as it is the product of intellectual and moral effort."[30]

In my view, Clement's undeveloped Christology, in comparison to the later Nicene formulations, presents Christ not as the perfect redeemer of humanity, but as a perfect guide and example to self-redemption, not without the aid of grace of course. Still one gets a picture of a virtuous Christian life that ends with a divine status to the degree of contemplative ascent and achieved godlikeness. The emulation of divine attributes in this life, with the final attainment of the divine status in the afterlife, resembles Greco-Roman ideas of *apotheosis*.[31] This resemblance, however, is only in principle and not in essence because Clement founded his idea of deification in the event of Logos's incarnation. In Russell's view, Clement attempted to harmonize the ecclesiastical and Philonic traditions. He was not able, however, to resolve the tensions, on the one hand, the transcendent nature of God, and, on the other hand, the destiny of humans to become divine. The church is indebted to the efforts of Cyril of Alexandria in achieving this synthesis.

Origen of Alexandria (ca. 185–253 CE)

Origen of Alexandria taught a progressive deification, whereby believers become partakers not only of Christ but also of God (*Philokalia* 13.4). Following his famous predecessor, Clement of Alexandria, Origen frequently used similar cognate terms, such as θεοποιέω and ἀποθεόω, to describe deification.[32]

---

29. Osborn, *Clement of Alexandria*, 280.

30. Russell, *Doctrine of Deification*, 139.

31. Russell, *Doctrine of Deification*, chap. 2.

32. Russell, *Doctrine of Deification*, 141; Collins, *Partaking in Divine Nature*, 58. Origen of Alexandria, *Origenes Werke*.

Less commonly used were Clement's favorite terms ἐκθεόω and ἐκθειάζω, perhaps due to the association of the terms with pagan deification.[33]

Origen, similar to Plato, believed that pre-existent human souls distanced themselves from the love and contemplation of God and were placed in material bodies for purification and restoration (*Princ.* 2.8.3).[34] As Benjamin Blosser convincingly argues, among the reasons why Origen preserved this Platonic idea in his theology was a desire to protect divine justice and the free will of the human soul in the face of the inequality of human beings at their birth (*Comm. Jo.* 2.180–2; *Princ.* 1.7.4; 2.9.7; 3.3.4–5).[35] Thus, the Alexandrian Christian philosopher found the way to preserve human freedom and to avoid pagan determinism and God's responsibility for the presence of evil. He did this by identifying both the pre-incarnate free choice and actions of souls (*Cels.* 1.32). Origen stated, "There were certain causes of prior existence, in consequence of which the souls, before their birth in the body, contracted a certain amount of guilt in their sensitive nature, or in their movements, on account of which they have been judged worthy by Divine Providence of being placed in this condition" (*Princ.* 3.3.5).[36]

Other reasons to propose pre-existence of souls were to show that God was active and exercised his power even before the creation of the world, as well as to defend the pre-existent humanity of Christ, who shares the same human nature with people, remaining an unfallen perfect *nous* to redeem the fallen ones.[37] Moreover, Blosser contends that for Origen, like for Philo, the idea of pre-existent souls did not connote bodiless existence before the primordial fall and incarnation, but only a different type of embodiment in celestial bodies.[38] That is because only the Trinity is truly an incorpo-

---

33. Russell, *Doctrine of Deification*, 339–40. As Russell points, the term ἐκθεόω was virtually abandoned by the church fathers after Origen until it became prominent again in the writings of Pseudo-Dionysius (around sixth century CE) under the influence of the Neoplatonists.

34. Gross, *Divinization of Christian*, 142. According to P. Tzamalikos, however, the idea of soul's pre-existence was not a settled issue in the early church. Therefore, one should not regard Origen's innovative approach to anthropology as a sign of heresy, but as a pioneering work of an inquisitive mind. Tzamalikos, *Origen*, 23.

35. Blosser, *Become Like Angels*, 161–62. Greggs thinks that the inequality of created beings points to the individuality of human agents for Origen. Greggs, *Barth, Origen, Universal Salvation*, 58.

36. Edwards, in my opinion, unconvincingly argues that Origen did not hold the doctrine of soul's pre-existence and fall before incarnation. It seems that Edwards' arguments are limited to deliberate quotations from the *De Principiis* and disregard or misinterpret passages like this. Edwards, *Origen against Plato*, 89–97.

37. Blosser, *Become Like Angels*, 212.

38. Blosser, *Become Like Angels*, 175, 192.

real being (*Princ.* 1.7.5; 2.2.2).[39] Further, "pre-existed" souls does not mean "eternal" or "uncreated," because only God and the *logoi* in his mind are uncreated (*Princ.* 1.1.3; 1.7.1). The fall of Adam was not a fall of a bodiless soul into flesh, but the degradation of a luminous body into a carnal one. Contrary to a Platonic belief in transmigration or reincarnation of souls, Origen thought that the transfer of a soul into another human body, an animal or plant would preclude the primary role of incarnation, which is the rational and voluntary restoration of an individual and a return to God (*Comm. Jo.* 6.7; *Princ.* 1.8.4; *Cels.* 3.75; 5.29; 8.30).

Like Clement, Origen distinguished between the natural image and beyond-natural likeness of God. Our innate kinship with God resides in one's mind from its creation, while likeness to God is an ever-growing spiritual resemblance to the divine persons that will reach its consummation in the *eschaton*. In his *De Principiis* 3.6.1, Origen wrote,

> [W]hile the first human being did indeed receive the dignity of God's image in the first creation, the dignity of his likeness is reserved for the consummation. This is so that human beings would work to acquire it by their own industrious efforts to imitate God; for in the beginning only the possibility of perfection is given them by the dignity of the "image," while in the end they are to acquire for themselves the perfect "likeness" by the carrying out of works.

A person can realize the potential contained in the divine image through assimilation to the Image, the Logos of God. Thus, the godlikeness of a person is a spiritual outgrowth of an innate capacity. The likeness to God and a name "god," nevertheless, do not make a human person equal in "power or nature" with the triune God, but merely divine in resemblance with him by grace (*Hom. Exod.* 6.5).

In his commentary on Romans, the Alexandrian interpreter presented salvation as God's justifying gift, which believers actively appropriate. In Scheck's account, Origen understood justification in Romans as both Christ and the divine attribute that believers receive when they accept Christ, and the whole Trinity dwells in them (*Comm. Rom.* 1.21.84–116; 4.9.192–98).[40] Thus, the justifying and deifying grace is not an external gift, but something that flows from the Spirit present in the saint. The sanctifying presence of the Son and the Spirit in a person does not preclude cooperation with grace. In his exegesis, the Alexandrian father concluded, "everywhere faith is joined with works and works are united with

---

39. Scott, *Origen and Life*, 154.
40. Scheck, *Origen and History*, 33.

faith" (*Comm. Rom.* 2.9.403-8; 2.9.62-3). According to Origen, justification by faith is the basis for the remission of past sins, fulfillment of the law in the Spirit, and reception of God's glory (*Comm. Rom.* 2.7.29-30; 3.4.154-8). "Faith," however, is not without hope, love, and obedience, but rather stands for the whole sanctification process.[41] Contrary to the gnostic groups, such as the Valentinians and Basilidians, who taught the determinism of human persons predestined to salvation or damnation from their birth, Origen posited a free human agent, who will be rewarded or judged in accordance with her deeds (*Comm. Rom.* 1.21.65-74; 5.10.169; 8.10.23-26).[42] Even the good works of unbelievers will receive a reward, albeit not eternal life. Thus, in the father's mind, the future aspect of justification presumes free will and merit after baptism on the part of the justified. Despite his teaching on a possibility of merit, Origen perceived no place for Christian boasting in works, but only in the cross of Christ (*Comm. Rom.* 3.6.81-101). Further, although works do not save believers, faith alone will not justify them at the final judgment either, because the merciful Savior is also the just Judge. Origen commented, "Let the faithful be edified lest they think that the fact alone that they believe can suffice for them, but let them know that God's righteous judgment will pay back to each one according to his own works" (*Comm. Rom.* 2.4.140-43).

Like Clement, Origen considered two categories of Christians: spiritual infants and the mature, who comprehend the spiritual meaning of the Scriptures and are capable of receiving the gnosis of God.[43] The spiritual progress of the soul consists of three stages. It starts with purification from sinful passions. Origen insisted that deification requires a virtuous life in the Spirit and orthodox beliefs in the context of prayer on the part of the perfected. Continuous moral perfection is a condition to grow in spiritual wisdom. Contrary to Plato, Origen believed that loving action precedes contemplation, and there is no divine knowledge without virtues (*Sel. Ps.* 5.13; *Cels.* 7.44).[44] To discard fleshly desires, for the Alexandrian, did not mean to discard the human body eventually. Therefore, in this life, Christians have to

---

41. Scheck, *Origen and History*, 52. "For Origen, justification is more than a non-imputation of past sins. It is an effectual and progressive sanctification in which sin is expelled and grace (sc. Christ), in all its aspects, is established in the believer's soul."

42. Scheck, *Origen and History*, 21. Scheck, following Reasoner, pointed out that Origen can be considered as a precursor of the New Perspective on Paul, because he drew a distinction between Jewish ethnic rituals as "works of the law" and good deeds in general. Scheck, *Origen and History*, 49. Reasoner, *Romans in Full Circle*, 25.

43. Gross, *Divinization of Christian*, 146.

44. Tzamalikos, *Origen*, 171.

master control over fleshly desires and subjugate them to the soul, which in its turn should be subjugated to the spirit (*Comm. Jo.* 1.229; 20.183).

This preparatory stage allows the soul—"purified and separated from bodily matter"—to comprehend the spiritual doctrines of the Logos contained in the Scriptures (*Princ.* 1.1.7). In this second stage, mature Christians strive to become knowledgeable in a deeper understanding of the Holy Writ. For this, the reader of the Scriptures needs to go beyond the text's literal meaning toward a spiritual knowledge inspired by the Spirit. God can be accessible to human reason, but only through the work of the Spirit, who reveals the knowledge of the Logos in the Old and New Testaments. Only through the Scriptures can believers perceive "being or that which transcends being, the power and nature of God" (*Comm. Jo.* 19.6.37). Perfection in scriptural apprehension is a prerequisite for advancing from the state of servanthood to sonship.

Finally, in the third stage, the divine wisdom leads the deified into communion and participation with the Father. A Christian call is to conform to God by means of intellectual growth in wisdom and knowledge of the Father in an immediate "face to face" manner (*Princ.* 3.6.1; *Comm. Jo.* 1.16.91–2).[45] The soul, which is intellectually nurtured on the Bread of Life, partakes in the eternal Logos and becomes an immortal and spiritual child of God (*Or.* 6.11). According to Origen, the real knowledge of God is possible only through union with God, for "to know is to mingle and to unite" (*Comm. Jo.* 19.1). With this knowledge, the soul regains the original warmth and love to God that it possessed before incarnation. Unlike God, who is living, immortal, and rational by nature, a human creature is a god, albeit through participation and appropriation of the divine faculties, θεοποιούμενος (*Comm. Jo.* 1:1). Thus, participation is the dominant mode in the process of deification.

Participation between the Creator and creatures is possible only through the Logos incarnate. The Son, sharing the Father's incorporeality and immutability, being eternally generated from the eternal Father, is at the same time the mediator between the one transcendent God and the multitude of finite creatures (*Princ.* 4.4.1–2; 1.2.2–3).[46] All material and intelligible things had existed in the form of eternal principles or *logoi* within the divine Wisdom before they were created in actuality (*Princ.* 1.2.2; *Comm. Jo.* 6.22). While the Son participates in the essence of God the Father, who is the absolute uncreated being, Christians, as created beings, can participate

---

45. Widdicombe, *Fatherhood of God*, 62.
46. Widdicombe, *Fatherhood of God*, 90.

EARLY APPROACHES TO *THEOSIS*

in God's qualities accidentally through the Logos. Believers experience a similar process of generation in the likeness of the Son:

> If the Saviour is continuously begotten by the Father,—says Origen in *Homilies on Jeremiah* 9.4—so also, if you possess the "spirit of adoption," God continuously generates you in him [the Savior] according to each of your works, each of your thoughts. And being begotten, you thereby become a continuously begotten son of God, in Christ Jesus.[47]

Therefore, Origen considered Christology as an essential aspect of soteriology.

Since God is incorporeal, Origen explained biblical passages where God is "seen" anthropomorphically in the sense of "him being known."[48] Human beings can contemplate God by nature, αὐτόθεος, and become gods by grace and adoption. This is possible because of their assimilation to the archetype, the Son of God by nature, αὐτόλογος, "who has drawn from God the power that enables them to be deified" (εἰς τὸ θεοποιηθῆναι αὐτούς) (*Comm. Jo.* 2.2.17; 2.3.204).[49] The Logos is the archetype of the "gods who are formed according to the true God, like images of a prototype" (*Comm. Jo.* 2.2.18). One cannot know God as Father—the highest of possible knowledge—until he or she participates in the Son (*Or.* 6.33). Christians become adopted sons of God, brothers of the Son, and enter into familial relationships with God as Father. According to the church father's optimistic anthropology, Christians progress in a degree of sonship from partial to perfect sonship, advancing in virtue and spiritual knowledge (*Comm. Jo.* 20.34.298–304). This spiritual progress reflects the change of human nature into the divine undiverted filiation. In distinction to Clement, Origen believed that those who achieve the knowledge of the Father via the mediation of the Son receive the knowledge of God's ineffable nature. Origen considered that "there will be one activity for those who have come to God by the Word, who is with him, which is to contemplate God, so that they might all become perfect sons of God, being thus transformed in the knowledge of the Father, as now only the Son knows the Father" (*Comm. Jo.* 1.16.92). This quotation indicates that knowledge of the Father is the highest and superior experience of the Creator that became possible after union with God.

---

47. Widdicombe, *Fatherhood of God*, 98.

48. Stroumsa, "Incorporeality of God," 351. The idea of contemplation of the invisible God gave rise to the future mystical anthropomorphism of God in the writings of Evagrius and Pseudo-Dionysius.

49. Russell, *Doctrine of Deification*, 142.

For Origen, Christ, besides being the Redeemer and Savior, is mostly the Teacher of divine mysteries, because of his enlightening activity. On the transformation of the human nature into the divine through Jesus's teaching, Origen says,

> In Him [Jesus] the divine nature and the human nature have begun to be closely joined together [συνυφαίνεσθαι] in order that, by its closeness with what is more divine [τῇ πρὸς τὸ θειότερον κοινωνίᾳ], the human nature might become divine, not only in Jesus, but also in all those who, with faith, embrace the life which Jesus taught and which leads to friendship and closeness with God (Cels. 3.28; PG 11:956d).[50]

As this quotation suggests, Origen believed in the deification of the human nature of Christ, who became an example of the deified life for his followers. Further, like Clement, Origen stated that Christ's divine life is not transmitted to believers, but is taught and needs to be embraced and imitated by faith. Christians are deified by grace in the likeness of Christ's human soul, which itself was deified in the likeness of the Father by nature. Blosser points to another image of Christ's saving activity, where Christ's "soul becomes a 'ladder' by which other souls advance back to the God, whom they have abandoned through sloth."[51] Believers should adhere to the spiritual guidance of Christ, who, "remaining always in uninterrupted contemplation of the depths of the Father" (Comm. Jo. 2.2.18), leads his followers into a similar contemplative state. Through the imitation of divine attributes, a human person regains original likeness to God and excels in the genuine knowledge of the Father (Princ. 4.4.4–10).

The mind's purification and philosophical ascent happen when it transcends all material things, its corporeal existence, and, in pure vision, contemplates the glory of God, as manifested the shining face of Moses (Comm. Jo. 32.27.338-9). Exploring the way Origen understood Paul's transformation language into the likeness of the divine glory in 2 Cor 3:18, Russell defines *theosis* in the following words, "Far from being static, contemplation is a dynamic activity, leading to an ever greater participation in the glory of God. It is a divine gift, conforming the recipient to the divine likeness, enabling him to know God and be known by him, and therefore deifying

---

50. Gross, *Divinization of Christian*, 144–45. Greggs correctly remarks a theological difficulty in Origen's affirmation of mingling between Christ's human soul and the Logos that become one after union (Cels 3.41; 6.47). Greggs, *Barth, Origen, Universal Salvation*, 61.

51. Blosser, *Become Like Angels*, 215. Comm. Matt. 13.26.

him."⁵² What distinguished Origen from his philosophical contemporaries is an accent on the necessity of grace to enter into and develop relationships with the Trinity, because "it is by the grace of God and not by their own merit that they [will] have been placed in that final state of happiness" (*Princ.* 2.3.3).

Although to acquire the divine status humans need to connect with the Father, Russell considers that a trinitarian depiction of *theosis* is not foreign to Origen, "By a parallel process of filiation, which is participation in the Son, and spiritualization, which is participation in the Spirit, the Christian can arrive at deification, which is ultimately participation in the Father."⁵³ The whole Trinity takes part in the dynamic process, wherein people progressively experience transfiguration into gods (*Princ.* 1.3.8). More specifically, by sharing in the Trinity's life, the saints become spirits, christs, and gods (*Comm. Jo.* 6.42; 10.92).

In the ἀποκατάστασις, the final restoration of all things, not only will the saved become one with God and see him "face to face" as the Son, but also the lost will be restored (*Princ.* 3.5.7; *Comm. Jo.* 1.16). Although sonship presupposes certain changes in the human nature, nevertheless, persons preserve their identity after the union. Both Gross and Scott disagree with Jerome and Justinian that Origen believed in the abolition of human identity in its mingling with God.⁵⁴ Only God exists incorporeally due to the simplicity of his nature while all rational creatures are corporeal and composite (*Princ.* 2.2.2; *Comm. Jo.* 1.20.119; 13.25.149). Saints preserve their individuality in eternity due to their participation in Christ (*Princ.* 2.6.3; 6.4.2).⁵⁵

Unlike gnostics and Neoplatonists, Origen believed in the bodily resurrection, when people would receive their due judgment for sins or blessedness for believing in Christ (*Cels.* 2.77; *Dial.* 25–6). Blosser considers that Origen also departed from the Platonists, rejecting disembodiment and fusion of believers with the Creator in the afterlife.⁵⁶ Christians experience the first or partial resurrection when they die to demonic powers and rise with Christ through baptism (*Hom. Luc.* 24). This union with Christ, being established in the sacrament, initiates a moral transformation that will be finalized at "the blessed and perfect resurrection" (*Comm. Jo.* 10.35.231–2). The substance of the resurrected body will depend on one's merits and the soul's new environment—heavenly, ethereal like stars or corporeal and

52. Russell, *Doctrine of Deification*, 144.
53. Russell, *Doctrine of Deification*, 149. See *Princ.* 1.3.5.
54. Gross, *Divinization of Christian*, 149; Scott, *Origen and Life*, 152–53.
55. Greggs, *Barth, Origen, Universal Salvation*, 80.
56. Blosser, *Become Like Angels*, 218, 248–49.

"dark" (*Cels.* 3.42; 7.5; *Princ.* 3.6.5; 2.10.3–8).[57] Thus, the terrestrial body will undergo transformation into the eternal, celestial, spiritual one, like ethereal Christ's body after his resurrection (*Cels.* 3.41), but a body nonetheless. Human individuals will regain their original likeness to angels since they share the same spiritual nature with the only difference in rank. Thus, *apokatastasis*, or redeification, means not only a return to the original subordination of creatures to the Creator but also a superior state, a harmonious union with God. The eternal life, in Origen's understanding, is an ever-growing contemplation of divine things in God's presence (*Comm. Jo.* 2.28; 13.3). All mystical experience in this life is incomplete and merely a foretaste of the eternal and perfect contemplative life thereafter.

In conclusion, I argue that Origen's presentation of human deification resembles Clement's *apotheosis*. It is not so much participation in Christ that deifies a person, as the imitation of the same deifying process that Christ's human soul and body experienced here on earth. The Logos incarnate is the perfect guide for saints in attaining to the divine life. The pre-existence of souls and their restoration into a star-like existence in the heavenly abode echoes Greco-Roman religious ideas. Notwithstanding the element of grace in Origen's soteriology and involvement of the whole Trinity in human salvation, the saving perfection of believers depends on continuous rational participation in the Logos and gaining merit.

Evagrius Ponticus (346–399 CE)

Evagrius Ponticus, a spiritual follower of Origen, believed that divine things are incomprehensible to the mind, which is trapped in passionate material images. To ascend to God, one needs to acquire a dispassionate intellect and attain true *gnosis* by means of contemplation that will lead to theology (*Praktikos* 84). In this respect, Casiday appropriately argues that Evagrius should be acknowledged as a spiritual guide toward progressive moral perfection, rather than a thinker, who presented a finalized system of speculative reasoning.[58]

57. Scott, *Origen and Life*, 154–57. Nevertheless, even those who enter the afterlife as sinners will face temporal punishment, which will lead them toward final restoration (*Princ.* 1.6.3; 2.10.7–8; *Or.* 27.15).

58. Casiday, *Evagrius Ponticus*, 25–27. In his astute article, Casiday correctly chides those contemporary patrologists (e.g., Hans Urs Von Balthasar and Antoine Guillaumont) who anachronistically apply the sixth-century Origenist condemnations to the fourth-century writings of Evagrius. Casiday, "On Heresy." The lack of deification terminology in Evagrius may be explained by a desire to dissociate with Apollinarius, who used it extensively. Collins, *Partaking in Divine Nature*, 64.

Evagrius followed Origen's idea of the pre-incarnate reasonable beings, *logikoi*, who, by their free choice, moved away from God's love and finally degraded into the ranks of good and evil spirits and human souls (*Kephalaia Gnostika* 1.49–51; 2.64; 3.22–24; 6.36). Thus, for the ascetic writer, the fall is a movement from the passionless contemplation of God into theological ignorance and descent from the immaterial state into the corporeal one, in the case of human beings.[59] God assigned to these orders of rational beings different types of material bodies and realms of existence. Nonetheless, these creatures are capable of ascending to a higher order and, eventually, reuniting with their Creator, by reacquiring the lost divine knowledge (*Kephalaia Gnostika* 1.82; 2.75; 3.38; 6.57).[60] The soul's restoration would presuppose a retracing to "essential contemplation" of God and bodiless existence. Only the Logos remained in constant contemplation of God. The Word incarnated to reveal the truth of salvation and to guide human beings into union with God.

Evagrius, being one of the greatest theoreticians of the monastic life, presented the spiritual goal in three stages.[61] The first stage is πρακτική, or a battle with passions and demons, which threatens and distracts the stillness of monastic life (*Antirrhetikos* 4). Despite the danger, the self-understanding and ascetic training of a monk are unthinkable without evil spirits's attacks.[62] In contrast, good angels encourage virtuous desires, by which the ascetic ascends above human rational and psychological constraints (*Praktikos*, 24, 80, 84). The aiding role of angels, who administer grace, reveal knowledge, and illumine the mind in the initial stage of the monastic life, is later assumed by the Holy Spirit at the more advanced stage.[63] In an ascetic aspiration toward moral perfection, deified persons place themselves in opposition to all that is sinful and material, which hinders intellectual progress. In the practice of *hesychia* or the state of stillness and tranquility of mind, a monk achieves and maintains control over passions. *Hesychasts*, similarly to Stoics, withdraw from circumstances (including marriage and contacts with relatives) that trigger anxieties and destroy internal emotional

---

59. Rasmussen, "Like a Rock?"

60. For the background discussion see Stewart, "Imageless Prayer," 176; Sinkewicz, *Evagrius of Pontus*, xxxviii–xxxix.

61. Stefaniw, *Mind, Text, and Commentary*, 289.

62. Harmless, *Mystics*, 145–46.

63. Scully argues that the reason Evagrius gives more prominent role to angels than to the Holy Spirit in his ascetic texts is not Evagrius's neglect of the Spirit (who received fully orthodox account in his *On the Faith* and the *Great Letter*), but an understanding of the angelic preparatory help at the initial steps with the prevalence of the Spirit at the more advanced stages. Scully, "Angelic Pneumatology."

balance (*Foundations* 2; *Eulogios* 12.11).⁶⁴ In this sense, *apatheia* is not a negation of emotions or goals, but a divine quality of immovability and independence from external forces other than God.⁶⁵ Compassion and care for others complement a radical austerity of monastic life. To counter boredom and acedia of the ascetic life monks have to include manual labor in their usual practice. *Hesychia* aims at attaining the state of partial impassibility in this life, which in its turn, leads to love and the practice of gnosis. As Harmless keenly puts it, "The ascetic life is not about negativity, denying oneself this or that, but about learning to love. Ultimately, the ascetic life makes one free to love others, free of subtle compulsions and hidden agenda."⁶⁶ Ascetics should not terminate their practice of moral perfection, even at the later stages, because the subjugation of vainglory and pride is never obsolete. In this life, monks can achieve perfect *apatheia*, which is not permanent due to constant changes and movements inherent in this world.⁶⁷

The second stage is θεωρία φυσική, a contemplative life that can coincide with the first stage (*Praktikos* 36).⁶⁸ It is a sort of natural philosophy that starts with the contemplation of the created order and its visible objects and gradually ascends to the vision of intellectually invisible beings and principles. The ascetic contemplates ontological principles of existent beings, i.e., *logoi*. The monk approaches Christ—the blueprint of all creation, who contains all *logoi* in himself—by contemplating the world's beauty. According to Evagrius, the one who is capable of natural knowledge is not the one who only controls his passions, but who also cultivates virtues, such as faith, hope, and love (*Eulogios* 10.11; *Praktikos*, Prologue 8). Gnosis does not supplant love but instead is perfected by love.⁶⁹ Practical and theoretical endeavors are not sequential, but simultaneous. Along with noetic comprehension of nature, the ascetic needs to comprehend the Scriptures that contain the hidden teachings of the divine wisdom (*Gnostikos* 18–21, 34). Through meditation on the Bible's teaching, one has access to the "chamber in which we behold the holy and hidden Father" (*Letters* 4.5). For Evagrius, the ascetic and contemplative life is unthinkable without immersion in the Bible. *Apatheia*, or the stillness of the soul, together with the contemplation

---

64. Sinkewicz, *Evagrius of Pontus*, xxi–xxii.

65. Corrigan, *Evagrius and Gregory*, 199. Corrigan argues that this ethical aspect of Evagrian thought is closer to Plato and Aristotle than to Stoics.

66. Harmless, *Mystics*, 148–49.

67. Rasmussen, "Like a Rock?," 160.

68. Russell, *Doctrine of Deification*, 239.

69. Corrigan, *Evagrius and Gregory*, 199.

of creation and biblical exegesis are the preconditions for the ultimate monastic goal, the contemplation of God.

The final stage is θεωρία θεολογική or an unmediated prayerful contemplation of the Trinity. For Evagrius, theology is not so much theoretical reasoning as the practice of unceasing prayer and intuitive vision, wherein theologians meet God. The ascetic stated, "If you are a theologian, you will pray truly; and if you pray truly, you will be a theologian" (*On Prayer* 60). In essence, the "pure prayer" is a constant repetition of short sayings, whereby ascetics, starting with the scriptural images of God, must eventually surpass material and word-images of the divine in their minds (*On Prayer* 66, 69–70, 117–20; *Reflections* 20). The contemplation dispatches the mind from physical things toward metaphysical, namely toward the immediate intellectual vision of God himself, which is the eschatological beatitude of the mind beyond verbal expression (*Gnostikos* 13, 41; *On Prayer* 3). In this stage, the aid of the holy angels is no longer necessary and is even distracting, because they appear as an image (*On Prayer* 95). During occasional moments of pure prayer, the mind can observe its own state, which is a "place of God" (*Thoughts* 39–40). The mind becomes luminous, like "sapphire-blue light," being illuminated by the light of the Trinity (*Thoughts* 39; *Reflections* 2.4).[70]

This vision of God is beyond any words, images or forms that the intellect may associate with the divine being. Nevertheless, the speechless prayer or imageless contemplation does not mean the dissolution of the mind or ecstasy. It is attaining to the true intellectual state. Evagrius said that "undistracted prayer is the highest mindfulness of the mind" (*On Prayer* 34a).[71] At this advanced stage, the deified are no longer in need of creation for mediating the divine knowledge, because the Son and the Spirit, as "the hand and finger" of God, directly administer the knowledge of the Trinity (*Letter to Melania*). It should be noted that these stages have no strict chronological sequence but can overlap as the following text indicates, "Our struggle is for the contemplation of that which is and of the Holy Trinity, and the demons wage a great war against us to hinder us from knowing" (*Epistle* 58.2). Moreover, whatever the monastic life achieves, it is never in isolation from God's grace (*Monks* 134).

The future destiny of all existent beings is to become like the Logos and return to incorporeal and contemplative communion with the One. Like

70. Sinkewicz, *Evagrius of Pontus*, xxxvi; Stewart, "Imageless Prayer," 195–98. The images of "the place of God" and "sapphire-blue light" from Exod 24:10–11 and Ezek 1:26, 10:1 are metaphorically applied by Evagrius to the mind. The mind of an ascetic is "the throne of God" in Isaiah's vision (6:1), which receives the imageless imprint of God (*Thoughts* 41).

71. Translated from *Philokalia* by Harmless, *Mystics*, 152.

Origen, Evagrius perceived the final restoration of all fallen creatures, including the evil spirits, in *apokatastasis* and their subjugation to God the Father (*Kephalaia Gnostika* 5.83; 6.15; 6.27). Unlike Origen, the ascetic from Pontus identified no place for corporeal existence after the resurrection. Even though Evagrius did not consider material bodies evil, he, nonetheless, expected the immaterial existence of the mind. Evagrius stated, "If the perfection of the *nous* is immaterial knowledge, as it is said, and if immaterial knowledge is solely the Trinity, it is evident that in perfection there will not be anything of matter. And if that is so, the nous forevermore naked will come to vision of the Trinity" (*Kephalaia Gnostika* 3.15).[72] At times Evagrius employed an image of torrents dissolved in the sea to express the mind's destiny, "When like torrents to the sea the minds return to him [God], he completely changes them to his own nature, colour, and taste: in his endless and inseparable unity, they will be one and no longer many, since they will be united and joined to him" (*Letter to Melania* 27). One is left to wonder whether the monk described one's temporal mystical experience of God or final personal absorption into God. Sinkewicz thinks that it is the former:

> [T]he intellects neither lose their individuality nor their created nature, they are divinized by this union with Christ and through him with the Word and the divine Unity and Trinity itself. Reunited with one another in the *henad*, they will have entirely laid aside their number, names, and location along with the corporeal matter associated with these.[73]

In 553 CE, the leaders of the church posthumously condemned—however rightly or wrongly—Origen's influence on Evagrius in the areas of the pre-existence of souls, their acedia and consequent degradation into the ranks of angels, humans, and demons, as well as his inadequate Christology and speculative *apokatastasis*. Russell finds Evagrius's noetic immaterial version of deification problematic and rightly condemned by the ancient churchmen, "This gnosticizing approach to deification, which sees the goal of the spiritual life as total assimilation to Christ through the shedding of

---

72. Stefaniw argues that the subordination of physical things to spiritual in Evagrius is not a gnostic dualism, but a matter of the ultimate superiority of the later. Stefaniw, "Evagrius Ponticus."

73. Sinkewicz, *Evagrius of Pontus*, xl. In a footnote, Sinkewicz provides quotations that support incorporeal eternal existence, "When the minds have received the contemplation that concerns them, then the entire nature of bodies shall also be removed, and thus the contemplation that concerns it shall become immaterial" (*Kephalaia Gnostika* 2.62; see 1.26; 2.17; 2.77; 3.66).

the material element that accounts for individuation, was decisively rejected by the fathers of the Fifth Ecumenical Council."[74]

Even if Casiday is right that one is not authorized to read Evagrius anachronistically in light of later Origenist condemnations, I think it is proper to call the ascetic's understanding of soteriology *apotheosis* for two reasons. First, for Evagrius, salvation is predominantly an ascetic endeavor toward virtuous perfection and contemplative ascension, understandably not without the help of grace. Second, the Evagrian deification is not participating in the deified human nature of Christ, but the progressive eradication of corporeal features, such as body and passions, with an eschatological ideal of a solely intellectual union with God.

Christosis

Irenaeus of Lyons (ca. 130–200 CE)

Irenaeus of Lyons believed that all believers could attain divine life due to the incarnation and participation in the sacraments, and not because of gnostic, esoteric knowledge as promoted by his opponents.[75] He developed the idea of deification in Pauline terms, calling the gods of Psalm 82:6 the adopted sons of God, who "mingled with the Logos" (*Haer.* 3.6.1; 3.19.1).[76] This adoption is possible due to the incarnation of the eternal Son, who unites himself with all humanity and in whom all believers participate in the uncorrupted life by baptism. Irenaeus raised a rhetorical question, "How could we have shared in adoption if the word of God had not entered into communion with us and become flesh himself?" (*Haer.* 3.18.7). Despite the absence of the term "deification" in his writings, Irenaeus's soteriology presents this gradual process toward a beatific vision of God and assimilation to him in likeness via the incarnate Logos.[77] The divine economy from the beginning to the end assumed the exaltation of humankind from dust to partaking in the divine life and glory.[78]

In the bishop of Lyons's anti-Valentinian understanding, creation is an act of the whole Trinity, whereby the Father creates through the Son in the

---

74. Russell, *Doctrine of Deification*, 241.

75. Russell, *Doctrine of Deification*, 105; Collins, *Partaking in Divine Nature*, 55–56.

76. Irenaeus of Lyons, *Irenaeus*.

77. Gross, *Divinization of Christian*, 130. Osborn helpfully identified four concepts that encompass Irenaeus's thought: the divine Intellect, economy, recapitulation, and participation. Osborn, *Irenaeus of Lyons*, 21–22.

78. Minns, *Irenaeus*, 70.

Spirit, as "through his word and wisdom" or "through the hands of God" (*Haer.* 2.30.9; 4.20.1; 5.28.4).[79] According to a patristic tradition discussed above, Irenaeus perceived a distinction between the image and likeness of the triune God. The divine image, which is the human nature proper that could not be lost, is different from the likeness, which is an accidental potential for assimilation to God that was lost and regained through the Word's incarnation and the Spirit's salvific activity (*Haer.* 3.18.1; 5.6.1).[80] For Irenaeus, unlike the Alexandrian fathers, the image of God is not a bodiless mind. Rather, people were created in the image of the Logos incarnate, because the Logos was incarnated from eternity.[81] The human intellect, free will, and life itself distinguish them as the image-bearers of the Trinity (*Haer.* 4.20.1). Further, the created human persons had a vocation to grow in their likeness to God, partaking in the divine immortality.

The first human couple was endowed with a capacity to see God and gradually to attain perfection and likeness to him, thus becoming gods (*Haer.* 4.20.5). Adam and Eve were immature children, whose calling was to grow in spiritual maturity, obedience, and sonship through their natural free choice and education (*Epid.* 12; *Haer.* 4.38).[82] Our progenitors would have become gods if they had continued to participate in the Son's life and freedom. Instead, they misused those gifts, becoming mortal slaves by "eating in disobedience" (*Epid.* 2; *Haer.* 3.18.6; 5.23.1). Having the potential to transform the image into the likeness of God, Adam and Eve forfeited it by their immature choice to seize the true knowledge of good and evil that they were not yet ready to grasp (*Haer.* 4.39.1). Minns summarizes the meaning of the fall well, "For it was not disobedience of an arbitrary command, but disobedience of the divine economy itself, a refusal to accept that they were only creatures and not gods, and that likeness to God was to be had only by God's gift, and only when they had grown strong enough to bear it" (cf., *Haer.* 4.38.4).[83]

Nonetheless, for Irenaeus, the fall was not a fatal accident because it provided a realistic understanding of human constraints and new ways toward maturity, i.e., through the coming of Christ (*Haer.* 5.2.3). As Steenberg rightly states, for Irenaeus, the fall was the "loss of potential, rather than the

79. Steenberg, *Irenaeus on Creation*, 103.

80. Osborn, *Irenaeus of Lyons*, 212. Osborn, however, thinks that Irenaeus retained no consistent distinction between image and likeness and at times could use them interchangeably, e.g., in his polemic against the Valentinians. On the inconsistency of this distinction in Irenaeus see also Minns, *Irenaeus*, 73.

81. Gross, *Divinization of Christian*, 122–23.

82. Irenaeus of Lyons, *Proof*.

83. Minns, *Irenaeus*, 76.

loss of actualized realities,"[84] and, consequently, not as tragic as for most of the church fathers. Thus, it is more appropriate to talk about humanity's "weakness," rather than its "total depravity." Satan is a "strong man" against immature first Adam and his descendants, but he will not prevail against the fully mature second Adam (*Haer.* 3.8.2; 3.18.6). Irenaeus optimistically perceived Adam's hiding in Eden not as an escape or deception of God, but as repentance of a child confused by the recent realization of his disobedience and its consequences (*Haer.* 3.23.5). One can see the repentance and humility of the first couple in making an "uncomfortable cover" out of fig leaves that signifies potential restoration in the future. Even death itself as an overthrow of human life is, in some sense, God's provision for sinful humanity to break with the lasting power of sin and regain life with God (*Haer.* 3.23.6).[85] Through the experience of death, the resurrected human creatures will be able to comprehend God's gracious gift of immortality and be grateful to him forever (*Haer.* 3.20.1-2).

Christ became the mediator and accommodator between the Uncreated God and created people so that mortal beings could receive the Son's immortal life. More precisely, as Steenberg notes, Irenaeus taught that the incarnation is not merely an act of the Son, but also an undertaking of the whole Trinity (*Haer.* 3.17.2; 4.28.2).[86] Christ is the archetypal visible image and likeness of the invisible God, of whom people are imperfect images (*Haer.* 4.6.6). To restore fallen humankind and advance it toward its ultimate goal, Jesus Christ had to be fully human and fully divine. Indeed, Christ recapitulated Adam by being born of the Virgin Mary, as Adam had been created from virgin soil (*Haer.* 3.21.10; *Epid.* 32).[87] The "one race" principle allowed Irenaeus to claim that Christ, the second Adam, recapitulated and redeemed humanity, by assuming the same human nature (*Haer.* 3.12.9; 5.14.2). According to Osborn, recapitulation, for Irenaeus, meant correction, perfection, inauguration, and consummation of restored humankind.[88] Humankind received a new head, the incarnate Son, who redeemed it through his obedient death on the cross and graciously endowed it with his incorruptibility (*Haer.* 3.18.7; 5.16.3).

84. Steenberg, *Irenaeus on Creation*, 168.
85. Steenberg, *Irenaeus on Creation*, 190-92.
86. Steenberg, *Irenaeus on Creation*, 107. Steenberg defends Irenaeus against charges in adoptionism (which seemingly evident in a passage like *Haer.* 3.9.3), by stating that for the incarnate Son to be truly redeemer, he had to manifest full trinitarian involvement at Jesus's baptism along with the Father and the Spirit. Steenberg, *Of God and Man*, 36-37.
87. Steenberg, *Irenaeus on Creation*, 108-10.
88. Osborn, *Irenaeus of Lyons*, chaps. 5-6.

Christ corrected and reconciled the fallen human race in his own sinless human life. As a real man, the Son defeated the devil and liberated fellow-humans from sin and death (*Haer.* 5.21.3; 5.24.4). The immortal God delivered mortal beings from a life of corruption, by uniting with them in the same flesh, conquering death and sharing with them his immortal life as a divine healer (*Haer.* 3.19.1; 3.20.2). Irenaeus used the language of "accustomization" to express the reality of divine-human reciprocity and participation (*Haer.* 3.20.2). Enmity with God that was brought by Adam is gone because the new Adam on the cross reconciled and unified estranged parties (*Haer.* 4.24.1; 5.17.3). Moreover, Christ not only restored and balanced the loss of Eden but also brought immature humanity toward glorious maturity in communion with God (*Haer.* 4.38.1–3; 4.39.2). Therefore, salvation, for Irenaeus, is the actualization of potential and growth toward perfection in Christ. The bishop of Lyons calls Christ's redemptive work on the cross "the remission of our debt" and "healing" (*Haer.* 5.17.2–3). In the introduction to book 5 of *Against Heresies*, Irenaeus wrote, "The word of God, our Lord Jesus Christ, through his immeasurable love, became what we are, that he might bring us to be even what he is himself." In another place, the apologist expands the idea of recapitulation by the Son:

> The Word of God became human and the One who is the Son of God became the Son of Man, united with the Word of God, in order that humankind might receive adoption and become sons of God. For we could not receive incorruptibility and immortality in any other way than by union with incorruptibility and immortality. But how could we have been united with incorruptibility and immortality, if incorruptibility and immortality had not first become what we are, in order that what was corruptible might be swallowed up by incorruptibility, what was mortal might be swallowed up by immortality, and in order that we might receive the adoption of sons? (*Haer.* 3.19.1).

Due to filial relationships with the incarnate Logos, believers can participate in Christ's divine attributes, such as immortality and incorruption. This divine-human exchange reflects Paul's language in 2 Cor 8:9—Christ exchanged his richness for our poverty so that we can become rich—and does not presuppose an essential change in believers because their sonship is based on the grace of adoption, rather than metaphysical upgrade. Through participation in the Son by nature, believers can become sons by adoption (*Haer.* 3.19.1). In Russell's words, recapitulation is an event, whereby Christ "accommodated himself to our infant state so as to enable us to grow and mature until we reach the stage when we can accept God's gratuitous gift of eternal existence, for 'the permanence of incorruption is the glory of the Uncreated'" (*Haer.* 4.38.3).[89] Since heretics rejected Christ's humanity, they have no access to incorruption and immortality available to believers. Thus, Christians, in God's words, "are gods and sons of the Most High," while heretics and those who want to bridge the divine-human gap too quickly, having the same potential with the faithful, "shall die like men" (Ps. 82:6; *Haer.* 4.38.3). The Irenaean approach to the divine-human participation is not a threat to either of the parties, whose natures remain eternally distinct and the gap unbridgeable.[90] Accordingly, "promotion into God" (*Haer.* 3.19.1) will never mean the equality of uncreated and created beings, "but man receives advancement and increase towards God. For as God is always the same, so also man, when found in God, shall always go on towards God. For neither does God at any time cease to confer benefits upon, or to enrich man; nor does man ever cease from receiving the benefits, and being enriched by God" (*Haer.* 4.11.2).

In his stimulating monograph, Ben C. Blackwell points out that Irenaeus emphasized the ontological distinction between the deified and the Deifier. Nonetheless, because of the Logos's incarnation and the indwelling of the Holy Spirit, believers experience communion with God and partake in the life of the Trinity. Blackwell identifies three central soteriological concepts in Irenaeus: the adoption by, the vision of, and union with God that constitute divine-human relationships. Blackwell states,

> Irenaeus commonly mentions that believers participate in life, immortality, and glory, and also more directly in God, Christ or the Spirit. Accordingly, believers do not just share in divine attributes but they share in God himself, particularly through the Spirit. Though participation bespeaks an intimate unity, it also presupposes a type of separation, which for Irenaeus is the separation between Creator and creation. The ultimate expression of union, communion, and participation is becoming like God by means of Christ and the Spirit. Believers partake in life and incorruptibility through the close relationship with God but remain distinct from him.[91]

More precisely, Irenaeus advocated two-way divine-human interaction: God the Father descends to an individual through the Son and the

---

89. Russell, *Doctrine of Deification*, 107.

90. Canlis, "Being Made Human," 444. "Without participation, humanity either must be divinized to the loss of creatureliness, or cease to exist entirely ('lest man, falling away from God altogether, should cease to exist')" (*Haer.* 4.20.7).

91. Blackwell, *Christosis*, 62.

Spirit, while an individual ascends to the Father through the Spirit and the Son (*Haer.* 4.20.5; 5.18.2; 5.36.2-8). Christians possess immortality potentially through baptism when they become gods by adoption, but they need to actualize it through moral progression by their free choice and nourishment in the Eucharist. Union with the Logos gradually recovers the divine likeness in human partakers, whereby they practice their freedom wisely and have access to the immortal life (*Haer.* 3.18.7). The church father presents a trinitarian dimension of this soteriological transformation in the following words, "the Spirit preparing human beings for the Son of God, the Son leading them to the Father, and the Father granting them incorruption and eternal life, which for those who see God results from the vision of him" (*Haer.* 4.20.5). People, being created by "the hands of God" in the beginning, will also be perfected by the same "hands," Son and Spirit, according to God's economic plan of history and human evolution (*Haer.* 5.16.1). Irenaeus was the first who advanced deification as the result of baptism and adoption by God.[92] The Spirit gradually accustoms believers to incorruptible life, to be the full God-bearers (*Haer.* 5.8.1). Obedience to the Spirit and partaking in the Eucharist are essential ways for deification that was initiated at baptism (*Haer.* 4.18.5; 5.11.1).

Incorruption is not natural to humans. Rather, it is inherited by the soul and the body through participation in the life of the Spirit at baptism, and it becomes apparent at their resurrection (*Haer.* 2.34.4; 5.2.3; 5.7.1).[93] Since, for Irenaeus, to be a complete human person means to possess a body, soul, and Spirit, eternal existence after resurrection presupposes restoration of the mortal bodies in union with their spiritual counterpart (*Haer.* 5.2.3; 5.13.3; 5.6.1). In fact, there would have been no point in the Son's incarnation if he did not intend to resurrect human bodies. Therefore, a mortal and corrupted flesh will be swallowed by immortality and incorruptibility of adopted divine sons, who, while in the flesh, will shine with the divine glory (*Haer.* 5.9.4; 5.10.2; 5.13.3-5). Before history ultimately consummates in the eternal reign of the Father, the intermediate earthly reign of the Son will inaugurate the first resurrection of the saints. They will continue to excel in the image of Christ "beyond the angels" and accustomization to the divine nature (*Haer.* 4.11.1; 5.35.1; 5.36.3). Since only God is a pure

---

92. Russell notes that, unlike Justin Martyr, who connected deification with Jewish obedience to the Law, Irenaeus linked deification with Paul's notion of sonship, whereby believers become gods by adoption. Russell, *Doctrine of Deification*, 106.

93. Osborn, *Irenaeus of Lyons*, 137. God's design in creation and perfection of human flesh "is better seen at the end than at the beginning ... man is a developing creature within a process which runs from creation to consummation." Osborn, *Irenaeus of Lyons*, 251-52.

Being, the restored human race will always remain in the state of becoming, transforming into the likeness of the Trinity (*Haer.* 4.11.1–2).[94] God's economy aims to restore not only humankind but also the whole created universe. Therefore, for the bishop of Lyons, Christ's recapitulation must also have physical consummation in the unmediated reign and fellowship of the Creator with his handiwork.

To summarize, the Alexandrians and Evagrius viewed Christ as the perfect example to imitate and the ideal to which believers will conform in eternity beyond their natural capacities, while for Irenaeus, Christ is the person in whom all humanity is restored. The incarnate Word, being the head of the human race, encompasses and heals human weakness. In him, slaves of sin, death, and corruption receive freedom to righteousness, immortality, and incorruption. The Son, being the perfect human archetype, brings imperfect images to the perfect likeness of God, when they share his divinity, and he assumes their humanity. The reciprocal participation of Christ and believers is the Irenaean way to deification that Blackwell, in a fitting way, named *christosis*.[95] For the bishop of Lyons, *christosis* is not something learned through contemplative or ascetic devotion but experienced by faith and obedience to Christ, who confers himself and his gifts to the adopted children of God (*Haer.* 5.36.3). In identification and communion with Christ in baptism and Eucharist, believers partake through the Spirit in the divine attributes of immortality, holiness, and perfection (*Haer.* 5.1.1). It is in Christ that we see a descent of divine to human and an ascent of human to divine accommodated. People were created in the image of Christ, and they reach assimilation to the divine perfection through the second Adam, in whom they become adopted children of God. Thus, I agree with Blackwell that deification, for Irenaeus, is primarily Christocentric.

Cyril of Alexandria (378–444 CE)

Cyril of Alexandria inherited most of his Christology and soteriology from Irenaeus via Athanasius. In christological disputes with Nestorius, Cyril elaborated personal view on orthodox beliefs about the person of Christ and their implications for anthropology, salvation, and worship. Union with the incarnate Son, in the archbishop's mind, facilitated deification by participation in

---

94. Minns, *Irenaeus*, 82–84.

95. Blackwell, *Christosis*, 265–67. Canlis points to the importance of preserving the gift with the giver, saying, "In Christ, we have life, immortality, our humanization, and more. These things are not 'given' by Christ as much as we are incorporated into him." Canlis, "Being Made Human," 451.

the deified flesh of Christ and the Spirit. Christians become adopted sons of God, appropriating by grace what the Son is by nature. This transformation, however, is not merely static or in name only, but also dynamic, in a real exchange of attributes with the Savior and moral restoration. These conclusions Cyril drew from his Christocentric reading of Scriptures.

According to Cyril of Alexandria, every created being originated from the Logos, while human beings also derive from him their intelligence and will. Contrary to Origen, Cyril called soul's pre-incarnate sin "silly nonsense" (*Comm. Jo.* 9:2–3, Pusey, 2.137).[96] Adam was created incorruptible not by nature, but as a gift from God. Being passionless, the first couple contemplated God in constant vision. The human soul, endowed with the divine qualities of incorruptibility, free will, and the Spirit himself, manifested divine likeness. From the beginning, Adam possessed the Spirit and participated in the divine life. After the fall, Adam became weak, mortal, and lost not only the Spirit but also access to grace and incorruptibility.[97] A gradual forfeit of the Spirit by the human race stained and darkened divine image and likeness, but they were not entirely lost (*Comm. Jo.* 1:32–3; Pusey 1.183).[98] By considering the incarnate Word, one can comprehend what the original ideal and goal of human existence were. The restoration of the divine likeness to its initial state became possible due to the incarnation of the divine Logos and reacquisition of the Spirit by redeemed humanity.

For Cyril, this decisive re-appropriation of the Spirit by humankind occurred in the baptism of the second Adam. Christ received the Spirit not for himself, but for those whom he represented and who are called to imitate him in the salvific reception of the Spirit in baptism (*Comm. Jo.* 1:32–3; Pusey 1.184; *Comm. Luc.* 3:21–2; 4:1–2, Reuss, 62–5).[99] To be fully human, in Cyril's logic, is to possess the Holy Spirit. Hence, through participation in their representative and re-joining with the Spirit, the baptized are re-created in their original state and partake in the divine nature. Moreover, Christ is not only the first human after Adam who received the Spirit, but also the one who bestows the Spirit to his disciples (*Comm. Jo.* 20:22–3, Pusey, 3.131–41).

In a traditional patristic manner (with Athanasius and Gregory of Nyssa), the incarnation, the union of divine and human natures, played for Cyril the defining role in the deification of humankind, making it

---

96. Cyril of Alexandria, *Sancti Patris Nostri*.

97. Gross, *Divinization of Christian*, 219–22.

98. Keating, *Appropriation of Divine Life*, 26–27.

99. Cyril of Alexandria, *Lukas-Kommentare*. Keating, *Appropriation of Divine Life*, 34–35; Collins, *Partaking in Divine Nature*, 72.

incorruptible.[100] The deified flesh of Christ, being united with the divine Logos, deifies those who partake of it in eucharistic communion. Cyril's Christology constituted single personal subject in Christ, namely the Word, while retaining the full representation of the human nature as body and soul, with its will and emotions in harmonious cooperation and submission to the Word (*Comm. Jo.* 8, PG 73:703d). To show that the Word indeed united with human nature in an inseparable and unconfused union (ἕνωσις), Cyril often used the term ἴδιος in phrases such as his "own flesh," "own soul," "own blood."[101] To express the ineffable union of the two natures in Christ, he used an analogy of a human person that indivisibly consists of a material body and a spiritual soul (*Ep.* 46, *ACO* 1.1.6, 158.3). Thus, Cyril claimed that after the mystical union and interpenetration of the two natures in Christ, one could not speak of separate actions of the divine Logos and the man Jesus, but only the divine-human acts of the Logos.[102] In contrast to Nestorius, Cyril taught that the distinction of natures in Christ after the incarnation exists "merely in thought" and in "mental intuition" not in reality (*Ep.* 46, *ACO* 1.1.6, 162.1.4f; *Ep.* 40, *ACO* 1.1.4, 27.8–16).[103] Christ could not have saved humanity if he would not be fully human, or if he were merely the embodied Word. The Arian Christ, as a lower created deity, could not be the proper mediator between God and creation and, consequently, a proper savior. The Nestorian Christ, likewise, was a deified person in an external union with the Son. Therefore, he could be only an example of such union to believers, not the redeemer and deifying agent.[104] Hence, for Cyril, Christ is both the one in whom human nature was sanctified and deified as in a human representative and the one who became a model of virtuous life. The archbishop expressed these two roles of Christ in the following words, "that he might sanctify our nature, and that he might be found our pattern and guide for a godly way of life" (*Comm. Jo.* 16:7, Pusey, 2.618). Only in the indissoluble union could the two Christ's natures mutually exchange properties, "communicatio idiomatum" (*Ep.* 3, *ACO* 1.1.1; 27.1.14f.).[105]

---

100. Gross, *Divinization of Christian*, 223–27. As Keating correctly puts it, "The re-creation, sanctification, and divinization of human nature is completed first in Christ himself." Keating, *Appropriation of Divine Life*, 20.

101. Loon, *Dyophysite Christology*, 517–18; Russell, *Cyril of Alexandria*, 26–27.

102. McGuckin, *St. Cyril of Alexandria*, 200.

103. Gebremedhin, *Life-Giving Blessing*, 36; Loon, *Dyophysite Christology*, 531–43.

104. Russell, *Doctrine of Deification*, 199.

105. Gebremedhin, *Life-Giving Blessing*, 40. This concept led Cyril to conclude that Christians worship to the flesh of the incarnate Logos as well as to the Logos himself, because it became an essential part of the one Lord (*Ep.* 17, *ACO* 1.1.1; 37.1.6f). On other theological premises of this concept in Cyril's dispute with Nestorius see

The divine-human exchange of attributes in Christ is the ground for redemption. This exchange is not symmetrical in the sense that believers do not become gods by nature as Christ became a human by nature. Rather, humankind united with the God-incarnate, who enhypostasized the assumed human nature. In Cyril's words,

> But the Son, somehow mingling [ἀνακιρνάς] himself, as it were, with us, bestows upon our nature the dignity which is properly and particularly his own, calling him who begat him "Father" in common with us. And because of his likeness with us, he receives into himself that which belongs to our nature (*Comm. Jo.* 20:17, Pusey, 3.122–3).

Christ, being by nature one with the Father and one with the human race, became the mediator or the "common frontier" (μεθόριον) (*Comm. Jo.* 10:15, Pusey, 2.232–3). Keating remarks that Cyril advocated both the real humanity of the Son, who became "one of us," and the ideal restored humanity of the Son, who became our representative and the firstfruit.[106] The Word's flesh, although superior to human flesh in general, was uniquely united with the Word. Still, it exists in "an external relationship" (σχετικῶς) with the Father, not consubstantially (φυσικῶς) (*Comm. Jo.* 17:22–23, Pusey, 3.2).[107]

Although Cyril followed much of the Athanasian language of deification, he preferred the language of participation in the divine life—although not to the exclusion of the former term—citing 2 Pet 1:4 more than any other church father.[108] In his commentary on John 14:20, Cyril presented the Son's reciprocal participation with created beings:

> And he [Christ] wears our nature, refashioning it to his own Life. And he himself is also in us, for we have all become partakers [μέτοχοι] of him, and have him in ourselves through the Spirit. For this reason we have become "partakers of the divine nature"

McGuckin, *St. Cyril of Alexandria*, 191–92.

106. Keating, *Appropriation of Divine Life*, 49–50.

107. Keating, *Appropriation of Divine Life*, 186–200. Keating states that Cyril upheld both the distinction of Christ's flesh from the rest of human beings and, nonetheless, Christ was a pattern of human existence and deification. Christ was both the "agent and recipient of redemption."

108. Russell, *Doctrine of Deification*, 192–93. Cyril began to avoid deification terminology probably because of Jewish accusations against Christians worshipping a deified man, as well as reaction against Apollinarian and Nestorian Christologies. He preferred Pauline terminology of sonship, co-inheritance with Christ, transformation from glory to glory. Keating, *Appropriation of Divine Life*, 193–96.

(2 Pet. 1:4), and are reckoned as sons, and so too we have in ourselves the Father himself through the Son (Pusey, 2.485–6).

Russell notes two levels of human participation in the divine, "Our participation in God has a twofold aspect, an ontological one in which we are raized from non-existence to createdness, and a dynamic one in which we advance from createdness to transcendence. Our dynamic participation begins when we receive the Spirit in baptism."[109] Hence, creatures participate in the Word's life and light ontologically and in the Word's moral attributes dynamically by faith and personal union with Christ (*Comm. Jo.* 1:9, Pusey, 1.96).

In the Alexandrian's mind, there are two types of divinity: one that is "by nature" and "in reality" versus "by adoption" and "by imitation" (*Comm. Jo.* 1.9, Pusey, 2.230–5). In other words, Cyril distinguished between the "natural union" of human and divine natures in Christ, and human "union by the relationship" with the divine Son. The anti-Arian theologian supposed that in abrogating this distinction one would arrive at blasphemous error because believers cannot claim to be one with the Father as the Son is one with the Father (*Comm. Jo.* 14:11, Pusey, 2.443–4).[110] In *Thesaurus* 4, Cyril discussed the difference between a believer's divine sonship by participation and Christ's divine sonship by nature:

> For we have been adopted through entering into a relationship with God and have been deified by him. For if we are called sons of God through having participated in God by grace, what kind of participation do we attribute to the Word, that he should become Son and God? We are [sons and gods] by participation in the Holy Spirit; to think this of the Son would be absurd (PG 75:45a; cf., 15:284b; 33:569c).[111]

Believers receive divine sonship not only through union with the incarnate Son but also striving to imitate God in the holiness of mind and will (*Comm. Jo.* 8:37, Pusey, 2.72). Christ is the means and pattern of ontological and moral kinship between human and divine agents. This potential kinship with God that was opened to all in the incarnation, however, needs to

---

109. Russell, *Doctrine of Deification*, 191; Macaskill, *Union with Christ*, 69; Keating, *Appropriation of Divine Life*, chap. 4.

110. Keating, *Appropriation of Divine Life*, 180–81. "For Cyril the term κοινωνία does not imply that our own essence (οὐσία) becomes mixed (ἀναμιγνύοντες) with the divine nature; rather, it refers to the likeness of our wills (εἰς τὴν τῶν θελημάτων ὁμοιότητα)."

111. Russell, *Doctrine of Deification*, 194.

be appropriated individually by faith and obedience (*Comm. Jo.* 10:14–15, Pusey, 2.233).

Unlike Irenaeus, who advanced the "physical theory" of deification, i.e., that the Logos's incarnation is the basis for redemption and deification of human nature, Cyril believed that Christ's death is equally essential for deification because it causes the death of our death and the beginning of life. The Alexandrian archbishop, in a biblical way, presented Christ's "saving passion" as redemption, ransom, justification, liberation, etc. (e.g., *Comm. Jo.* 5:3, Pusey, 2.1; *Ep.* 1, *ACO* 1.1.1, 22.24).[112] Cyril, however, was not concerned with reconciling his physical theory of deification with the redemptive necessity of Christ's death.[113] Moreover, as Russell correctly notes, the Cyrillian synthetic accomplishment consisted of combining the "realist theory" of the ontological transformation of human nature through the incarnation and the "ethical theory" of Christ's example.[114] The "partakers of the divine nature" (2 Pet 1:4) are not simply passive recipients of the deifying gifts of Christ, but also active partakers and imitators of Christ's virtuous life because he is a pattern, who accomplished everything for believers "as man" (*Comm. Jo.* 16:33, Pusey, 2.657). Cyril commented on John 17:4-5, "Christ is for us a pattern [τύπος] and beginning [ἀρχή] and image [εἰκών] of the divine way of life [τῆς ἐνθέου πολιτείας], and he displayed clearly how and in what manner it is fitting for us to live" (Pusey, 2.672).[115]

The divine image and likeness in sons of God by grace are restored and perfected not only by participation in the divinity of the Son of God by nature but also by means of sacraments and the practice of free will in choosing the good, growing in righteousness, holiness and other virtues (*Dogm. Sol.* 3-4, Wickham, 192-3).[116] In other words, faith in Christ necessarily leads to spiritual illumination and blameless obedience to God (*Comm. Luc.*

---

112. Loon, *Dyophysite Christology*, 573.

113. Gross, *Divinization of Christian*, 225.

114. Russell, *Doctrine of Deification*, 192.

115. Keating, *Appropriation of Divine Life*, 125-27. As Christ overcame his temptations and sufferings by the power of the Holy Spirit, so he became a model of victory for believers by the same Spirit (*Comm. Jo.* 11:33-4, Pusey, 2.280; 6:38-9, Pusey, 1.487).

116. Cyril of Alexandria, *Cyril of Alexandria*. Russell analyzes Cyril's contribution to Athanasian theology, stating that since in Christ not only the human body is deified but also the soul, it means that the transformation of the will and attainment of virtues is essential for deification. Also for the first time the Eucharist received due emphasis in the process of assimilation to Christ. Russell, *Doctrine of Deification*, 192. See also similar view in Macaskill, *Union with Christ*, 70-71. Keating identifies approximately twenty passages, where Cyril used θεοποιέω and θεοποίησις. Keating, *Appropriation of Divine Life*, 10.

EARLY APPROACHES TO *THEOSIS* 51

18:15-17, Smith, 484).[117] The divine-human relationships aim to restore people into the likeness of the personal God, whereby mortal and sinful beings become incorruptible and holy. Through the grace of baptism, believers unite and partake in Christ. More precisely, Cyril claimed that believers are baptized "into the Holy Trinity itself" because through the salvific rite of baptismal initiation they receive the gift of the Spirit, partake in the incarnate Son and are indwelled by the Father (*Comm. Jo.* 1:12-14a, Pusey, 1.136-137). Hence, the baptismal waters are efficient to purify and sanctify one's body as a requisite for circumcision of the Spirit and participation in the holy flesh of the Son (*Comm. Jo.* 7:24, Pusey, 1.639).[118]

In the Eucharist, one receives Christ's life-giving body that vivifies and sanctifies both body and soul. Cyril commented on John 6:33, "So [Christ] too, through the working of the Spirit [διὰ τῆς τοῦ Πνεύματος ἐνεργείας] gives life to the soul, and not only this, but even maintains the body itself for incorruption [αὐτὸ τὸ σῶμα συνέχων εἰς ἀφθαρσίαν]" (Pusey, 1.458). Since the Word's flesh, which manifests the divine δύναμις and ἐνέργεια, is the bread of life, the Eucharist possesses vivifying virtue for spiritual and somatic spheres of human existence (*Comm. Jo.* 3:6, Pusey, 1.473).[119] For Cyril, Christ is both the food and the agent of spiritual nourishment, who feeds his people through the Holy Spirit and his own flesh. Believers participate in Christ in a twofold manner: in a spiritual way through the Spirit's indwelling and in a physical way by means of partaking in the Word's flesh (*Comm. 1 Cor.* 6:15, Pusey, 3.263-4). The Eucharist is participation and mingling with the deified flesh of the Word that brings healing from corruption and nurtures saints for immortality (*Comm. Jo.* 3:6, Pusey, 1.535). Gebremedhin summarizes it well:

---

117. Cyril of Alexandria, *Commentary upon the Gospel*.

118. Keating, *Appropriation of Divine Life*, 54-63; Russell, *Cyril of Alexandria*, 19-20.

119. Gebremedhin, *Life-Giving Blessing*, 50. Gebremedhin defends the idea that Cyril sided with those church fathers who considered Christ, not the Spirit, as both the host, the consecrator, and the food of the Eucharist. This fact is expressed in Cyril's comments on epiclesis of the Logos during the Lord's Supper in Luke 22:19-20 (PG 72:912a; also in Cyril's *Letter to Tiberius the Deacon*, PG 76:1097bc). Gebremedhin, *Life-Giving Blessing*, 61-70. Gebremedhin thinks that Cyril wanted to preserve Christ's both spiritual and corporeal presence in the Eucharist, and not to divide the incarnate Son in two entities as Nestorius did. Gebremedhin, *Life-Giving Blessing*, 85. In contrast to Gebremendhin, Keating contends that the seemingly Logos-dominated Eucharist in Cyril should not be viewed as an attempt to balance the Spirit-dominated baptism, because the life-giving role of the Spirit is essential in both sacraments. Keating, *Appropriation of Divine Life*, 97-99; McGuckin, *St. Cyril of Alexandria*, 187.

Through the Eucharist the faithful become concorporeal [σύσσωμοι] with Christ. They become partakers of the nature of God through the Holy Ghost. The faithful are mixed [συνανακίρνασθαι] with Christ on a level befitting man. The former union is effected through the Holy Spirit and the latter through the body and blood of Christ. Christ is in the faithful not only by a relation conceived of through a certain disposition alone, but also by a natural participation [μέθεξις φυσική]. Just as melting two pieces of wax by fire results in one thing out of two, so are those who participate in the body and blood of Christ united to Him and He to them.[120]

Since for Cyril participation in the deified nature of Christ is always accompanied with the instrumentality of the Spirit, the "physical theory"—the mechanic transfer of Christ's qualities to the human race—is equipoised by spiritual incorporation. As Adam was supposed to maintain the gift of the Spirit by obedience, so Christians have to abide in the Spirit by voluntary submission to God in righteous living (*Comm. Rom.* 11:22, Pusey, 3.242). In spiritual transformation, Christians transcend their human limitations and share in the incorruptible life of the Trinity while remaining creatures.

The trinitarian character of the divine image in human beings is a distinctive feature of Cyrillian anthropology. According to this father, participation is communion with a personal God, which is accomplished by the Holy Spirit on the ground of the hypostatic union of human and divine natures in Christ.[121] In commenting on John 17:20-21, Cyril wrote, "And the Son is the exact image of the Father, and his Spirit is the natural likeness of the Son. For this reason, molding anew, as it were, into himself the souls of men, he stamps them with the divine form and seals them with the image of the Most High" (Randell, 546).[122] Thus, the deified reflect by participation not only the image and divinity of the Son but also those of the Father. The Alexandrian father continued his commentary by saying that Christians participate in the Son's divine nature by "the transcendent formation [μόρφωσις] of the Holy Spirit"[123] and by taking part the immortal

120. Gebremedhin, *Life-Giving Blessing*, 90. *Comm. Jo.* 11, PG 74:560b; *Glaphyra Gen.* 1, PG 69:29bc; *Comm. Matt.* 26:27, PG 72:452d; *Comm. Jo.* 10, PG 74:341cd.

121. Blackwell, *Christosis*, 106. "Neither Irenaeus nor Cyril seemed concerned with abstract qualities. Rather, they emphasize the personal presence of God as the source of divine attributes within humanity." Keating expresses Cyril's trinitarian framework well, "Cyril's narrative of divine life is not only Christologically centered; it is also pneumatological in execution and trinitarian in shape." Keating, *Appropriation of Divine Life*, 204.

122. Cyril of Alexandria, *Commentary on the Gospel*.

123. Cyril of Alexandria, *Commentary on the Gospel*.

EARLY APPROACHES TO *THEOSIS* 53

Christ shared in the life-changing Eucharist. Earlier in his commentary on John 15:1, he stated:

> For what reason, then, does He call the vinegrower His Father? It is because the Father is neither idle nor inactive with regard to us, while in the Holy Spirit the Son is nourishing us and keeping us in the good. Our restoring is as the work of the entire holy and consubstantial Trinity, and it is through all the divine nature, and in all that is done by it, that the will and the strength pass. For this reason, . . . our salvation is truly the work of the unique Deity. And although to each person seemingly is attributed something of what is done in our regard or carried out in the creature, we do not believe less that all is from the Father by the Son in the Spirit [πάντα ἐστὶ παρὰ τοῦ Πατρὸς δι' Υἱοῦ ἐν Πνεύματι]. Therefore you will be fully in the truth in thinking that the Father nourishes us in piety by the Son in the Spirit. In the same way He functions as the vinegrower, that is to say, He observes, watches over, and takes care of our restoration by the Son in the Spirit (PG 74:333d–336b).

Similarly, Cyril ascribed the deifying role to the Spirit, who transforms partakers of the divinity not ontologically, but ethically. Cyril stated, "[F]or we are justified by faith and are proved to be partakers of the divine nature by participation in the Holy Spirit" (*Comm. Jo.* 14:4, Randell, 239). Participation in the Spirit leads to moral progress and illumination of the soul (*C. Nest.* 3.2, Schwartz, 60.16–20). Indeed, the Spirit's divinity is supported by the fact that saints are deified and called "temples of God" and "gods" by the indwelling of the third person of the Trinity, which would be absurd if the Spirit were not God (*Dial. Trin.* 7.639e–644e).[124] Participation in the Spirit makes possible the partaking in the divine nature of the Son and the Father (*Thes.* 13, PG 75:225c).

Despite his central thesis, Blackwell strikingly concludes, "Thus, Cyril presents a thoroughly Trinitarian presentation of the divine-human interaction, with a strong emphasis upon the work of Christ and the Spirit in deification."[125] Due to the transformative work of the Spirit and personal

---

124. Cyril of Alexandria, *Dialogues sur la Trinité*, 166, 180; Gross, *Divinization of Christian*, 230.

125. Blackwell, *Christosis*, 90. "With regard to participation in the divine nature and 2 Pet 1.4, Cyril uses this to describe both participation in the Trinity and participation in the attributes of the Trinity. He repeatedly writes that participation in the divine nature is a participation in the Spirit, who allows participation in Christ and God. Based on the consubstantial union of the three members of the Trinity, the presence of the Spirit mediates the presence of the other two members. In addition, Cyril also speaks of participating in the attributes of the Trinity, in particular, incorruption, sanctification,

union with the Son, a Christian becomes a son of the Father or even a god not by nature but by grace.

Deification is a continuous process that will be perfected after Christ's second coming when the deified will be full of divine gnosis and light.[126] The exaltation of human nature, however, was already inaugurated in Christ's ascension, whereby Christ as man is seated and reigns with the Father, anticipating the ascension of all humankind to the incorruptible life (*Comm. Jo.* 16:7, Pusey, 2.619). While Christ is enthroned in heaven, he is present with his followers through the life-giving Spirit. In his commentary on John 1:13, Cyril stated:

> Those, he says, who through faith in Christ have been called to the sonship of God, have put off the inferiority of their own nature. Radiant with the grace of him who is honouring them, as if dressed in brilliant white clothing, they advance to a status that transcends nature. For they are no longer called children of the flesh but rather offspring of God by adoption (cf., Rom. 8:14–15; 9:8).[127]

According to Cyril, participation in divine attributes even transcends human nature. The elevated human condition, which Cyril described as "heavenly human beings" and "dignity above our nature," appropriates Christ's natural qualities by the grace of adoption as far as it is possible for human nature (*Comm. Jo.* 17:20–1, Pusey, 2.737; 12:26, Pusey, 2.314). Nonetheless, the "transcendence of nature" in the afterlife, as Evagrius perceived it, for Cyril, did not mean the abrogation of human createdness, body, and nature as such.[128] Rather, it is an ability to partake of the life and virtues of the Uncreated (*Comm. Jo.* 1:13, Pusey, 1.105). There is no point in the Son's incarnation and resurrection if the human bodies will not be resurrected and remain corruptible.

After comparing Irenaeus's and Cyril's soteriology with Paul's soteriology, Blackwell prefers the term *christosis*, rather than *theosis*, for the description of the apostle's teaching about salvation, "However, while deification, or theosis, can generally serve as a helpful description of Paul's soteriology, perhaps *christosis* is a better term to describe Paul's specific soteriological emphasis."[129] Indeed, Cyrillian soteriology with strong christological lenses

---

and sonship."

126. Gross, *Divinization of Christian*, 233.

127. Cited in Russell, *Cyril of Alexandria*, 101.

128. On the importance of Cyril's eschatology for his christology and anthropology see O'Keefe, "Incorruption, Anti-Origenism, and Incarnation."

129. Blackwell, *Christosis*, 264.

can appropriately be defined as *christosis*. However, as Blackwell himself acknowledges, a trinitarian dimension in Cyril's soteriology can be appropriated through *triadosis* that was prominent in the Cappadocian fathers, to whom we now turn.

Triadosis

The majority of patristic scholars consider the Cappadocians—the two brothers, Basil of Caesarea and Gregory of Nyssa, together with their friend, Gregory of Nazianzus—as the most influential trinitarian theologians of the fourth century. All three were highly indebted to Origen's exegetical methodologies and theological formulations, bringing their synthesis in the midst of christological and pneumatological debates of the period.[130] Despite God's incomprehensibility and ontological distinction between created and uncreated, the Cappadocians believed that divine-human communion is possible because of kinship with Christ and the work of the Holy Spirit.[131] The idea of the Father's monarchy became the basis for the Cappadocians to argue for natural equality and personal distinction within the Trinity.[132] Soteriological questions, such as trinitarian baptism[133] and the deifying role of the Son and the Spirit, were central in their doctrinal elaboration on the Trinity. Gregory of Nazianzus's statement "the unassumed is unhealed" (*Ep.* 101.7) became the basic formula for subsequent christological explorations. Nevertheless, the Cappadocians diverged from each other on a number of points and emphases, e.g., the duality and unity of Christ, the interrelationship of persons within the Trinity, as well as the Spirit's role in creation and deification.[134] Likewise, the degree to which the soul is capable of contemplating the source of all existence, namely God (whereby a human being receives incorruptible existence together with the transformation of the body into a spiritual one), is differently nuanced by each of the Cappadocians. Hence, each father had a distinct theological impact, which has to be studied in its own right.

130. Beeley, *Gregory of Nazianzus*, 293.

131. Macaskill, *Union with Christ*, 72.

132. Gregory of Nyssa, contrary to Basil and the other Gregory, emphasized the Platonic priority of the divine essence over hypostases, thus reducing the significance of the Father's monarchy. Beeley, *Gregory of Nazianzus*, 307–8.

133. On the Cappadocians's treatment of baptism see Ferguson, "Exhortations to Baptism."

134. Beeley, *Gregory of Nazianzus*, 296–99.

Basil of Caesarea (330–379 CE)

Basil of Caesarea was one of the prominent defenders of orthodoxy against Arianism before its official triumph at the Council of Constantinople in 381.[135] His remarkable education and ascetical efforts in earlier periods stimulated Basil's theology and church leadership as a bishop. As is often the case, precise terminology played a crucial role in the theological debates, in which he was involved. As will be seen below, Basil did not resolve all the trinitarian conundrums, but he laid the ground for later creedal formulations.

The trinitarian views, as well as their terminology, evolved through several stages in the life of the bishop of Caesarea. As Hildebrand notes, over two decades during his tenure as bishop and scholar Basil progressed to distinctly pro-Nicene definitions, from ὁμοιούσιος to ὁμοούσιος and from πρόσωπον to ὑπόστασις.[136] To avoid the Sabellian identification of the Father with the Son, the Cappadocian initially rejected ὁμοούσιος as a term that confuses personal distinctions between them (*Ep.* 361).[137] In his *Against Eunomius*, written around 364, the bishop of Caesarea still preferred ὁμοιούσιος terminology, defending the unknowability of one divine οὐσία and the essential equality of the Son with the Father against the Eunomian subordinationism. The fundamental distinction between Eunomius and Basil consisted in the epistemological question of knowing God in his essence. Basil, in contrast to Eunomius, wanted to preserve the unknowability of God's essence and, at the same time, some way of knowing God through his attributes or "activities" (ἐνέργειαι).[138] The Cappadocian wrote, "The activities are various, the essence simple. But we ourselves say that we know our God from the activities, but do not venture to draw near to the essence itself. For his activities come down to us, but his essence remains unapproachable" (*Ep.* 234.1).[139] The diversity of names or concepts (ἐπίνοια), such as life, light, and goodness, that theologians assign to the nature of God do not distort its simplicity, because these concepts, for Basil, are exclusively mental realities and do not correspond to different aspects of God.[140] At this stage, Basil did not yet identify the trinitarian persons

---

135. For a detailed biography of Basil see Rousseau, *Basil of Caesarea*.
136. Hildebrand, *Trinitarian Theology*, 31; Turcescu, "Prosōpon and Hypostasis."
137. Basil of Caesarea, *Basil*.
138. Radde-Gallwitz, *Basil of Caesarea*, 124.
139. Cited in Torrance, "Precedents for Palamas' Essence-Energies," 54.
140. Radde-Gallwitz, *Basil of Caesarea*, 153.

EARLY APPROACHES TO *THEOSIS* 57

with a technical term *hypostasis*.[141] Rather, he spoke about distinct properties (ἰδιώματα) peculiar to the Father and the Son—such as unbegotten and begotten—within the one Godhead (*Con. Eun.* 2.28; *Ep.* 214.4).[142] The Father can be known only through his image, who is the Son. Therefore, the Son always existed and shared the same divinity, because "like is naturally known by like" (*Con. Eun.* 1.17). The Father and the Son, being identified in essence, also share the same power and activity, because power belongs to nature (*Con. Eun.* 1.23; 2.32). To explain the Father's superiority in Jesus's saying that "the Father is greater than I" (John 14:28), Basil introduced the idea of causal superiority, i.e., the *monarchia* of the Father, not substantial superiority (*Con. Eun.* 1.25).[143] He determined the necessity of the Father's monarchy language by the fact that uncaused hypostatic equality within the Trinity would require the language of triplet brothers or tritheism, rather than Father, Son, and Spirit. Around 375, Basil hammered out more consistent definitions of οὐσία and φύσις, ὑπόστασις and πρόσωπον—though not entirely rigid definitions—that later became the key terminology for creedal statements about unity and plurality within the Trinity.

Naming people "gods" in the Scriptures (John 10:34-35), was traditionally interpreted by fathers as the deification of believers. Since *theosis* is a process accomplished by the Spirit, Basil affirmed it as an argument for the divinity of the Spirit. The third person of the Trinity has to be God to deify virtuous believers (*Con. Eun.* 2.4; 3.5). Through the Spirit's efficacy, the soul is restored beyond its primal beauty of the likeness to God, so that a person becomes a god (θεὸν γενέσθαι) (*De Sp. S.* 9.23).[144] The Holy Spirit applied Christ's redemption to believers, infusing his grace into the deified.

141. Indeed, Turcescu groups Basil's usage of ὑπόστασις in *Against Eunomius* under four main headings: substance, subsistence, substratum, and person. Turcescu, "*Prosōpon* and *Hypostasis*," 377.

142. Hildebrand, *Trinitarian Theology*, 65. In fact, in *Against Eunomius*, Basil used οὐσία and ὑπόστασις interchangeably. The plurality in God is expressed by means of "unbegotten and begotten *ousia*." Hildebrand, *Trinitarian Theology*, 75. *Epistle* 9 bears witness to a gradual change in Basil's language by the preference of *homoousios*, but even after the full endorsement of the Nicene term, he continued occasionally to use *homoios*. Finally, the distinction between οὐσία and ὑπόστασις clearly appeared in Basil's attempt to combat the Marcellian heresy (the Sabellians of his day) that confused the divine essence and persons (*Ep.* 125). Hildebrand, *Trinitarian Theology*, 80–85.

143. Awad contends that the idea of the Father's monarchy as the source of Godhead introduced by Basil is flawed and inconsistent with other Cappadocians, being "patrocentrically semi-hierarchical." Instead, Awad argues, Gregory of Nazianzus presented a more balanced approach to the Trinity *ad intra*, which is the Father's monarchy as the cause of the Son's and the Spirit's hypostases. Awad calls this approach "reciprocally koinonial" by nature. Awad, "Between Subordination and Koinonia."

144. Russell, *Doctrine of Deification*, 209.

58   TRIADOSIS: UNION WITH THE TRIUNE GOD

The Spirit, being present in the soul, deifies it into the divine likeness, as iron in fire receives some of the fire's qualities.

Only occasionally, Basil used θεοποιέω and θεοί in respect of Christians in his writings.[145] Becoming a god, however, would presuppose no ontological change on the part of Christians lest they become consubstantial with God (*Con. Eun.* 2.4; 3.5). Instead, their "divinity" was analogous to the deified human nature of Christ. Unlike Athanasius, who associated deification with adoption by God in baptism, and Gregory of Nazianzus, who assumed that believers participate in the life of the Trinity through the Spirit,[146] Basil correlated deification with perfection in virtuous life and participation in God's holiness. For the bishop of Caesarea, the continuous contemplation of God and union with him in love is the goal of human existence before and after the fall. According to Basil, the main objective of ascetic aspirations is to attain likeness to God as far as it is possible for a human being. Also, it means to participate in the Spirit's holiness, to imitate Christ's virtues, and to glorify God (*Reg. fus. tract.* 20.2; 43.1; *De Sp. S.* 1.2; *Con. Eun.* 3.2).[147] Hence, Russell thinks that in Basil, unlike in Plotinus, the soul does not recover its former divinity, but receives qualities beyond its original capacities through illumination by the Spirit.[148] The highest point of deification that can begin even in this life is the vision of God, through mingling with the divine Spirit according to human capacity (*Ep.* 233.1). One can "taste" God, who is in heaven, by means of the Eucharist (*Hom. in Ps.* 33.6). Such partaking, however, is a mere foretaste before the final deification of the soul and body after the resurrection (*Ep.* 233.1).

Gregory of Nyssa (ca. 330–395 CE)

Gregory of Nyssa, also known as Gregory Nyssen, was instructed and inspired by his brother Basil in theological thinking. Unlike his older brother, he never pursued a monastic life and was reluctantly appointed as a bishop in Nyssa.[149] Gregory did, however, greatly succeed as a rhetorician and

145. Russell, *Doctrine of Deification*, 208.

146. The lack of clear confirmation of the Spirit's full divinity leads Beeley to conclude that Basil's pneumatology was not much different from the unorthodox position of Eusebius of Caesarea. While Gregory of Nyssa's pneumatology is stronger than that of Basil, it is still less developed, as in Gregory of Nazianzus. Beeley, *Gregory of Nazianzus*, 300, 305. I find this judgment unconvincing in light of those passages, where Basil discussed the deifying role of the Spirit (*Con. Eun.* 2.4; 3.5).

147. Russell, *Doctrine of Deification*, 211.

148. Russell, *Doctrine of Deification*, 210.

149. For an excellent biography of Gregory see Meredith, *Gregory of Nyssa*.

promoter of the orthodox faith at the Council of Constantinople in 381 as well as a defender of the Spirit's full divinity, employing philosophical ideas contrary to Basil's suspicion of philosophy.

Undoubtedly, Gregory of Nyssa, like the other two Cappadocians, developed what Lewis Ayres called the pro-Nicene "grammar" of trinitarian ontology and personhood.[150] To explain the simplicity of God's nature and the multiplicity of persons, Gregory adopted Plotinus's idea of the coexistence of cause and things caused by it. He wrote, "That is indeed why the one as cause of its [two] causeds we say is one God; since indeed it co-exists with them" (*Ad Graec.*, GNO 3.1.25.6-8).[151] In his *To Ablabius: On not Three Gods*, Gregory discussed the ontological relationships (σχέσις) within the Trinity, whereby the uncaused Father is the immediate cause of the Son and mediate cause of the Spirit (GNO 3.1.55-56).[152] In the letter *To Those Who Discredit His Orthodoxy*, Gregory expressed his belief in the Father's monarchy:

> But as many as *walk by the rule* of truth (cf., Gal 6.16, Phil 3.16) and piously acknowledge the three *hypostases* in their distinct properties, and believe that there is one Godhead, one goodness, one principle (μίαν ἀρχήν), one authority and power (cf., 1 Cor 15.24), and thus neither set aside the sovereignty of the *monarchy*, nor fall away into polytheism, nor confuse the *hypostases*, nor synthesize the Holy Trinity from heterogeneous and dissimilar elements, but receive in simplicity the dogma of the faith, placing all *their hope of salvation* (1 Thess 5.8) in *Father, Son and Holy Spirit* (Mt 28.19)—these in our judgment are of the same mind with us, with whom we also pray to have part in the Lord (cf., Jn 13.8) (*Ep.* 5.9).[153]

Nyssen argued for the indivisibility of nature in general with its intrinsic power. Hence, the acts of individual divine hypostases do not imply three Gods, but one, because these hypostases share in the same divine nature and power. Since God's nature is incomprehensible, one cannot define it by a list of attributes. These conceptions (ἐπίνοια) would explain something one perceives about the divine nature, but not what this nature really is.[154] Similar to Plotinus (*Ennead* 5.1), Gregory utilized the ideas of

---

150. Ayres, "On Not Three People."

151. Gregory of Nyssa, *GNO*. Cited in Corrigan, *Evagrius and Gregory*, 135.

152. As Maspero indicates, Gregory followed the traditional ἐκ—διά—ἐν scheme to represent the monarchy of the Father. Maspero, "Ad Ablabium," 5.

153. Gregory of Nyssa and Silvas, *Gregory of Nyssa*, 139 (emphasis original).

154. Ayres, "On Not Three People," 26.

power (δύναμις) and activities or operations (ἐνεργείαι) that surround God's nature, making it manifested and, at the same time, unknown to observers.[155] Gregory insisted that different operations come from separate causes, but these causes constitute different powers (δύναμις), not οὐσία, as Eunomius argued.[156] Therefore, God's diversity of power and operations does not fracture his essential unity, as, for example, the diversity of operations does not fracture a single mind. Moreover, Father, Son, and Holy Spirit participate in one divine act and not as three distinct agents, co-operating towards a single goal. Similarly, in his *Against Eunomius III*, the Cappadocian affirmed that the community of will (ἡ κοινωνία τοῦ θελήματος) of the Father through the Son in the Spirit indicates independent psychological existences in the Trinity and at the same time the unity of the divine essence (τῆς οὐσίας ἑνότητα) (GNO 2.403.4–7; NPNF 5.132).[157] This concept makes Gregory's model of divine personhood distinct from that of human personhood, wherein the co-operation of individual human persons, who share the same nature, constitutes distinct actions, not one. In *To Ablabius*, Gregory stated, "The Father is God: the Son is God: and yet, by the same proclamation God is One, because no difference either of nature or of operation is contemplated in the Godhead" (GNO 3.1.55; NPNF 5.336). Thus, as long as there is only one power and activity that operate in the three divine persons, one should conclude that the three persons constitute the same undivided nature of Godhead.

During the anti-Arian christological controversy, Gregory painstakingly defended Christ's natural equality with the Father. As Ramelli convincingly elaborates, Gregory's arguments against Arianism were much in line with Origen's anti-subordinationism.[158] Gregory, likewise, championed the full humanity of Christ, including the human mind, against Apollinarius, who considered the νοῦς sinful and, thus, inappropriately ascribed to Christ (*Antirrh.* 7; GNO 3.1.141). Gregory exposed himself to criticism in the pantheistic dissolution of Christ's human nature, which was "absorbed by the omnipotent divinity like a drop of vinegar mingled in the boundless sea" (*Antirrh.* 42; GNO 3.1.201; *Ad Theoph. adv. Apoll.*; GNO 3.1.126; *Con. Eun.* 3.4; GNO 2.150). His desire to win Apollinarians's favor, however, is

155. Ayres, "On Not Three People," 28.

156. Barnes, "Divine Unity and Divided Self," 51.

157. Schaff, *Nicene and Post-Nicene.*

158. That is especially evident in Gregory's *In Illud: Tunc et Ipse Filius*, where he interpreted 1 Cor 15:28 as the submission of the human nature of Christ to the Father in usual Origenist way. "Origen already used the Cappadocian formula μία οὐσία, τρεῖς ὑποστάσεις, and the adjective ὁμοούσιος in reference to the Son in respect to the Father." Ramelli, "Origen's Anti-Subordinationism."

balanced by later writings, where the bishop of Nyssa preserved not just the human body of Jesus, but also the human mind and will, "If (Jesus) is endowed with a soul, but not with a mind, how is he human? For a human being is not an animal without intelligence" (*Ep.* 101.34; *Antirrh.* 23, 31). Notwithstanding the fact that Gregory utilized the controversial language of "mixing" and "mingling" (μίξις, κρᾶσις) to describe the union (ἕνωσις) of the Logos with human nature, for the church father, these terms always presumed relationships (σχέσις) and, hence, the natural and numerical distinction of the natures.[159]

Since, for Gregory of Nyssa, the idea of simplicity and uniformity is the ideal way of existence that characterizes God's being, he presented a hypothesis that God in his thought created humankind without sexual distinction, and its propagation would have been in an angelic manner (*De Op. Hom.* 16–17).[160] However, in reality, God created the first couple sexed, because the Creator foresaw their fall and the misuse of freedom. Mind, reason, and free will as well as other divine perfections—that belong to God essentially (ὄντως) and to humans as gifts—constitute the divine image (*De Op. Hom.* 4, 12).[161] The ever-increasing receptive capacity to accommodate God's perfections constitutes the likeness of God in humankind (*Anim. et Res.*; PG 46:105a–b). Gregory believed in the original immortality of the soul and body and impassibility of Adam (*Or. Cat.* 5).[162] Although the first couple possessed divine characteristics, these were not their natural qualities, but received and, thus, came from alteration, unlike the unchangeable divine nature. Humanity killed their deiform state in an attempt to change and sinned against God (*Or. Cat.* 6; *Cant.* 8).[163] Although humankind has lost incorruptibility and impassibility, the attributes of the image, like intelligence and freedom, are marred, but not lost (*De Virg.* 12).

This restoration was made possible through the Son's incarnation, "[God] mingled with our nature in order that, by virtue of its mingling with the divine, our nature might become divine" (*Or. Cat.* 25). The transformation of the human nature in Christ is the basis for the deification of all humankind, whereby human changeability, mortality, and corruption are continuously changing into the unchangeable, immortal, and incorruptible *idiomatum* of

---

159. Daley, "Divine Transcendence," 71–72.
160. Gross, *Divinization of the Christian*, 177.
161. Gross, *Divinization of the Christian*, 178–79; Balás, Μετουσία Θεοῦ, 142.
162. Gross, *Divinization of the Christian*, 179–80; Gregory of Nyssa, *Catechetical Oration*.
163. Gross, *Divinization of the Christian*, 181.

the Son.[164] Gregory of Nyssa stated that the "blending" of Christ's natures humanized his divine nature and divinized his human nature. He allegorized Christ as both sheep and Shepherd, "[the Word] received into himself all our nature, so that through the blending with divinity that which is human would be co-divinized (συναποθεωθῇ), and with this beginning the whole composite of our being would be co-sanctified (συναγιαζομένου)" (*Antirrh.* 15; GNO 3.1.151; *Antirrh.* 16).[165] Gross concluded that Christ, according to Gregory, assumed humanity to deify it:

> It also seems quite incontestable that this realism is at the root of his physical theory of deification, which served the saint both in affirming the individuality of the human nature of Christ and in maintaining that, in His incarnation, the Logos assumed *the* human nature, the entire humanity, deifying it through this assumption.[166]

Russell, however, disagrees with Gross. Russell argues that participation in God, for Gregory, is the imitation of the divine attributes. Hence, Russell writes,

> Gregory of Nyssa appears to have been wary of the slightest tendency to compromise the utter transcendence and unknowability of God by the use of the terminology of deification. For him the terminology of participation provides an alternative means of expressing our ever deepening relationship with God through union with his energies, while his nature or essence remains totally beyond our comprehension.[167]

According to Russell, the bishop of Nyssa believed the deification of human nature occurs not through the incarnation of Christ in a Platonic mechanic way, but through faith, repentance and participation in the sacraments.[168] I contend that Gregory's soteriology should be read in a synthetic way, i.e., the sacraments and faith are the means of appropriation and

---

164. According to Russell, Gregory rarely used "theosis" terminology with respect to the deification of Christ's human nature and the divine transformation of a human person. Unlike Gregory of Nazianzus, Gregory of Nyssa used θεοποιέω only twice as well as twice συναποθεόω. The reason for avoiding this terminology, according to Russell, might have been the misuse of it by Apollinarius, who taught the deified body of Christ. Russell, *Doctrine of Deification*, 226, 230.

165. Bouteneff, "Soteriological Imagery," 82–83.

166. Gross, *Divinization of the Christian*, 184 (emphasis original).

167. Russell, *Doctrine of Deification*, 232.

168. Russell, *Doctrine of Deification*, 230.

participation in the deified humanity of Christ.[169] Hence, deification is not automatic, but still real participation in the Son. Gregory wrote, "After being stripped of themselves [in baptism], they put on the divine nature [τὴν θείαν ἐπενδύεται φύσιν]" (Con. Eun. 3; PG 45:609a).[170] Here the theologian stated that deification is not a mere moral transformation, but sharing in Christ's divinity. Believers can transcend their nature by becoming the sons of God through the deifying gift of baptism, rather than through their philosophical or ascetical aspirations, not to the exclusion of the latter. In the same manner, by partaking of the Eucharist, one partakes in the immortal body of God that transforms one's body according to the divine-like body of Christ (Or. Cat. 35, 37). When the participants of the Eucharist are mingled with the immortal and incorruptible humanity of Christ, they become the immortal and incorruptible partakers of the deifying incarnation of the Lord (Or. Cat. 35). Thus, through baptism and the Eucharist, both soul and body are deified and immortalized correspondingly.

For Gregory of Nyssa, the concept of the soul's proper desire for God and non-attachment to visible things plays a significant role in a deifying ascent toward the Creator.[171] In the bishop's view, the problem is not with desire as such, which is a part of the human constitution, but with its inclinations toward lower things. Thus, desires need not be extinguished for the sake of rational deification but instead purified and reoriented through ascetic practices. *Apatheia* is the unrestricted proclivity of mind and heart to God and not a desire-less state of being. Laird called it "a noetic-erotic movement toward God."[172] In commenting on the *Song of Songs* 6, Gregory linked the image of marriage with the unintelligible union of the human mind with the ineffable Bridegroom, who abides in the divine darkness (γνόφος). A process, which starts with images in mind and passionate desire for God and then leads toward an imageless and dispassionate contemplation of God in the Holy of Holies, describes the paradoxical nature of this union.[173]

Gregory likened the soul's contemplation to Moses's mystical experience of the divine darkness, "Moses' vision of God began with light;

169. Balás assumes that "in virtue of the ontological solidarity of the human nature, we all have been saved, at least potentially and virtually." Balás, Μετουσία Θεοῦ, 150.

170. Cited in Gross, *Divinization of the Christian*, 185.

171. Laird, "Under Solomon's Tutelage," 78.

172. Laird, "Under Solomon's Tutelage," 79.

173. Laird, "Under Solomon's Tutelage," 84. Laird expresses the paradox well, "Abandoning everything she [the bride/soul] has comprehended, she finds her Beloved, not by the grasp of comprehension but by the ungrasping grasp of faith." Laird, "Under Solomon's Tutelage," 88.

afterwards God conversed with him in a cloud. Then, becoming higher and more perfect, he saw God in darkness" (*Cant.* 11; GNO 6.322). In fact, "the luminous darkness" is the inalienable context of God's invisible presence, in which the mind unites with the incomprehensible and penetrates the impenetrable (*V. Mos.* 1.46.4–5; 2.162.1; 2.163.9–13).[174] The divine darkness, as Laird convincingly argued, is not an expression of God's absence, but an epistemological claim about God's fundamental incomprehensibility to the mind and accessibility to faith: the soul experiences "a sense of presence" (*Cant.* 11; GNO 6.324.10–11).[175] Along with the theme of darkness, Gregory discussed the subject of the divine light that precedes entering into God's darkness and follows it as the ever-increasing light that divinizes one's virtues (*Cant.* 11; GNO 6.322.9; *V. Mos.* 2.162). The ancient Greek thought, i.e., like knows like, is displayed in Moses's mystical transfiguration into the likeness of God so that he became invisible like the object of his contemplation (*V. Mos.* 1.46.6–10). The mind is passive in the presence of God, and cognitive capacities are transcended in the darkness of unknowing. Nevertheless, it is not completely bypassed, but engages in knowing something about God, is indwelled by God, and "bedewed with insights" (*Cant.* 11; GNO 6.325–326).

Since intellectual attempts to behold the divine essence are unachievable, it is faith that comes to aid and grasps the Beloved in the unconfused union of the infinite God and a finite creature.[176] Faith, however, is not merely an apophatic ascent and union with the Word, but also a way of transferring some of the divine knowledge to the mind, making the person the Word's mouthpiece to people around (*Cant.* 1, 3; GNO 6.32.9–33; 6.91.7–92).[177] Gregory's *Homilies on the Song of Songs* 4, 12, 13 used another trinitarian image to present the oxymoronic character of the human experience of God. The archer (the loving God) shoots an arrow (the Son), moistened in the Spirit, into the soul. The soul wounded by love, however, experiences an ecstatic joy and incomprehensible boasting from this beautiful and healing blow from God. Further, the wounded bride herself becomes an arrow in the loving arms of the Bridegroom, ready to be shot forth from the bow. This image of intimate union between the bride and the Bridegroom reveals the personal aspect of mystical union with personal God.[178]

174. Laird, *Gregory of Nyssa*, 49.
175. Laird, *Gregory of Nyssa*, 198.
176. Laird, *Gregory of Nyssa*, chap. 3.
177. According to Laird, Gregory's *apophasis* is accompanied by *logophasis*. Laird, *Gregory of Nyssa*, 170–71.
178. This is contrary to Balás, who claims this aspect is not prominent in Gregory. Balás, Μετουσία Θεοῦ, 159–60.

Despite Plotinus's influence, Gregory rejected the absorption of the human identity into God. When the Cappadocian applied the term "god" to people, it was always in an analogical sense, as Moses was a god to Pharaoh (*V. Mos.* 2.35). Gregory's language of "mingling" and "fusion" notwithstanding, the human nature is not absorbed or dissolved in the divine but acquires additional qualities. The gradual progress of the soul toward God is infinite because of God's ultimate transcendence (*V. Mos.* 1.7–8). Similarly, God granted Moses the vision of the Beauty to satisfy his desire, but not to the extent that Moses would cease to long for more vision (*V. Mos.* 2.231–3).

The τέλος of the purified soul is to go beyond contemplation into the presence of God. In the ecstatic vision, the soul contemplates God's ineffable beauty without passions or even reason, being deified as much as it is possible for creatures. After the resurrection, asexual and perfect bodies will gain honor, glory, and other divine qualities. Thus, saints will return to their original simplicity. In *On the Soul and the Resurrection*, Gregory described deification as the union of love and transfiguration:

> So when the soul has become simple, uniform and exactly godlike, it finds the truly simple and immaterial good, that which alone is really worthy of love and desire, and attaches itself to it and mingles with it through the motion and activity of love, conforming itself to that which is always being grasped and found" (*Anim. et Res.*; PG 46:93c).[179]

The soul ascents in four stages: 1) purification from passions in the divine light, 2) the contemplation of intelligible things in the cloud, 3) in darkness, the soul becomes the mirror of divine perfection,[180] and 4) the ever-growing grasp of the Trinity in the Spirit's illumination throughout eternity. Deification, for Gregory of Nyssa, is a process that is based on the dynamic relationships between virtuous life and the experiential knowledge of the Trinity that comes through faith.

Gregory of Nazianzus (ca. 329–390 CE)

Gregory of Nazianzus, also known as "the Theologian," was a friend of Basil and Gregory of Nyssa. He attained a brilliant education in philosophy and rhetoric, which he used as archbishop of Constantinople and later as bishop of Nazianzus. Gregory's main concern was the divinity of the Son and the Spirit because that was the ground for their deifying activity (*Or.*

---

179. Translated by Radde-Gallwitz, *Basil of Caesarea*, 220.
180. Russell, *Doctrine of Deification*, 231.

31.4; 34.12). Thus, soteriology became the starting point and driving force for his Christology and pneumatology. Arguably, Gregory of Nazianzus surpassed his friends in a clear and consistent presentation of the Trinity and deification. Despite this fact, he rarely employed the traditional language of participation, incorporation into Christ, adoption, and did not quote 2 Pet 1:4. The most frequent verb he used for deification was θεόω, the noun θέωσις (the term not mentioned by any extant Christian writing before Gregory and later espoused by Dionysius the Areopagite and Maximus the Confessor), and the adjective θεοποιός.[181]

Gregory believed in the divine origin and intellectual affinity of the reasonable soul to the divine Mind, even "a divine emanation" in poetic terms (*Carm.* 34.27).[182] Human beings were created with the prospect of growing into the likeness of God so that deification is effectively a natural condition of human life. Adam, being a mature "seer" in the world of created things, was still a novice in the world of intelligible things designated by "the tree of knowledge." He would have become a "seer" of divine things (θεωρία) if he passed the test. Due to the fall, people turned away from the upward movement to God, precluding their eschatological fulfillment in joining with their Creator (*Or.* 38.12).

The purpose of the Logos's incarnation was to redeem humanity. One needs to understand Christ's identity in the context of the complete salvific narrative, namely, his incarnation, redemptive death, and resurrection. In addition, one needs to read Gregory's emphasis on the full divinity of Christ in light of his anti-Arian and anti-Eunomian apologetics. In contrast to Apollinarius, Gregory confirmed that to heal the human race Christ assumed real human flesh, will, and *nous*, and at the same time was the fully divine Son (*Ep.* 101.32, 50–55). Nazianzen stated, "What He was He laid aside; what He was not He assumed; not that He became two, but He deigned to be One made out of the two. For both are God, that which assumed, and that which was assumed; two Natures meeting in One, not two Sons (let us not give a false account of the blending (σύγκρασις)" (*Or.* 37.2).[183] Hence, after the union of two natures, Christ is a single being, the Son of God in human flesh, preserving his full divine and human capacities. Gregory ascribed the divine and human attributes of Christ to the same incarnate Logos, not to his corresponding natures.

---

181. Russell, *Doctrine of Deification*, 214–15; Beeley, *Gregory of Nazianzus*, 117; Collins, *Partaking in Divine Nature*, 67.

182. Gross, *Divinization of Christian*, 194.

183. Cyril of Jerusalem and Nazianzen, *Cyril of Jerusalem*.

The deification of humanity would not be possible without this two natures union of Christ, wherein the eternal God condescended in a self-humiliating act to take on himself the infirmity of our bodily existence, retaining his natural equality with the Father (*Or.* 37.3; 38.13). The Cappadocian held a view that Christ's incarnation and redemptive death are equally necessary for human salvation. In Jesus's death, Satan and death are defeated, so that believers are "saved by the sufferings of the impassable one" (*Or.* 30.5; 39.13; *Carm.* 1.1.10.6-9). Human salvation and deification require God incarnated and God crucified (*Or.* 45.28-29). Deification achieved by Christ in his own flesh does not automatically imply the *theosis* of every particular human being. Instead, it became the ground for the divine-human union and transformation of believers into godlikeness through participation in Christ's saving life, death, and resurrection (*Or.* 38.4, 18). This participation includes recognition and meditation on the genuine identity of Christ, the God-man. Gregory of Nazianzus boldly stated, "recognize that you have become a son of God, fellow heir with Christ, if I may be so bold, even very God" (*Or.* 14.23). The mutual intermingling of divine and human natures in Christ allows for a similar change in people, into gods by grace, who become like God and wholly filled by God (*Or.* 29.19; 30.3-6). Thus, Christ is both deified as a man and deifier as the Logos.

Likewise, the Holy Spirit, who by grace deifies a person, should be fully God. Unlike Basil of Caesarea and Gregory of Nyssa, who gradually arrived at a conclusion on the full divinity of the Spirit, Gregory, from the time of his episcopal appointment in Nazianzus in 372, preached the equal divinity of the Spirit along with the Father and the Son.[184] Gregory placed the Spirit on the divine side of the Creator-creation ontological divide and anathematized those who proclaim the Spirit to be a creature and servant (*Or.* 34.8; 41.6). The Holy Spirit is consubstantial with the Father and the Son, but, unlike them, is neither unbegotten nor begotten. The Spirit is not deified like Christ but shares the deifying activity with the Son (*Or.* 41.9-14). To defend the divinity of the Spirit, Gregory utilized the idea of the progressive revelation of the Trinity in salvation history. Starting from the Father in the Old Testament, the revelation expanded through the Son's salvific ministry in the New Testament and consummated with the descent and indwelling of the Spirit in the apostles (*Or.* 31.26-27). Further, the regenerating and deifying activity of the Spirit in baptism is the sure proof of divinity, because only God can accomplish both (*Or.* 33.17; 34.12; 39.17; 41.9; *Carm.* 1.1.3.1-4). Also, if the Spirit receives equal honor and worship

---

184. On Gregory's complaint about Basil's depreciation of the Spirit, see *Ep.* 58.7. Beeley, *Gregory of Nazianzus*, 156-58, 167, 198. See also discussion in Kelly, *Early Christian Doctrines*, 260-61.

with the Father and the Son, "how is it not God?" asked Gregory in *Oration* 31.28. The ontological ground for the deification achieved by Christ now receives actualization through the sanctifying and transforming role of the Spirit. Thus, the Spirit is the perfecting agent (τελειοποιός) of the Father's work for the world that was accomplished in the Son as in the archetype (*Or.* 31.29; 32.6; 34.8).

Although the establishment of the Son's and the Spirit's divinity, as well as their relationship within the Trinity, necessitated the use of particular categories, the Theologian's epistemology of God's nature reflected a traditional apophatic, but, nonetheless, certain existential approach.[185] God is unknown to people outside of his economic revelation as the Trinity. In *Oration* 25.15–18, Gregory expressed the nature of intratrinitarian relations, whereby the monarchy (μοναρχία) of the Father as the one without source (ἄναρχος) is contrasted with the timeless generation of the Son begotten of the Father and the Spirit, who eternally proceeds (προελθόν, προϊόν) from the Father. In other words, the Son's and the Holy Spirit's origination is not subsequent to the Father in time. It is because the Father was a father from the beginning (ἀπ' ἀρχῆς), and the sending forth (ἔκπεμψις) of the Spirit did not add anything to the Godhead (*Or.* 20.7; 29.3). Gregory emphasized not so much the divine equality of the persons, as the uniqueness of their interrelationships. The economic superiority of the Father (as is seen, for example, in John 14:28) does not mean that the Son and the Spirit are lower deities, but that the Father is the eternal source of their personal existence (*Or.* 30.7; 31.30). In *Oration* 40.43, the bishop is even hesitant to use the term "origin" (ἀρχήν) in respect to the Father, lest someone concludes the inferiority of the other two persons.[186] Thus, the Father as the single principle and cause of the Son and the Spirit is the ground of unity in one God, not the source of the divine nature common to all three persons.[187] The monarchy of the Father does not contradict the equality and consubstantiality of the Son and the Spirit, but, in fact, is the reason for their equality, because the Father shares his divine nature with the other persons of the Trinity. Contrary to some modern Orthodox commentators, like Meyendorff, Beeley accurately affirms that, for Gregory, "the first principle of the Trinity is neither 'personhood' nor the divine essence per se, but God the Father, who, as unbegotten Divinity, is both *hypostasis and* divine essence."[188]

185. Hence, as Beeley correctly argued, the immanent and economic Trinity are not two separate teachings in Gregory, but mutually revealing aspects of theology proper. Beeley, *Gregory of Nazianzus*, 200–201.

186. Egan, "ἄτιος/'Author,' αἰτία/'Cause' and ἀρχή/'Origin,'" 104.

187. Beeley, *Gregory of Nazianzus*, 207; Awad, "Between Subordination," 192–98.

188. Beeley, *Gregory of Nazianzus*, 212 (emphasis original).

In respect to the immanent Trinity, the Cappadocian argued, contrary to Eunomius, that God's essence, as it really is, is unknown to people or angelic beings exclusively by the fact of its unbegottenness. God's infinitely transcendent nature is incomprehensible (ἀκατάληπτον) and beyond any attempt of conception (ἐπίνοια) and measure by finite creatures (*Or.* 18.16; 30.17; 38.7-8).[189] In his *Oration* 28, Gregory insisted that, far from knowing God in his entirety, the limited knowledge a person may hope to receive is the "back parts of God" and "things around him" (περὶ αὐτόν) (*Or.* 28.3). Therefore, the human comprehension of God will always remain partial, no matter how perfect it can be from a human standpoint, and the search for the more excellent knowledge of the Trinity is the eternal destiny of the deified (*Or.* 26.19).

This apophatic theology should not discourage intellectual aspiration toward the deified contemplation of Christ (*Or.* 38.7). Gregory, although advocating the divinization of creatures, which "mingle" with the divine light, and constant growth toward God, never perceived the loss of human identity.[190] Gregory wrote, "What greater destiny can befall our humility than that humanity should be intermingled with God, and by this intermingling should become divine (θεόν)?" (*Or.* 30.3). He repeatedly clarified that he meant assimilation to the Trinity as far as it is possible for creatures (κατ' οἰκονομίαν), not dissolution in the divinity.[191] In the first *Oration*, Gregory stated the traditional patristic dictum about the divine-human exchange, "Let us become as Christ is, since Christ became as we are; let us become gods for his sake, since he became man for our sake" (*Or.* 1.5).

Deification, for Gregory of Nazianzus, includes ascetic ascension to God, leaving behind earthly passions. Striving toward monastic life, he praised asceticism, using the technical term "theosis" for the first time:

> . . . who are immortal through mortifying themselves; who are united with God through release [from the body]; who are separated from desire and are joined to that love which is divine and dispassionate; to whom belongs the fountain of light and who enjoy even now its radiance; to whom belong the angelic psalmodies, the night-long services and the departure of the intellect to God, rapt up before its time; to whom belong

---

189. Beeley, *Gregory of Nazianzus*, 95. Gregory even called God a superessential being (ὑπὲρ τὴν οὐσίαν) (*Or.* 6.12), the point later employed by Gregory Palamas.

190. Russell, *Doctrine of Deification*, 214.

191. Lossky chided Gregory of Nazianzus for inconsistency in his view on the possibility of the intellectual vision of God's nature. Lossky, *Vision of God*, 69-70, 89. McGuckin, correctly in my view, defended Gregory's dynamic tension between unknowability and self-disclosure of God. McGuckin, "Vision of God."

purification and being purified; who know no limit in ascending or in being deified (μηδὲν μέτρον εἰδότων ἀναβάσεως καὶ θεώσεως) (*Or.* 4.71).

Gregory followed Origen when he claimed that those deified should be purified and illumined in order to progress in the knowledge of the blessed Trinity (*Or.* 27-28; *Carm.* 1.1.1.1-5, 7-9; cf., *C. Cels.* 6.44).[192] The degree of mystical knowledge corresponds to the degree of continuous spiritual purification (κάθαρσις) and the transformation of life, which finds its aid in Christ's purifying and deifying activity (*Or.* 2.14-15; 27.3; 38.7-13; 44.8). The Christian is called to imitate Christ in moral ascent, in becoming like God. Gregory believed that "[c]onduct (πρᾶξις) is the steppingstone to contemplation (θεωρία)" (*Or.* 20.12).[193] The baptismal rite is traditionally associated with cleansing from sin, the re-creation of sinners into new humanity by the Spirit, and deification (*Or.* 40.7-8). A task of a Christian priest is to grow in virtue toward deification and to lead others toward the same state of becoming a god (*Or.* 2.73). Gregory's perspective on divine and human cooperation in purification leads Beeley to conclude that "Gregory understands God's grace to be fully productive of salvation and human virtue, so that Christian purification is both the result of human effort and ascetical discipline and at the same time entirely the gift of God."[194]

Moreover, Beeley, contrary to Russell, states that, for Gregory, deification is not a matter of the baptismal analogy or moral imitation of God, but real and progressive participation in the divine being in a mysterious way as much as humanity is capable of such a sharing.[195] A purified soul is capable of the mystical vision of the divine glory, which Gregory called the gift of illumination (*Or.* 28.3). The light of the Trinity, like the sun, illumines all created things, especially reasonable beings, which by faith become godlike through the real and ever-growing deifying vision (θεοειδεῖς) and union with the Trinity (*Or.* 21.1; 38.11; 39.9; 40.5). Gregory the Theologian considered the soul's earthly transformation the beginning of eschatological deification, "To become god, having been made a god, it is true, but filled with the supreme light, of which we only taste the firstfruits here below, and even at that, with smallness: such will be the reward for your sorrows" (*Carm.* 10.140-143; PG 37:690). Once the purified reach the state of eternal perfec-

---

192. Russell, *Doctrine of Deification*, 216; Beeley, *Gregory of Nazianzus*, 65-90.

193. Gregory of Nazianzus, *Select Orations*.

194. Beeley, *Gregory of Nazianzus*, 85. Beeley correctly notices that Gregory's view was a conscious precursor of later Pelagian controversy.

195. Beeley, *Gregory of Nazianzus*, 119; Russell, *Doctrine of Deification*, 213-14, 222-25. Note similar contention in relation to Gregory of Nyssa above.

tion, they will be able to know fully as they are fully known (1 Cor 13:12), being Spirit-enhanced to gaze at the greater illumination of the divine light (*Or.* 28.17). Hence, in Gregory, one finds the fully developed doctrine of the Trinity that interweaves with soteriology, and more precisely, with deification as participation in the life of Father, Son, and Holy Spirit.[196]

As has become apparent in this study, the Cappadocians explored the orthodox image of the Christian God: three persons, one nature. To avoid charges in tritheism or subordinationism, the fathers emphasized the monarchy of the Father, who is the logical and personal cause of the natural equality of the Son and the Spirit within Godhead. The image of God's personhood is the Trinity. Communication between human and divine occurs on the level of persons. Deification is a transformation of person, not essence. Thus, transformation into the likeness of God is a transformation into the likeness of the Trinity or, as I call it, *triadosis*. These church leaders strongly believed that deification is the action of the whole Trinity, whereby both Son and Spirit bring believers into the likeness of the triune God. Partaking in the divine light of knowledge, virtues, and goodness is the way of sharing the life of the whole Trinity. Hence, I suggest reading the Cappadocian soteriology through trinitarian lenses that point the reader to *triadosis* as the ultimate image of the human-divine relationships.

Energeosis

The distinction between God's essence and energies, which was developed in the fourteenth century, marks a distinctively Eastern Orthodox contemporary account of *theosis*. Gregory Palamas (1269-1359 CE), a leader of the Athonite monastic community and later the archbishop of Thessalonica, attempted to resolve the ontological gulf in communication between created and uncreated beings by declaring that the relationship between Creator and creation occurs on the level of the divine *energies*, not on the level of natures or merely ethics. He became a defender of the hesychastic monastic movement that advocated participation in the uncreated energies of God. Palamas's teaching on deification as participation in the divine energies was

---

196. Beeley appropriately concludes, "His doctrine of the Trinity not only originates and culminates in a soteriological imperative, but it is soteriological through and through—from its epistemic character as the theology of the divine economy; through the central idea of the monarchy of God the Father, which generates the Son and the Spirit as both distinct from and equal to the Father; to the literary form and conceptual qualifications of Trinitarian statements; to the participatory character of the whole enterprise." Beeley, *Gregory of Nazianzus*, 232.

ardently debated at his own time and after his death.[197] As Williams indicates, Palamas usually employed θέωσις, ἐκθεωσίζω, θεοποιός, θεουργός, and θεούμενος for his account of deification.[198]

To understand Palamas's approach, one needs to consider his historical setting and main theological presuppositions. The first assumption was the traditional patristic notion that God has uncreated, unknowable, unapproachable, and hence, imparticipable nature. As Gregory wrote in his *Triads*, "For God is not only beyond knowledge, but also beyond unknowing" and, consequently, "not only incomprehensible but also unnameable" (*Triads* 1.3.4).[199] Due to God's transcendence, he is "above being" and cannot be an object of intellectual inquiry (*Triads* 2.3.17). In *The One Hundred and Fifty Chapters* 78, Palamas conceived an unbridgeable ontological gap between Creator and creation, "Every nature is utterly remote and absolutely estranged from the divine nature. For if God is nature, other things are not nature, but if each of the other things is nature, he is not nature: just as he is not a being, if others are beings; and if he is a being, the others are not beings."[200] The language itself is inadequate to express the ineffable essence of God. Even angelic beings perceive God not through mental or sensational activity, but in "the ineffable vision, and ecstasy in the vision" of pure prayer (*Triads* 1.3.18). God's essence can never be contemplated by the created intellect and is unattainable for the human mind aided by secular education. Thus, Palamas employed negation language to express what God is not. However, even the apophaticism will not draw a contemplative mind closer to the inexpressible God. This is because "[t]he ascent by negation is in fact only an apprehension of how all things are distinct from God; it conveys only an image of the formless contemplation and of the fulfillment of the mind in contemplation, not being itself that fulfillment" (*Triads* 1.3.19). Even the term "essence" is misleading, because it presupposes certain no-

---

197. Russell, "Theosis and Gregory Palamas," 360. The hesychastic movement with Palamas as a representative was met with ardent opposition from Barlaam the Calabrian, who considered it as an absurd teaching. After the defeat of Barlaam, Gregory Akindynos became the head of the anti-Palamite movement. After Akindynos's condemnation, he was replaced by Nikephoros Gregoras. Russell and Tollefsen regard Palamas as a faithful heir and appropriator of such Greek fathers as Gregory of Nyssa, Dionysius the Areopagite, and Maximus the Confessor. Tollefsen, *Activity and Participation*, 193.

198. Williams, *Ground of Union*, 104. Williams helpfully lists images (i.e., virtue, knowledge, vision, contemplation, light, glory, grace, adoption, participation, and union), which are both natural and transcend human capacities and help to define what *theosis* is or is not. Williams, *Ground of Union*, 106.

199. Gregory Palamas, *Triads*.

200. Gregory Palamas, *Gregory Palamas*.

tions and categories, while God is beyond all affirmation and negation; he is "superessential nature" (*Triads* 3.2.11; 3.2.7). Logically, the corollary of human inability to talk meaningfully about God's essence would be silence and absolute ignorance. That would be the case unless God decided to reveal himself. This divine self-disclosure can be appropriated only through a direct illumination from God and participation in the divine life.[201]

Gregory's second assumption was that the hesychastic visions of the *divine light* by monks were real and immediate. He set up himself to clarify the nature of the divine light and the character of mystical experience, in which the deified person can participate. For the defender of the hesychasts, the mystical vision of the divine light is superior to Greek philosophical knowledge and even to the Scriptures (*Triads* 2.3.18). Hence, contemplative vision is beyond knowing and unknowing (*Triads* 1.3.4). Even though words are infinitely limited to express the vision of a transcended God, words are used to describe this experience only in analogies, symbols, and allusions (*Triads* 1.3.4; 2.3.20). The disciples on the Transfiguration Mountain gazed at the light of Jesus's glory not by natural senses or intellect, but by utterly transformed perception, being ecstatically disengaged from all perceptible things through the power of the Holy Spirit (*Triads* 1.3.17). Analogously, the vision of the divine light occurs when God ecstatically descends to meet with monks, who ecstatically ascend to perceive God, not outside of their body, but beyond any natural means (*Triads* 1.3.47). In the spiritual vision, a monk is united with the light, so that he becomes the light and perceives the light through the light (*Triads* 2.3.36). Nonetheless, the light of this mysterious vision does not reveal the essence of God; rather it reveals God's transcendence and hiddenness. Palamas articulated the paradox of this supernatural experience as "a grace invisibly seen and ignorantly known" (*Triads* 2.3.8). Anastos summarizes the paradoxical nature of deifying vision well, "In deification God then appears as an 'intellectual light' to the uncreated created subject who is in a state labeled as one of 'inaction surpassing action,' a state in which the subject 'comprehends incomprehensibly.'"[202] The apophatic theology of the hesychast did not preclude him from claiming the contemplation of the divine glory, which is not essence, but, nonetheless, divine and visible in an ecstatic vision (*Triads* 1.3.5).

Philosophically, the divine light is a divine attribute. Gregory was confident that this aspect of God is open for participation to created beings, while the divine essence remains wholly unperceived. Palamas's critics could not agree that God's attributes have the same ontological status as God's

201. Russell, "Theosis and Gregory Palamas," 365.
202. Anastos, "Gregory Palamas' Radicalization," 340.

nature because attributes do not exist by themselves outside of nature and are distinguishable only in thought.[203] For Palamas, God's transcendence is not absolute, because he willfully made himself manifested to creation in his acts and attributes. Gunnarsson correctly contends that Palamas's arguments are not sustainable on a philosophical plane because mystical experience cannot be substantiated due to the limitations of the human intellect, using philosophical categories.[204]

Theologically, Palamas argued that the deifying light on Mount Tabor was of God's essential quality, but was not God's essence as such. The light was both symbolic and real. Moreover, it was enhypostatic, i.e., it had no other hypostasis than that of Christ himself (*Triads* 3.1.28; 3.1.16; 3.1.23). Gregory claimed that "[t]his hypostatic light, [is] seen spiritually by the saints," who know it by personal experience (*Triads* 2.3.8). Palamas called the divine light "the deifying gift" of the Spirit. He writes, "It is 'enhypostatic' not because it possesses a hypostasis of its own, but because the Spirit 'sends it out into the hypostasis of another,' in which it is indeed contemplated. It is then properly called 'enhypostatic,' in that it is not contemplated by itself, nor in essence, but in hypostasis" (*Triads* 3.1.9).[205] Once contemplators appropriate this light, they, to some degree, become "uncreated" hypostases of this light.[206] Thus, the logic was this: God's essence is manifested in a mystical vision through the person of Christ, who manifested this essence through his divine light. Russell justifiably concludes, "The Taboric light was not simply an external phenomenon, but an 'enhypostatic' symbol (*enhypostaton symbolon*), meaning that the light was real even if it did not have an independent existence, or hypostasis, of its own."[207] Hence, the Taboric light allowed the participation of created beings in the divine, while at the same time transcending human perception.

Based on these assumptions, Palamas concluded that participation in God is possible and *the divine energies* are the medium for such participation. According to Palamas, hesychasts in their contemplation of the divine light, enabled by the uncreated grace, participated in the divine energies, not essence (*Triads* 3.1.33). The divine energies are divine activity, manifestations,

---

203. Russell, "Theosis and Gregory Palamas," 366.

204. Gunnarsson, *Mystical Realism*, 190.

205. McGuckin, *Transfiguration of Christ*; Collins, *Partaking in Divine Nature*, 100. Hussey thinks that in order to express the personal nature of God's light, but at the same time to discard the idea that the light has its own independent hypostasis, it is better to use ἐνυποστάτως (enhypostasized), rather than the usual ὑποστατικός (hypostatic). Hussey, "Persons-Energy Structure," 25.

206. Hussey, "Persons-Energy Structure," 27.

207. Russell, "Theosis and Gregory Palamas," 367.

EARLY APPROACHES TO *THEOSIS* 75

attributes, gifts, names and everything that is used for describing God.[208] These energies are eternal and inseparable from the essence of the Uncreated. The energies are natural symbols of God's nature, and therefore are coexistent and uncreated.[209] In his *Triads* 3.2, Palamas defines the difference between the essence and energies of God. Founding his claim on a Cappadocian and Maximian idea of the divine participable realities, Palamas asserted the existence of the uncreated energies alongside the imparticipable divine nature. Such divine reality is the deifying grace of the Holy Spirit that is not self-subsistent, but at the same time is not originated.[210] Russell expresses Palamas's dichotomy of the transcendent and immanent God, "In his essence (*ousia*) God was beyond even Godhead but in his operations or energies (*energiai*) he came into an intimate relationship with the contingent order, so that the worthy could participate in him through attaining a vision of the divine light."[211]

This approach allowed the church father to maintain the distinction between God's unshareable essence and accessible divine qualities, energies. Energy is an external manifestation of nature, not of a hypostasis. Palamas inherited this fundamental principle from Maximus the Confessor, who assumed that if every person in the Trinity possessed individual energy, there would be three essences in Godhead, i.e., tritheism.[212] Further, since God is one, the Trinity possesses only one energy common to the Father, Son, and Holy Spirit, "God is identical within himself since the three divine hypostases are related to one another and coinhere in one another naturally, wholly, eternally and inaccessibly, but at the same time without mixture and without confusion, just as they have also a single energy" (*Cap*. 112). Consequently, God's creative activity is not the combined acts or effects of the three persons, but the single creative act (*Cap*. 112, 140). Although God operates through one divine energy, personal aspects of one energy are not blurred into Unitarianism. As Hussey maintains, the anti-Barlaamite employed the patristic formula "*from* the Father, *through* the Son *in* the Holy Spirit" to demonstrate that the same energy presupposes involvement of all three persons in a single divine act.[213] Since the

208. Indeed, Tollefsen prefers the term "activity" to the traditional "energy." Tollefsen, *Activity and Participation*, 187.

209. Gavrilyuk, "Retrieval of Deification," 650.

210. Russell, "Theosis and Gregory Palamas," 368–69.

211. Russell, *Doctrine of Deification*, 304.

212. Hussey, "Persons-Energy Structure," 28.

213. Hussey, "Persons-Energy Structure," 28. Tollefsen speculates that the singular activity of God becomes plural because it "is pluralized in accordance with the divinely predefined receptive potentiality and capacity of creatures." Tollefsen, *Activity and*

divine energies are not operations of different persons in the Godhead, but of one God, the partaker of the divine energies partakes in union with the whole Trinity, not only the incarnate Son.[214] God's essence, however, does not exist independently from but is manifested and enacted by an individual hypostasis. Hence, the essential divine property is revealed through the one will and act of the Father through the Son in the Holy Spirit. Even though the divine energies are not self-subsistent beings, they are permanent and stable, because their existence depends on the nature of God. These energies are also personalized because they equally manifest the three divine persons (*Triads* 3.1.18; *Cap.* 114).

Moreover, Palamas extended this concept to another level, suggesting that energies are transmissible from person to person, without changing the nature of a person. Hence, saints could produce miracles and even "the sanctifying bestowal of the Spirit" (*Triads* 2.2.13; 3.1.33). Gregory went as far as to claim that the deified subjects, being united with Christ, could themselves enact and operate the divine energies, "Only those beings united to It are deified 'by the total presence of the Anointer'; they have received an energy identical to that of the deifying essence, and possessing it in absolute entirety, reveal it through themselves" (*Triads* 3.1.33). By partaking in God's energies, creation remains distinct from God and avoids pantheistic notions of equality.[215] Joost van Rossum accurately underlines a subtle difference in Palamas's categories: the *distinction* between essence and energy does not mean *separability*.[216] Thus, in Chalcedonian terms, God's essence is inseparably distinct from his energies.

During the hesychastic controversy, Gregory disagreed with Barlaam the Calabrian about the nature of the divine vision. The Calabrian accused Palamas of teaching the heresy of Messalians, a previously condemned group that claimed a physical vision of God's essence.[217] Barlaam argued that everything that is not God's essence is created and has a beginning. Therefore, energies are created symbols of unapproachable divine nature,

---

Participation, 201.

214. Del Colle, *Christ and Spirit*, 10.

215. Macaskill, *Union with Christ*, 49.

216. Rossum, "Deification in Palamas and Aquinas," 368. Rossum incorrectly states that in *Triads* 3.1.33 Palamas taught about "equality" of essence and its energy in contrast to their "identity." Rossum, "Deification in Palamas and Aquinas," 371. The phase τὴν ἴσην ἐνέργειαν τῇ θεούσῃ οὐσίᾳ probably means not "the energy is equal to the deifying essence," but "the same energy of the deifying essence." The point is not in the equality of essence and energy, but in linking energy with its essence.

217. Gregory Palamas, *Triads*, 9.

and participation in the divine is impossible (*Triads* 2.3.12).[218] Palamas responded that although the deifying light is not the essence of God, it is not created or merely symbolic, but essential and means relationship (*Triads* 3.1.29). At the same time, God remains wholly other and transcendent, and the only way of relating to him is through his uncreated energies. The deifying union with God is not a natural transformation of human reason, as Barlaam claimed, but the supernatural transformation of body and soul into the divine by grace, so that the deified share the glory of Christ in a visible way (*Triads* 3.1.33; 1.3.5). Further, the defender of the Athonite monks claimed that since Barlaamites accept *theosis*, they could only participate in the created God. Russell specifies what Palamas meant when he insisted on participation in God via the divine energy in the *Dialogue between an Orthodox and Barlaamite* 46, "But if we speak of the divine energies, we can overcome this problem without making God composite or compromising the transcendence of the divine essence, for the whole of God is present in each of his energies. Those who participate in the energies therefore participate in the whole of God."[219] Theosis, according to Palamas, is not just a divine gift. It is union with God the Holy Spirit, as he makes himself available via a participable mode of relations to the believer, though not in his essence. Since saints share God's attributes, they become *homotheoi* ("wholly one with God") like the deified human nature of Christ, and also *anarchoi* ("without beginning") and *ateleutetoi* ("without end").[220] By participating in the participable uncreated divine energies of the Holy Spirit, saints participate in the whole of God, while God's essence remains unattainable. Participation in God's divinity is the purpose God intended when he created people. Palamas's critics charged him with creating divinities out of deified human beings.

Palamas faced another opponent in the person of Gregory Akindynos, who criticized the Palamite concept of energies as polytheistic innovations. Akindynos insisted that introduction of the uncreated divine energies, in fact, creates multiple divinities: the unknown Deity and known divinities, i.e., polytheism. Hence, for Akindynos, if the vision of God is possible, it could be only by means of created divine attributes because no division in the uncreated God is possible. The skeptic wrote,

---

218. Bradshaw argues that Barlaam's insistence that only the divine essence is uncreated reflects Augustine's approach in the *De Trinitate*. Bradshaw, *Aristotle East and West*, 233–34.

219. Russell, "Theosis and Gregory Palamas," 369–70.

220. Russell, "Theosis and Gregory Palamas," 370.

[T]he "new theologian" [Palamas] not only in long written discourses but also by word of mouth has been proclaiming two uncreated divinities, not to say actually a great many, "one higher and the other infinitely lower"; one invisible and the other visible even to the bodily eyes of certain men; one activating and the other activated; one nameless and the other having a name; one being the essence and the other not; one incapable of being shared and the other capable of being shared. The latter he calls deification (θέωσιν) and power and energy and grace and illumination and form and essential and natural glory of God, being separate, as he says, from his essence and nature (*Letter* 27.81–91).[221]

Akindynos associated the desire of deification with the fall of Lucifer and Adam (*Letter* 49.45–52). Palamas responded to this caricature in his *The One Hundred and Fifty Chapters*, arguing that believers were created to become gods only by participation in a shareable aspect of God, i.e., the divine energies (*Cap.* 105). Through participation in the divine energies, saints change their natural human qualities and become like pure air and light, remaining human individuals (*On Divine and Deifying Participation* 21).[222] Palamas's opponents were not convinced by his arguments because there was no place for human participation in God in their apophatic theology.[223]

Palamas continued the traditional patristic teaching on the assumption of human nature by Christ and its deification (*Triads* 3.1.15).[224] The deification of Christ's human nature is the basis for the deification of those who unite with him through the regeneration of the Spirit. The uncreated grace of God accomplishes the appropriation of deifying gift by an individual believer through created means, such as sacraments.[225] In baptism, a person receives freedom from the power of sin and death. The new life of resurrection will proceed until its completion in the incorruptible life with God. Mantzaridis highlights the mutual signification of baptism and the Eucharist for deification, "Through baptism the 'image' in man is purified and

221. Russell, *Doctrine of Deification*, 307; cited from Gregory Akindynos, *Letters of Gregory Akindynos*.

222. Russell, *Doctrine of Deification*, 308.

223. Russell, *Doctrine of Deification*, 308; Gregory Palamas, *Triads*, 7. Gregory's final opponent was Prochorus Cydones who argued against the separation of energies from essence because that would create an independent reality alongside God. God's energies or attributes are analogies of God's essence, not external entity. God is light, but does not have light. Thus theosis, for Prochorus, is an analogy or symbolic. Russell, *Doctrine of Deification*, 309.

224. Mantzaridis, *Deification of Man*, chap. 1.

225. Mantzaridis, *Deification of Man*, 41.

the imitation of Christ commences, while the Holy Eucharist brings about his advance toward the 'likeness' and his full union with Christ."[226] In the Eucharist, Christ unites and intermingles with believers into one body, not only in his deified flesh and blood but also in spirit (*Homily* 56.6–7).[227] The communion of the faithful in the body of Christ makes them a "communion of deification" (*Demonstrative Discourse* 2.78).[228]

To contemplate the ineffable super-essential light of God, one needs purification by fulfilling commandments, attaining virtues and "pure and immaterial prayer" (*Triads* 1.3.19, 2.1.40, 2.3.17). In fact, the degree of deification and appropriation of the divine energy corresponds to one's virtuous life and sanctification (*Triads* 3.1.34; *Cap.* 69). The ascetic ideal, in Palamas's view, is dispassion, whereby natural passions are transformed, and the fragmented mind is reunited with its heart into obedience and worship to God. The deifying contemplation can occur only in a complete stillness of soul and "cessation of all intellectual activity," i.e., *hesychia* (*Triads* 3.1.36). In *apatheia*, hesychasts practiced the psychosomatic method of the "Jesus Prayer" in preparation for the mystical vision of the uncreated light.[229] The deified cooperate with the deifying grace in fulfilling God's commandments. It is spiritual progress that starts in this life and consummates in the afterlife.[230] Here is how Palamas presented the deifying grace and its superiority over the preparatory means of human efforts, "Every virtue and imitation of God on our part indeed prepares those who practice them for divine union, but the mysterious union itself is effected by grace" (*Triads* 3.1.27). The contemplative vision of God "face to face" by the deified, however, will never end, because it is an endless dynamic process and the revelation of the divine light is never exhausted (*Triads* 2.3.35, cf., 2.2.11).

"The doctor of uncreated energies" claimed that deification is the process, whereby saints transcend their human nature, "Those who attain it become thereby uncreated, unoriginate and indescribable, although in their own nature, they derive from nothingness" (*Triads* 3.1.31). Anastos attempts to find a way out of the Palamite ontological conundrum, where one participates in divine nature and, simultaneously, not participates, by pointing out that, for the leader of the hesychasts, God is above nature. According to Anastos, Palamas claimed that deification crosses an ontological gap

226. Mantzaridis, *Deification of Man*, 51.
227. Gregory Palamas, *Tu en hagios patros*.
228. Gregory Palamas, *Grigoriou tou Palama Syngrammata*.
229. Mantzaridis, *Deification of Man*, 93. The Jesus prayer is a continuous repetition of a short saying, "Lord Jesus Christ, Son of God, have mercy upon me" with minimized frequency of breath while focusing one's sight on one's navel as the residence of heart.
230. Mantzaridis, *Deification of Man*, chap. 3.

between God and humans through participation in the divine energies.[231] Russell agrees with Anastos that the deified is one with the Trinity in energies and distinct in hypostases, but disagrees that *theosis* means bridging the ontological gap.[232] Russell thinks that Palamas unpacked the traditional patristic teaching on the two natures of Christ, looking at the idea from a different perspective, changing a viewpoint, not the doctrine.

The above view created several problems, which, in my opinion, were not adequately resolved by its author. First, Gregory attempted to preserve God's inaccessibility by elevating God into a higher realm above essence: God is a superessential being (*Triads* 2.3.33; 3.1.23–24).[233] If this is the case, then God is not simplicity, but an irreconcilable duality of imparticipable transcendence and participable mutability.[234] Even if God is not simple due to the nature-persons duality in the Trinity, the divine energies bring further division into the divine being, which arguably contradicts traditional patristic thought. Second, Palamas had to deal with a tension between the eternal, uncreated energies and the finite world. If the energies are God's creative power, then the world has to be coeternal with them and with God. In response, Gregory had to concede that some energies (e.g., creative energy or at least its activity) have the beginning and end (*Triads* 3.2.8).[235] However, if some energies are temporal, it undermines their uncreated and coeternal qualification. Third, Palamas stated that each energy is "relative" and "refers to relationships with another, but is not indicative of substance" (*Cap.* 127). In the *Triads*, however, he claimed, in a more traditional way, that energies are the manifestations of nature, not persons. It seems to be a contradiction. To resolve it, Bradshaw suggests that the divine light, as one of the energies, is an aspect of mutual glorification between the Son and the Spirit, thus

---

231. Anastos, "Gregory Palamas' Radicalization," 347.

232. Russell, "Theosis and Gregory Palamas," 377n76.

233. Anastos, "Gregory Palamas' Radicalization," 347.

234. Contos, however, sees the problem in claiming God's absolute simplicity, because it would logically lead to the abrogation of a hypostatic distinction within the Trinity. Contos, "Essence-Energies Structure," 287. Torrance thinks that Palamas's οὐσία-ἐνέργειαι distinction presents no difficulty for the idea of the divine simplicity, as is the case with the οὐσία-ὑποστάσεις distinction in Cappadocian theology. Torrance, "Precedents for Palamas' Essence-Energies," 51. Mantzaridis acknowledges this difficulty for the divine simplicity. In response, the author wrongly, in my view, equated the procession of uncreated energies from God with the generation and procession of the Son and the Spirit from the Father, because energies are the manifestations of nature, not self-subsistent beings as the divine persons. Mantzaridis, *Deification of Man*, 106–7.

235. Rossum states that, for Palamas, ultimately God's free will makes the creative power manifested in time and space. Rossum, "Deification in Palamas and Aquinas," 376.

assigning energies to persons.[236] If energy is not "indicative of substance" but of person, then one has to ascribe only one energy in the incarnate Son as well as three energies in one God, which is unorthodox.[237]

Palamas's contribution to the doctrine of deification consists in his philosophical rationalization of what it means to become divine-like in light of monastic experiential phenomenon. For him, *theosis* is not only an ethical transformation but also ontological. The archbishop followed long patristic tradition, employing the Aristotelian "essence" and "energies" distinction and bringing the uncreated divine light to the discussion of deification. For Gregory, Taboric light is not a created symbol of God, but really God manifested, who shares his glory with contemplating observers, transforming them spiritually and physically. If one agrees with Williams that Palamas did not invent a new doctrine, but simply synthesized previous patristic poles of the divine-human ontological divide and participation of creation in the divine life, then one can appreciate Palamas's innovative approach in utilizing essence-energy terminology.[238] Undoubtedly, *theosis* as the transformation of believers in communication with the divine energies represents a trend of patristic theology that could appropriately be called *energeosis*. *Energeosis* is not a universally accepted Orthodox dogma and remains a controversial perspective today even among Eastern Orthodox theologians.[239]

Conclusion

In this chapter, I have argued that it is possible to trace four main viewpoints within Eastern patristic theologies on the doctrine of deification. The approach of the first group presented a Christianized version of Greek *apotheosis*. The Alexandrians and Evagrius perceived deification as the process of intellectual and ascetic ascent, whereby the deified contemplate and imitate the divine virtues by grace, to the full extent as possible for such creatures. Perhaps, to some degree, one can trace Origen's influence on all subsequent schools of patristic thought by his ideas and methodologies. These church

236. Bradshaw, *Aristotle East and West*, 273.

237. Borysov, "Doctrine of Deification."

238. Williams, *Ground of Union*, 164.

239. Williams, for example, observes that for such Orthodox theologians as Florovsky and P. N. Trempelas Palamas's doctrine received no universal dogmatic status and, in fact, was neglected in the Orthodox theologies since the late seventeen century until its retrieval by Russian Orthodox émigré in Paris. Williams, *Ground of Union*, 148–50. Some contemporary Orthodox dogmatic texts scarcely mention or even avoid Palamas's distinction. Karmiris, *Synopsis of Dogmatic Theology*; Pomazansky, *Orthodox Dogmatic Theology*.

fathers were optimistic about the ultimate blissful status of the deified in eternity that goes beyond their natural bodily capacities.

Irenaeus and Cyril, on the other hand, expressed a keen interest in the recapitulation of humankind in Christ's incarnation and the deification of the human nature in Christ. For both fathers, the imitation of Christ's virtues is insufficient outside intimate union with the deified nature of Christ through faith. The ideas of sonship, adoption, and filiation with God through Christ are prominent in Irenaeus and Cyril. Participation in the sacraments of baptism and the Eucharist is the means of incorporation into Christ and sharing in his deified humanity. Despite strong Cappadocian trinitarian influence, Cyril expressed an immense fascination for, and concern in, personal union with Christ. Thus, *christosis* became the predominant soteriological framework for these church fathers.

The Cappadocian fathers represent a third approach, by synthesizing their theological heritage and bringing their trinitarian formulations in agreement with the Nicene faith. They strived to preserve the apophatic character of God's incomprehensibility and kataphatic revelation of God as the Trinity in the Scriptures and the person of Jesus Christ. Ontological questions about the Trinity and intrapersonal relationships within Godhead led these fourth-century theologians to conclude that salvation is due to a single act of the whole Trinity, not only Christ's incarnation, his redemptive death, and resurrection. The deification and trinitarian concerns of the Cappadocians are thoroughly interwoven: it is true that trinitarianism drove deification, but the interest in deification equally drove more refined articulations of trinitarianism, precisely to distinguish our participation from that of Jesus. Therefore, deification is essentially *triadosis*: participation in the life of the Trinity and transformation according to the image and likeness of the tripersonal God.

Gregory Palamas illustrated how extreme apophatism could lead to impersonal participation in God. Palamas was so concerned with the unapproachable character of God's nature that even the divine persons remain unknown. The only point of contact with God, for Gregory, is the divine energies that manifest an otherwise unknown being of God. Deification mediated by God's energies becomes the manner Palamas theologized about soteriology. Thus, *energeosis* is a philosophical attempt to explain how ascetics can experience deification through supernatural contact with the visible divine energies of the invisible God. Palamas's contribution to modern Orthodox understandings of *theosis* is undeniable, but not necessarily universal, and thus has to be distinguished before the term *theosis* could be applied to Pauline study.

This chapter contributes to the study of *theosis* by taking the breadth of patristic view in the account. Unlike Blackwell, the survey goes beyond a narrow focus on Irenaeus and Cyril and takes into consideration a broader scope of ideas in a more extended period. By narrowing his focus, Blackwell inevitably skews what he finds in Paul: by looking for *christosis*, he finds *christosis* (and not the other things that he might have seen had he looked at the fathers more broadly). In contrast to Macaskill and others, I suggest the categorization of the patristic data into the four approaches, which are new and perhaps helpful for the systematization of ideas, while still recognizing the limitations of any categorization. Gorman, who utilizes the deification language, gives no historical account of this idea.

Finally, one should note the pervasiveness of the ontological concerns in the fathers, both in terms of the link between the ontology of the incarnation and Christian deification and in terms of the fundamental ontological distinction between participants and that in which they participate. These notions will play an important role in our analysis of Litwa in chapter 5. In the next chapter, I will address the appropriateness of *theosis* as a theme to Luther's and Calvin's soteriologies. The results of this inquiry will be compared with the views of a contemporary Eastern Orthodox theologian, John Zizioulas. By comparing Reformers with an Orthodox figure, I will indicate their similarities and distinctions. This will set the discussion of deification in respect to Paul's theology proper and soteriology in a more critical fashion.

Chapter 3

Reformers and Triadosis

Introduction

A MEDIEVAL SOTERIOLOGICAL CONUNDRUM between imparted and declared righteousness or between transformational and forensic justification saturated disputes between Roman Catholics and the Reformers. It seems, however, that subsequent generations of Protestants have had no more success than Luther and Calvin themselves in resolving this issue. On the one hand, a Roman Catholic doctrine of imparted righteousness paves the way to reality, in which a believer can become an independent owner of grace as some property, autonomous from God. On the other hand, a Protestant doctrine of the forensic imputation of Christ's righteousness can result in a "legal fiction," i.e., a person may become confident in God's election and the formal declaration of her as righteous, without being righteous in reality and seeing no need to depend on God's grace for sanctification. Contrary to the traditional interpretations of Luther's and Calvin's theologies, several recent studies have shown that neither Reformer separated Christ from the righteousness he imputed to believers, i.e., the giver from the gift.[1] To receive justification by faith is only possible through union with Christ or being "in Christ." Moreover, the Finnish Lutheran School and J. Todd Billings have convincingly demonstrated that *theosis* can be a heuristic lens in reading both Luther and Calvin, albeit with a careful definition of the term. This section will assess the "new perspectives on Luther and Calvin" in light of two participationist concepts: union with Christ and deification. First, however, the traditional Lutheran and Calvinist interpretations will set the stage for a fresh interpretation.

---

1. Cavanaugh, "Joint Declaration?"; Billings, *Calvin, Participation, and Gift*; Braaten and Jenson, *Union with Christ*.

Traditional Lutheran and Calvinist Interpretations

Luther, in his *Lectures on Galatians* in 1535, confidently wrote that the fundamental human inclination, the natural religion of the world, consists of earning everlasting life by good intentions, deeds, and merits:

> There is no difference at all between a papist, a Jew, a Turk, or a sectarian. Their persons, locations, rituals, religions, works, and forms of worship are, of course, diverse; but they all have the same reason, the same heart, the same opinion and idea.... "If I do this or that, I have a God who is favourably disposed toward me; if I do not, I have a God who is wrathful" (*LW* 26:396).

In his famous *Institutes*, John Calvin presented his view on the corrupted human heart and will that can freely desire only evil (2.1.8; 2.2.12; 2.3.5). Adam, being the "root" of human nature and receiver of divine "gifts," has lost those gifts and transmitted depravity to all his posterity (*Inst.* 2.1.6–7). The law in a general sense, in Calvin's view, is as good as the gospel, because both have divine origin and both in connection with Christ show the way of life acceptable to God. The fall, however, restricted the law's functions to constant threats and condemnation, because, apart from Christ, the law is lifeless (*Comm.* Gal 3:10, 12, 21; Phil 3:6). In Luther's words, the Mosaic Law was given to reveal human corruption, blindness about self-righteousness, incapacity to comply perfectly with God's standards, as well as "sickness, sin, evil, death, hell, the wrath of God" (*LW* 33:261–2) and to look for help in the gospel of Jesus Christ.[2] The Old Testament sacrificial system was grounded on and foreshadowed Christ's future sacrifice (*Inst.* 2.7.1–16; 2.9.4; 3.2.32). Thus, the faith and rituals of Israelites were not superseded but reinterpreted and confirmed by the coming of Christ, who was foreseen in them as the type. Luther called believing Old Testament Jews and gentiles Christians before Christ "just as much Christians as we are," (*LW* 45:97) while Calvin believed that the present day church existed in the Old Testament and participated in the Abrahamic covenant (*Inst.* 2.9.2; 2.10.1–20. 2.11.2–4; *Comm.* Gal 4:1).

Luther taught that God has decided to reveal himself in Jesus's preaching and ministry. Christ is the object of faith. By taking all sins committed by all people at all times, Christ became "the greatest thief, murderer, adulterer, robber, desecrator, blasphemer, etc., there has ever been anywhere in the world" (*LW* 26:277). Since Jesus is also the God of perfect righteousness, he

---

2. The primary role of the law for Luther, in Westerholm's words, is "to lead us out of 'tents' of our self-confidence and complacency into the presence of God." Westerholm, *Perspectives Old and New*, 29.

conquered sin and its consequences. Calvin claimed that the Son of God, being the perfect priest and a sin-offering at the same time, expiated human sins and, as the Mediator, brought reconciliation between a holy God and unrighteous people (*Inst.* 2.16.3; 2.6.2-4). Believers by faith exchange their sinfulness, death, and condemnation for Christ's righteousness, life, and grace. God justifies the ungodly sinners with His righteousness for the sake of Christ's redemptive death on their behalf. In his *Lectures on Galatians*, Luther stated that Christ's righteousness is imputed to those who entered into union with Him by faith apart from works so that this righteousness is both "alien" to them and becomes their own (*LW* 26:6-7, 223, 234). As Luther stressed a believer always remains *simul iustus et peccator* (simultaneously a righteous person and a sinner), "In myself outside of Christ, I am a sinner; in Christ outside of myself, I am not a sinner" (*WA* 38:205; 57:165; *LW* 26:232). Paul Althaus calls this state of incomplete righteousness "a fragmentary beginning." He writes, "The Christian is not yet completely the man of faith in whom Christ lives; he still remains the old man, the man of 'flesh.'"[3] Therefore, union of saints with Christ does not eradicate their distinction as a sinner and the Savior. If any part of human achievements were considered for justification at the final judgment, this would result in the haunting doubts of self-sufficiency in the human conscience.

According to Luther, when Paul defended justification by grace through faith without "works of the law," he referred to the Mosaic Law that epitomized any good work done for the sake of salvation, not merely the Jewish rituals abolished by Christ (*LW* 26:140; 33:268-269, 276-277; cf., *Inst.* 3.11.19-20).[4] In Christ, believers received freedom from the demand for perfect obedience imposed by the law. On the one hand, after the coming of Christ, the ceremonial laws are abrogated for Jews and gentiles alike, albeit Jews could continue to keep them, but not as a requirement for salvation. On the other hand, even in a Christian society, the need for discipline and the warnings of the moral law continue because of the "flesh" (*LW* 26:80, 317, 341, 350; 45:91-92). Similarly, Calvin supported the continuity of the Old Testament law in the Christian era, "We must never imagine that the law is in any way abrogated in regard to the Ten Commandments,

---

3. Althaus, *Theology of Martin Luther*, 240.

4. Westerholm highlights the point that, for both Luther and Calvin, "works of the law" meant not only ceremonial commands, but also any moral requirements. If Christ justified sinners apart from "ceremonial law," they still perish as moral transgressors. Against Augustine, Luther excluded works of faith as the basis for the final justification, as if one would attempt to come to God with his or her own righteousness, robbing God of his glory. Westerholm, *Perspectives Old and New*, 34-35. These points are contested by the New Perspective on Paul proponents.

in which God has taught us what is right and has ordered our life, because the will of God must stand for ever" (*Comm.* Gal 3:25; *Inst.* 2.7.12).[5] It is the Holy Spirit, who makes believers able to fulfill God's law, in however imperfect a way, supplementing the lack of perfection.

The illumination of the Holy Spirit arouses faith in Christ through gospel proclamation (*LW* 26:73). The salvific faith is not the cause of justification but the means of receiving it, unlike Christ, who is the only cause and administrator of salvation. For Luther, faith as a divine gift is not merely static or juridical, but is also dynamic and transforming, that "changes us and makes us to be born anew of God. It kills the old Adam and makes us altogether different men, in heart and spirit and mind and powers; and it brings with it the Holy Spirit. O it is a living, busy, active, mighty thing, this faith. It is impossible for it not to be doing good works incessantly" (*LW* 35:370).[6] Calvin echoes Luther with a paradox that justifying faith is never alone, "we are justified not without works yet not through works" (*Inst.* 3.16.1; *Comm.* Gal 5:6). Christians, by being engrafted in Christ, inevitably experience sanctification and produce works of righteousness pleasing to God. Hence, whatever good work a saint produces is the result of divine grace and transformed will that God rewards (*Inst.* 2.3.11-14; 3.15.3-4). Justification from the start until the final judgment is solely by grace through faith.

The subjective experience of salvation unavoidably follows the objective experience of salvation through justification by grace through the sanctification process and restoration of the *imago Dei*. Since sanctification is transformation process that includes practical holiness, for the Reformers, salvation seemed to run the risk of becoming a form of semi-Pelagianism—or using anachronistically E. P. Sanders's language— "getting in" God's family by faith and "staying in" by works. To avoid "the Galatian" heresy, the Reformed theologians subordinated sanctification to justification as a consequence of the latter, and not a condition of it (*Inst.* 3.11.6; 3.16.1).[7] Hence, Thomas Coates argues that both Luther and Calvin "taught that sanctification is an outgrowth of justification" and, therefore, subsidiary to the latter.[8] Moreover, there is no place for synergy: God

---

5. In the *Institutes*, Calvin wrote that the moral law is "the true and eternal rule of righteousness, prescribed for men of all nations and times, who wish to conform their lives to God's will" (4.20.15).

6. Coates considers that Luther's dynamic view of justification distinguished him from Calvin's static and judicial view. Coates, "Calvin's Doctrine of Justification," 201-2.

7. To be fair, Calvin regarded justification and sanctification as inseparable activities of God, as light and heat of the sun. This aspect will be explored below.

8. Coates, "Calvin's Doctrine of Justification," 201.

bestows righteousness on those who believe, while the Spirit accomplishes the sanctifying role in Christians.

Luther and Deification

A majority of German Lutheran scholars prefer to talk about God-human relations as an external cause and effect, rather than an internal communion of beings. The traditional Lutheran interpretation, attested in the Formula of Concord, separated, on the one hand, "justification by faith" as a sheer gift of forgiveness and imputed righteousness based on Christ's obedience and, on the other hand, the "divine indwelling" as merely a sanctification process that follows justification. Robert Kolb, however, following Gustaf Aulén and Ian D. Kingston Siggins, contends that Luther's soteriology should not be reduced to the Anselmian theory of substitutionary atonement to the exclusion of other themes, because the Reformer employed a broad range of images to describe the effects of Christ's work.[9] For instance, at the later stage in his career (1540), Luther calls Christ the "example" for Christians (*LW* 4:190-2; *WA* 43:273.20-274.12) or "victor" over many spiritual tyrants (*LW* 26:21-2; *WA* 40.1:65.12-7). In 1535, the papal opponent elucidated, "justification is in reality a kind of rebirth in newness," whereby God changes the identity of a Christian, i.e., it is not simply a legal proclamation (*LW* 34:113-4; *WA* 39.1:48.10-30). Kolb and Arand correctly call this reckoning of Christ's righteousness to believers "God's re-creative pronouncement," whereby the saved ones are both righteous and sinners simultaneously (*simul iustus et peccator*).[10] To these voices, Alister McGrath adds his own opinion on the mistaken systematization of Luther's view on justification, "Luther himself did not teach a doctrine of forensic justification in the strict sense. The concept of a forensic justification necessitates a deliberate and systematic distinction between justification and regeneration, a distinction which is not found in Luther's earlier works."[11] In fact, Luther wrote that the term "satisfaction" is "too weak to fully express Christ's

---

9. Kolb, *Martin Luther*, 118-19.

10. Kolb and Arand, *Genius of Luther's Theology*, 49.

11. McGrath, "Forerunners of Reformation," 225. A former Lutheran, Ross Aden, called this division between justification and sanctification "unfortunate." Aden, "Justification and Sanctification." For Melanchthon as the author of the Lutheran doctrine of justification in exclusively forensic sense, see Strehle, "Imputatio Iustitiae"; Seifrid, "Paul, Luther, and Justification," 229; O'Kelley, "Luther and Melanchthon." Green, however, finds no significant distinction between Luther's and Melanchthon's articulations of forensic justification. Green, "Question of Theosis."

grace and does not adequately honor his suffering" (*Summer Postil* (1544), WA 21:264.21-35).[12]

At the outset of this study on Luther and his affinity to the concept of deification, it should be stressed that I have no intention to minimize the external aspects of the Reformer's soteriology. Such notions as receiving the preached Word by faith, Christ's redemptive work on the cross, who is God *pro nobis*, the imputation and grasping of Christ's righteousness by faith, participation in the sacraments are the features of external soteriological experience. A reader of Luther encounters a strong expression of "alien righteousness" that constitutes the Reformer's doctrine of justification. In the *Smalcald Articles*, Luther stated that "nothing in this article [justification by faith] can be given up or compromised, even if heaven and earth and thing temporal should be destroyed . . . on this article rests all that we teach and practice" (*WA* 50:199).[13] It needs to be acknowledged that even among some theological works interested in participationist approaches the "alien" reality of Christ's righteousness is explicitly maintained.[14] Moreover, the father of the Finnish Lutheran School, which I will discuss in detail below, recognizes the aspect of "alien righteousness" in Luther, "In a human being, righteousness is 'alien righteousness'—even though in faith this alien reality really determines the believer's being, which it is intimately connected with (*formalis iustitia*). What is 'alien' here is not the elevated human love, but Christ himself and his real presence."[15]

The extended treatment of these external aspects is precluded by space only, not by their significance. Thus, the subsequent explorations of Luther's proximity to *theosis* with the aid of the Finnish scholars aim at highlighting

12. Kolb, *Martin Luther*, 121, 129. Kolb, however, is critical of the Finnish School findings, following Schwarzwäller's suspicion. Schwarzwäller, "Verantwortung des Glaubens," 146-48. Also Kolb and Arand, *Genius of Luther's Theology*, 48.

13. Althaus, *Theology of Martin Luther*, 224-33. Althaus correctly notices that "justification" for Luther meant both God's declaration of righteousness [justum computare], i.e., imputation, and the whole process of sanctification, whereby a person "essentially made righteous" (*LW* 34:320; *WA* 2:495; *LW* 27:227. Althaus, *Theology of Martin Luther*, 226, nn. 12, 13. Althaus concludes that this twofold meaning of the term was not a theological development in Luther but he used both in the same context. Thus, "[c]omplete righteousness in this sense is an eschatological reality."

14. For instance, Tanner, before citing Luther's comment on Gal 2:20, writes, "Christ retains his righteousness for his own even as that righteousness exists within us, if it becomes ours simply through attachment to him. . . . The righteousness that we possess in Christ remains alien to us in that Christ is what we can never be . . ." Tanner, *Christ the Key*, 103-4. Also Leithart maintains that the biblical definition of justification contains both forensic, external declaration as well as transformative, internal deliverance. Leithart, "Justification as Verdict."

15. Mannermaa, *Christ Present in Faith*, 26, 50.

the often downplayed participationist themes of the German theologian, not to the exclusion or juxtaposition of internal with external sides.

The Finnish Lutheran School objects to the unnatural split of the two soteriological concepts.[16] Here is how the originator of this school, Tuomo Mannermaa, defines the problem of traditional Lutheranism:

> In contrast to Luther's theology, forgiveness *(favor)* justification and the real presence of God *(donum)* in faith are in danger of being separated by the one-sidedly forensic doctrine of justification adopted by the Formula of Concord and by subsequent Lutheranism. In Luther's theology, however, both of these motifs are closely united in his understanding of the person of Christ. Christ is both the *favor* and the *donum*. And this unity is, to use Chalcedonian expressions, both inseparable and unconfused.[17]

In a similar vein, Richard A. Jensen correctly identified a problem in dividing external divine agency from the internal human agency, whereby humans are called to live up to the divine mercy shown to them. Thus, the driving force for Christians becomes not moral transformation originated internally from union with Christ, but personal efforts put forth in response to an external gift.[18] To understand Luther's soteriology, beyond more traditional concepts of justification by faith and imputation of Christ's righteousness, one needs to appreciate his teachings on "wonderful exchange" (fröhlicher Wechsel), faith as real ontological participation in Christ, Christ as object and subject of the gift.

According to the Finnish Luther research, Luther himself did not separate the external gift of Christ's righteousness from Christ himself who abides in the receiver of the gift. The wonderful exchange is the ground for the internalization of both gift and giver. Luther believed that Christ assumed not simple human nature in a neutral form, but became "immersed" into sinful human nature, becoming the "greatest sinner" (*maximus*

---

16. For the precursors of the Finnish Lutheran School see an article of Briskina, who is critical of the Finnish Luther research. Briskina, "Orthodox View."

17. Mannermaa, "Justification and Theosis," 28–29. Marquart, however, considers that Mannermaa misinterprets the Formula of Concord, which, in Article III, does not separate the two natures of Christ and confirms participation in the whole person of Christ for justification. Marquart, "Luther and Theosis," 202. Laato prioritized *favor* over *donum*, in contrast to Mannermaa's attempt to balance both Christ's atonement and Christ's presence in faith. Laato, "Justification." I find Laato's treatment of Luther's citations unconvincing. I think that the issue often depends on emphasis in a particular context, rather than on juxtaposition.

18. Jensen, "Theosis and Preaching."

peccator) (*LW* 25:277; *WA* 40.1:433; 26:434.12).[19] Further, Mannermaa states, "Christ is a kind of 'collective person,' or, as the Reformer formulates it himself, the 'greatest person' (*maxima persona*), in whom the persons of all human beings are united in a real manner. Christ *is* every sinner" (cf., *LW* 26:280; *WA* 40.1:20-5).[20] However, since Christ is also the divine Logos and wholly righteous, he became the "battlefield" of God's holiness with sin, death, and curse. Therefore, Christ's atoning death on behalf of sinners is at the same time a victory over sin, death, and curse. By being the person in whom all sinfulness and all righteousness is contained, Christ brings restoration to all sinners who participate in him (*LW* 26:282; *WA* 40.1:26-30). The "happy exchange" presupposes that a sinner participates by faith in the person of Christ, who is the divine grace, righteousness, life, and blessings. The corollary of this glorious "trade" is that "our sins are now not ours but Christ's, and Christ's righteousness is not Christ's but ours" (*LW* 31:189-91; *WA* 1:593.3-38). Put simply, Luther proclaimed, "In myself outside of Christ, I am a sinner; in Christ outside of myself, I am not a sinner" (*LW* 38:158; *WA* 38:205.25-31). In this equation, sinfulness and righteousness are not simply theoretical, but real. The church experiences Christ's attributes not merely as external gifts, but inwardly, because Christ and his body, the church, are one. In Luther's words,

> Christ is God's grace, mercy, righteousness, truth, wisdom, power, comfort, and salvation, given to us by God without any merit on our part. Christ, I say, not as some express it in blind words, "causally," so that he grants righteousness and remains absent himself, for that would be dead. Yes, it is not given at all unless Christ himself is present, just as the radiance of the sun and the heat of fire are not present if there is no sun and no fire (*LW* 14:204).[21]

Imputation and righteousness, being external divine gifts, never remain external to the justified, but become personal and internal because the giver himself enters the believer with his gifts. Justification by faith becomes a reality to the believer solely by Christ's real presence in the believer. Luther avoided a synergism of divine grace with human effort in a person struggling with sin. Grace gives to the Christian favor before God, while the

---

19. Mannermaa, "Justification and Theosis," 29. Not that Christ committed those sins, but he took all of them on himself.

20. Mannermaa, "Justification and Theosis," 30.

21. Luther employed an image of harmonious marriage to Christ and the church, whereby the bridegroom and his bride share both good and evil, being one flesh (*LW* 31:351; *WA* 7:54).

gift helps to overcome sin. Both grace and the gift are mutually dependent. Even though Christians received Christ's righteousness by grace and, can call it their own, it still depends on the continuous gift of faith obtained by *unio cum Christo*.[22] Believers can never be self-confident because their righteousness always depends on the person of Christ present in them. Union with Christ was such an intimate reality to the apostle Paul in Gal 2:20 that Luther acknowledged Paul's life as "alien life," whereby Christ becomes the operative identity, "Christ is speaking, acting, and performing all actions in him; these do not belong to the Paul-life, but to the Christ-life" (*LW* 26:170; *WA* 40.1:288). Against those who taught Christ's spiritual presence in believers, Luther affirmed real or ontological presence:

> Hence the speculation of the sectarians is vain when they imagine that Christ is present in us "spiritually," that is, speculatively, but is present really in heaven. Christ and faith must be completely joined. We must simply take our place in heaven; and Christ must be, live, and work in us. But He lives and works in us, not speculatively but really, with presence and with power [*realiter, praesentissime et efficacissim*] (*LW* 26:356-7; *WA* 40.1:545-6).[23]

Therefore, for Luther, the gospel is not so much about the cross and forgiveness of sins, as it is about union with Christ crucified and risen, whose indwelling alone can guarantee justification and sanctification.

According to the Finnish research of Luther's theology, faith is real ontological participation in Christ without distinguishing forensic and infused righteousness. Faith, not being a sort of work worthy of merit by itself, is the means to take hold of Christ, who is the real treasure and the source of salvation (*LW* 26:130; *WA* 40.1:229). Thus, the value of faith is its content, the person of Christ. Saving faith is not a mere legal instrument to change one's status before God; it is the key to a personal transforming bond between believers and their Lord. The imputation of the alien Christ's righteousness to the believer without a proper account of the intimate communion between Christ and the justified distorts the way Luther understood the justification. Luther, in his commentary on Galatians (1535), expressed a natural sequence, where believers receive righteousness after they accept Christ by faith, "As I have said, faith grasps and embraces Christ, the Son of God, who was given for us . . . When He has been grasped by faith, we have righteousness and life" (*LW* 26:129-30, 177; *WA* 40.1:228-9, 297).[24] Thus, God gives

---

22. Peura, "Christ as Favor," 60.

23. Cited in Marquart, "Luther and Theosis," 193.

24. Earlier in the text, Luther wrote, "Therefore the Christ who is grasped by faith

himself when he imputes Christ's righteousness, grants forgiveness, and confers other benefits. A proper balance between Christ's external and internal righteousness conveys the holistic view of justification in Luther.[25]

According to Luther, Christ is not simply the object of faith, but also the subject, because he is really present in faith. The justifying faith cannot be separated from the deifying faith due to Christ's real presence in that faith (*LW* 26:129–130; *WA* 40.1:228–9).[26] This faith in Christ transforms saints into god according to 2 Pet 1:4. The German Reformer wrote, "The one who has faith is a completely divine man [*plane est divinus homo*], a son of God, the inheritor of the universe . . . Therefore the Abraham who has faith fills heaven and earth; thus every Christian fills heaven and earth by his faith" (*LW* 26:100, 247–8; *WA* 40.1:182, 390). In his earlier writings, Luther taught that to possess the divine gift of grace is no less than to possess Christ himself (*WA* 21:458.11–24). In faith, the believer appropriates not only the effects of Christ, such as imputed righteousness and forgiveness of sins but also Christ himself and the transforming power of the Spirit by participation and union. To partake of Christ means to partake of God incarnate, which unavoidably leaves a divine imprint on the partaker. In *Sermo de duplici iustitiae* (1519), Luther stated, "Thus the righteousness of Christ becomes our righteousness through faith in Christ, and everything that is his, even he himself, becomes ours . . . and he who believes in Christ clings to Christ and is one with Christ and has the same righteousness with him" (*LW* 31:298; *WA* 2:146.8–15). God's righteousness does not exist as an abstract Platonic idea but always exists where God is present. God's righteousness can become human righteousness only when they enter into union with Christ, who becomes the basis for the continuing righteousness of still sinful Christians. As Paul L. Metzger accurately puts it, "We are not one flesh with Christ because we are declared righteous. Rather, we are declared righteous because we are one flesh with Christ."[27] To reverse this order would mean to

---

and who lives in the heart is the true Christian righteousness, on account of which God counts us as righteous and grants us eternal life" (*LW* 26:130; *WA* 40.1:229). Similarly, Seifrid states, "The imputation of righteousness, that is, acceptance with God, coincides with union with Christ. . ." Seifrid, "Paul, Luther, and Justification," 226.

25. As Johnson sums up, "Whereas for Luther justification dependsed [*sic*] upon the alien, *extra nos*, imputed righteousness of Christ, it also depended upon the familiar, *in nobis*, possessed righteousness of Christ." Johnson, "Luther and Calvin," 69.

26. Indeed, Aden suggests that Lutheran and Orthodox views can converge when the role of "deifying grace" is compared to that of "faith." Aden, "Justification and Sanctification," 105. Yet, unlike Aden, I insist, the conversation between the two groups could be more fruitful, if the basis for divine-human union was the persons of God, not the Palamite divine energies.

27. Metzger, "Luther and Finnish School," 206.

dispense with participation in Christ since the righteous cannot gain more than they already have. Hence, the Finnish researchers call this union with Christ "real-ontic" participation.[28]

This personal transformational communion with Christ approximates to the idea of *theosis*. By breaking the human efforts of self-divinization, God's "nihilizing work" precedes the giving of God's Word, which human person passively receives. Luther preferred to view divine-human relationships as the community of persons, of God and believer, rather than the community of wills or acts. Mannermaa maintains that the German Reformer came close to the Palamite notion of deification through the divine energies as Luther considered God's giving of himself. Participation in God is possible because all "properties of God, which are at the same time the essence of God, are present in their abundance in the person of Christ."[29] Therefore, by participating in Christ, one participates in God's essence through his properties. According to Mannermaa, "The *theosis* of the believer [for Luther] is initiated when God bestows on the believer God's essential properties; that is, what God gives of himself to humans is nothing separate from God himself."[30] God and his work are fully present in the believer through Christ. Luther cites 2 Pet 1:4 to show that Christians share divine properties because of Christ's presence in them:

> This is one of those apposite, beautiful, and (as St. Peter says in 2 Pet. 1) precious and very great promises given to us, poor miserable sinners: that we are to become *participants of the divine nature* and be exalted so high in nobility that we are not only to become loved by God through Christ, and have His favor and grace as the highest and most precious shrine, but also to have Him, the Lord Himself, dwelling in us in His fullness (WA 21:458.11–22, trans. Mannermaa).[31]

In 1525, in a classical, patristic way, Luther preached the possibility of sharing in the divine life, being fully filled with God, "In short, that everything he is and can do be in us fully and affect vigorously, so that we become completely divine, not having a piece or even a few pieces of God, but all abundance" (*WA* 17.1:438.14–28, trans. Mannermaa, 35). Simo Peura agrees with Mannermaa that Luther understood God's attributes or "names" as the nature of God.[32] Consequently, when imparted with the divine attri-

28. Kärkkäinen, "Salvation as Justification," 76; Kärkkäinen, *One with God*, 37, 46.
29. Mannermaa, "Why Is Luther so Fascinating?," 15.
30. Mannermaa, "Why Is Luther so Fascinating?," 10.
31. Mannermaa, "Justification and Theosis," 33–34.
32. Peura, "Christ as Favor," 49–50.

butes, believers participate wholly in God himself, i.e., they are deified, "For it is true that a man helped by grace is more than a man; indeed, the grace of God gives him the form of God and deifies him, so that even the Scriptures call him 'God' and 'God's son'" (*Sermon on the Day of St. Peter and St. Paul* (1519); *LW* 51:58; *WA* 2:247–8). Peura summarizes the Reformer's words, "This deification is based on God's indwelling, or inhabitation: a Christian is a god, God's child and infinite, because God indwells in him."[33] Therefore, to possess the divine qualities means to possess God himself to the degree that these qualities can be manifested in the believer. In his sermon on Christmas (1514), Luther incorporated the Irenaean-Athanasian formula of divine-human exchange, retaining the corresponding substantial difference between participants of the union:

> Just as the word of God became flesh, so it is certainly also necessary that the flesh may become word. In other words: God becomes man so that man may become God. Thus power becomes powerless so that weakness may become powerful. The *Logos* puts on our form and gestalt *(Form und Gestalt)*, our image and likeness, so that it may clothe us with its image, its gestalt, and its likeness. Thus wisdom becomes foolish so that foolishness may become wisdom, and so it is in all other things that are in God and in us, to the extent that in all these things he takes what is ours to himself in order to impart what is his to us (*WA* 1:28.25–32, trans. Mannermaa, 36).

Regarding the theoretical explanation of *theosis*, Luther preferred relational or personalist ontology, rather than substantial ontology, because he saw the danger of the latter being used by a sinful man for self-divinization.[34] In a sermon preached in 1526, Luther stated the famous patristic dictum, "God pours out Christ His dear Son over us and pours Himself into us and draws us into Himself, so that He becomes completely humanified [*vermenschet*] and we become completely deified [*gantz und gar vergottet*, "Godded-through"] and everything is altogether one thing, God, Christ, and you" (*WA* 20:229–30).[35] The preacher rejected the partial good of metaphysics for the sake of real knowledge of God through Christ's love and death. The created beings, which are contingent realities with the definite origin, exist only by continuous participation in God, who is the original and unconditional reality. Luther stated that, although all creatures participate in the being of God without mingling, Christians, participating

---

33. Peura, "Christ as Favor," 51. *WA* 4:280.2–5.
34. Juntunen, "Luther and Metaphysics," 129–30.
35. Cited in Marquart, "Luther and Theosis," 185.

in the person of Christ through intimate union with him and *communicatio idiomatum*, nevertheless, do not become one identity and essence with him.[36] According to Sammeli Juntunen, "Luther understands the participation of the believer in Christ as something so 'ontologically intense' that the actions which Christ works in a Christian can be considered the actions of this Christian in question himself."[37] This transfiguration of believers into Christlikeness occurs not in a mechanical manner, but in personal identification with the Savior. The Reformer contended that insofar as there is nothing outside of God—and human existence is a constant reception of life, reason, and material provisions from God—a Christian existence is a continuous reception of Christ's life through the gifts of sacraments, wherein Christ is present. Consequently, *theosis* is the appropriation of the divine life through personal relationships with Christ.

Since love is one of the essential divine qualities, faith allows a person to partake in the very being of God by partaking in Christ's love. To Luther, the significance of the faith-love relationship for *theosis* is evident because the law is fulfilled by love, not by faith directly. Faith brings the Spirit and love to the believer, using which he or she can fulfill the law. In the same way, love does not justify, but it testifies to the real presence of faith in the believer (*WA* 17.2:98.13–4). Mannermaa deduces that Christians possess two natures similar to Christ: that of Christ himself, who is present in faith and lives through them, and their own human nature, which manifests itself in Christ's love toward a neighbor.[38] Luther finished his tractate, *The Freedom of a Christian*, with these words, "We conclude, therefore, that a Christian lives not in himself, but in Christ and his neighbor. Otherwise he is not a Christian. He lives in Christ through faith, in his neighbor through love. By faith he is caught up beyond himself into God. By love he descends beneath himself into his neighbor. Yet he always remains in God and in his love" (*LW* 31:371). In one of his early sermons (1518), Luther stated, "Therefore human beings must become more than human beings" (*LW* 51:58; *WA* 2:247.39–248.8). The preacher could make such statement because the deified human beings are not simply restored to their original righteousness, but receive Christ and his divine righteousness.[39] Christians, being transformed into the likeness of Christ, express Christ's divine love by taking the burdens and weaknesses of others upon themselves, as Christ did.

---

36. Juntunen, "Luther and Metaphysics," 154–55.
37. Juntunen, "Luther and Metaphysics," 155–56. *WA* 3:257.10–4.
38. Mannermaa, "Why Is Luther so Fascinating?," 19.
39. Briskina, "Orthodox View," 21.

Peura considers that Luther's agonizing concern is not fully grasped by the question, "How can I find the merciful God?" but rather "How can one love God and neighbour as himself or herself?"[40] Luther realized that faith in God by itself could lead to a selfish, impure love and focus on God's goods, rather than loving God per se. A believer needs love. Pure love comes from God, who is pure love. According to the First Commandment, God is someone in whom a person fully believes, trusts, and looks for refuge. A person becomes similar to the object of his love. A human desire to earn and merit righteousness or any reward from God is sinful. It makes God into a servant and an idol while that person becomes God to herself. Peura indicates that God's revelation to sanctified believers is his trinitarian presence in love that can be appropriately called *theosis*:

> As we have seen, the threefold self-giving of God means that God reveals himself as the love that finally transforms us into God. God not only reveals his very nature to us, but he also gives himself to us as the triune God. The result is that we are made partakers of his divine nature and thus transformed into God. We can, therefore, speak about salvation as *theosis* in a genuine Lutheran sense of the word.[41]

The question that remained outside much of the discussion of the Finnish scholars is whether Luther's soteriology embraced a trinitarian framework or was distinctively christological in nature. It is appropriate to claim that, similarly to the Cappadocians, Luther's teaching on the Trinity has a strong soteriological underpinning. Although the Reformer did not argue for the divinity of the Son and the Spirit based on their deifying role (while he accepted creedal formulations of the first four ecumenical councils), he discussed the doctrine of the Trinity predominantly in the context of its role in salvation.[42] Powell argues that Luther's strong Christocentric reading of the Scripture influenced his trinitarian discussion. The human intellect is unable to perceive the hidden God, but Jesus revealed the divine self-giving nature and relationships within the Trinity.[43] In his *The Three*

40. Peura, "What God Gives Man," 76.
41. Peura, "What God Gives Man," 91.
42. *On the Councils and the Church* (1539), LW 41:121. Powell, *Trinity in German Thought*, 15. Helmer states that, for Luther, the account of the "inner-Trinity," wherein the word spoken by the Father and was heard by the Spirit, relays the narrative of Son's generation. In the "outer-Trinity," the movement proceeds in the opposite direction: the voice of the Spirit witnessing to Christ is followed by the Son's incorporation of believers into the Father's love. Helmer, *Trinity and Martin Luther*.
43. Powell, "Rethinking Trinitarian Theology," 46. Since Luther preferred biblical language to philosophical one, he was hesitant in using the term *homoousios*.

Symbols (1538) and *Treatise on the Last Words of David* (1543), Luther proclaimed the faith of Athanasius, when he stated that any work that is done by one of the trinitarian persons should be recognized as mutual acting of the other two persons or a three-fold work (*LW* 15:302; *WA* 54:57-8). In the same discussion, the German Reformer affirmed the distinction of the persons to avoid a mono-personal God of Jews, Moslems and Christian heretics.[44] Luther did not shy away from belief in the monarchy of the Father, from whom the divinity of the Son and the Spirit is originated. However, his formulation is distinct from the Eastern fathers with the introduction of the *Filioque* clause (*LW* 15:303; 34:216-7; *WA* 54:58; 50:274; 10.1:151.7-155.24, 183.13-186.8). He concludes, "God's one essence is definitely three distinctive Persons from eternity" (*LW* 15:307; *WA* 54:61). In this way, Luther accounted for the unity and diversity in the Trinity and rejected tritheism. In worshiping one God, believers at the same time worship three persons of the Godhead (*LW* 15:311; *WA* 54:64).

Every living creature participates in the creative life of the Father while believers attain their salvation in connection with the Son and the Holy Spirit. As Ngien illustrates, for Luther, Christ is fully God. Therefore, it is possible to say that the incarnate God suffered and died. Such conclusion, however, does not mean that the whole Godhead or the Father or the Spirit suffered and died.[45] This statement is nuanced by the idea of *perichoresis*, whereby the Father and the Spirit co-suffer with the Son due to the unity of nature and action. The role of the Spirit in the divine work of salvation consists in revealing Christ's redemption to people and causing them to believe in the gospel (*LW* 37:366; *WA* 26:505.38-506.12). The Holy Spirit mediates the gift of Christ to the believer through faith. Quite noticeable is Luther's parallel between Christ and the Spirit as divine giver and gift, "By this Holy Spirit, as a living, eternal, divine gift and endowment, all believers are adorned with faith and other spiritual gifts, raised from the dead, freed from sin, and made joyful and confident, free and secure in their conscience" (*LW* 37:365).[46] When Luther stated "God is to be found nowhere except in suffering and in the cross,"

---

44. Ngien, *Suffering of God*, 137-45. Ngien believes that Luther developed his view of the Trinity in close connection to soteriology.

45. Ngien, *Suffering of God*, 145-53. In the author's words, "Luther affirms theopaschitism but rejects patripassianism . . . because it collapses the distinction between the Father and the Son." The idea of suffering God distinguishes Luther from Calvin, who cautiously avoided absolute *communicatio idiomatum* of natures in Christ (i.e., *extra Calvinisticum*). See Habets, "Putting 'Extra' Back." See also an extended treatment of *extra Calvinisticum* and differences between the Reformers in Willis, *Calvin's Catholic Christology*.

46. Kärkkäinen studies the interconnection of the gift of faith and the gift of the Spirit. Kärkkäinen, *Luthers Trinitarische Theologie*, 105-7, 112.

he meant that self-giving, humble attitude, suffering, and death, which were expressed by Jesus, are natural predispositions of God (WA 1:362.18-9).[47] God's essence is inseparable from and manifested in the divine act of God the Son. Moreover, when one looks for God outside of Jesus, he or she can only find a terrifying and condemning God, even devil (WA 40.3:337.11).[48] It is possible that this dark side or *deus absconditus* precluded Luther from employing the patristic notion of *theosis* because ultimately God the Father remains unknown, imparticipable and even terrifying to humans. Only in Jesus believers encounter the self-revelation of God. It may indicate that Luther leaned toward a form of *christosis*.

In the *Large Catechism* (1529), Luther plainly expressed how God's saving power is revealed by all three persons and would remain unknown without at least one of them, "[W]e could never come to recognize the Father's favor and grace were it not for the Lord Christ, who is a mirror of the Father's heart. Apart from him, we see nothing but an angry and terrible judge. But neither could we know anything of Christ, had it not been revealed by the Holy Spirit."[49] All three persons give not simply gifts, but themselves to people completely: the Father, by his creation that serves people, the Son, by his suffering and reconciliation of sinners with the Father, and the Spirit, by revealing and maintaining the work of Christ in believers. Coming from a presupposition that salvation is an act of one God, Luther stated, "the Father is our Saviour and Redeemer, the Son is our Saviour and Redeemer, and the Holy Spirit is our Saviour and Redeemer, and yet there are not three saviours and redeemers, but only one Saviour and Redeemer" (*LW* 15:311; *WA* 54:64). Luther believed in complete divinity of the Word and its communicative nature, "Word is not merely wind or noise, but brings with it the entire being of the divine nature" and "His Word is so much like him [God] that the entire divinity is completely within, and whoever has the Word has the entire divinity" (*LW* 52:45-46; *WA* 101.1:186.16-188.7). Bayer concludes that, for the Reformer, the Trinity is relational in nature, and the Son revealed the intrinsic outgoing nature of the inner-Trinity:

> If the Trinity is a dialogue, if God, within himself, is communication, relationship, a relational three-ness, then he does not allow himself to be conceptualized in any way as a monad, as a monarchical being or subject. Instead, within himself he is in motion: speaking and hearing, speaking and answering, as

---

47. Luther, *Luther*, 290-91.
48. "Extra Iesum quaerere deum est diabolus" (on Ps 130:1). See also Bayer, *Martin Luther's Theology*, 336.
49. Published in Luther, *Book of Concord*, 440.65.

Father and Son, to whom the Spirit listens, so that what is heard can be communicated to us.[50]

Likewise, Marshall observes that Luther's soteriology went beyond a christological framework, "Luther's concepts of participation in the divine nature and deification are thus genuinely trinitarian, and not only christological."[51] Thus, Luther was conversant with the distinctly patristic trinitarian character of deification.

In conclusion, the doctrine of justification in Luther can—and should—be presented in terms of its forensic and effective aspects. The former means a declarative statement about one's status before God. The latter means the declarative act of God, who not only imputes Christ's righteousness but also makes one righteous in Christ. Mattes correctly concludes, "[a]n 'effective' dimension to justification is inescapable, crucial, and decisive for Luther," although both forensic and effective justifications are an external accomplishment or passive from the believer's point of view.[52] In a similar vein, Vainio, in a brilliant study, deduces that although justification and sanctification in Luther are different, they are not divorced, due to ontological participation in Christ:

> The forensic and effective aspects of justification are not to be understood in a cause and effect relationship. Justification consists of both the renewal of individual's relationship with God and a renewal nature of the human being (*renovatio1*). The basis of salvation is located outside of the person, but it becomes actualized in the person through faith.[53]

When one considers justification as a part of the single trinitarian act that includes all aspects of salvation from its initiation to consummation, it is appropriate, in my view, counting forensic declaration a part of a greater reality, which Luther together with the church fathers called deification.

The Finnish School, arguably, overstates the effective side of the doctrine and is at the risk of running aground of Luther's claims such as in his commentary on Psalm 117 (1530), "If this one teaching [the doctrine of justification by faith] stands in its purity, then Christendom will also remain pure and good, undivided and unseparated; for this alone, and nothing else,

---

50. Bayer, *Martin Luther's Theology*, 341. Moreover, "because Christ identifies himself with the sinner, reconciliation takes place *within* God as well." Bayer, *Martin Luther's Theology*, 342 (emphasis original).
51. Marshall, "Justification as Declaration," 7.
52. Mattes, "Luther on Justification," 265.
53. Vainio, *Justification and Participation*, 61.

makes and maintains Christendom" (*LW* 14:37; *WA* 31:255.5-8; cf., *LW* 28:6; *WA* 40.1:48).[54] But it is equally incorrect to strip Luther's doctrine of justification of its effective side altogether, that is, downplaying real union with Christ by faith, which brings the promise of the Holy Spirit.[55] It should be noted that effective justificäion presupposes no work, synergism of free will with grace, or merit on the part of believers. However, the fact that the active righteousness of Christ accomplished *pro nobis* and is accepted passively by faith becomes the basis for our forensic and transforming righteousness in union with Christ. This ontological participation in the person of Christ in no way violates human identity and allows avoiding the unnecessary legal fiction of forensic justification alone. Moreover, the juridical and moral elements of salvation in this approach become different sides of the same coin, on which the image of God, Jesus Christ, is imprinted.[56] As believers receive Christ personally, they are declared righteous and holy by grace, becoming righteous and holy in union with Christ and yet they remain sinners until the day of final redemption. Mannermaa succinctly concludes, "Forgiveness and indwelling of God are inseparable in the person of Christ, who is present in faith. In that sense, in Luther's theology,

---

54. Flogaus suspects that Mannermaa's reading of Luther's statement about Christ's presence in the believer concurs with Osiander's ontological participation in the divine essence. Nonetheless, Flogaus recognizes the theme of deification in Luther. Flogaus, *Theosis bei Palamas und Luther*, 337-42. I think, the Finns, in response could claim that, unlike Osiander, they interpret Luther as the one who believed in union with the person of Christ, not his natures. Kärkkäinen accurately points out areas, where "The New Perspective on Luther" needs to clarify its stance, such as the meaning of "real-ontic" union, Luther's views on free will and fall in comparison to the Eastern Orthodox views of synergy and divine energies. Kärkkäinen, "Salvation as Justification and Theosis," 79. Clark thinks that the Finnish School "Thomafized" and "Platonized" Luther by confusing justification with sanctification. Clark believes that, for Luther, union with Christ is a consequence of justification, but surprisingly Clark himself mixes the two, stating, "We are justified by virtue of our *legal* union with Christ." Clark, "Iustitia Imputata Christi," 286, 309. Saarinen is confident that the Finnish School preserves a sound balance between forensic and effective justification. Saarinen, "Justification by Faith," 257. Finding union with Christ at the core of Luther's theology, Collins is uncertain whether deification is also central to the Reformer. Collins, *Partaking in Divine Nature*, 148.

55. Contrary to Marquart, who is persuaded that Luther taught only passive or imputed righteousness of Christ that the Formula of Concord affirmed. Marquart, "Luther and Theosis." In my view, bringing the full trinitarian dimension into Luther's soteriology would avoid accusations of the Finnish School in "pneumatological Modalism" by such scholars as Wenz. Wenz, "Unio," 379. Bakken's otherwise fine study of the Spirit's role in *theosis* contains virtually no direct reference to Luther despite its title. Bakken, "Holy Spirit and Theosis."

56. See also Hinlicky, who comes to the same conclusion. Hinlicky, "Theological Anthropology," 61.

justification and *theosis* as participation in God are also inseparable."⁵⁷ Thus, the later Formula of Concord can be read in a way that Luther considered as damning, i.e., a separation of forensic justification from the transforming presence of Christ in the believer.

It is clear that Luther's preaching on justification by faith and legal righteousness stands in no contradiction to the patristic idea of *theosis*. I, however, disagree with Mannermaa that the Palamite notion of divine energies represents Luther's understanding of God's essential attributes. If, as Palamas stated, the divine energies are uncreated as the divine essence, then how is partaking in God's energies different from partaking in his essence. This conundrum was resolved neither by Palamas nor by his successors. Thus, it is doubtful that Luther thought in this way. Hence, I consider that both the Reformer and the church fathers espoused a kind of soteriology, in which believers are transformed into the likeness of the tripersonal God through Christ in terms of both justification and practical sanctification. More precisely, I contend that when one reads Luther's soteriology within the trinitarian framework, it allows to understand him on a par with the Cappadocian theme of *triadosis* via *christosis*, whereby the saved are incorporated into the life of the tripersonal God by grace.

Calvin and Deification

Some of the Calvin researchers consider that the notion of deification is foreign to the Reformer, who taught that there is an unbridgeable gap between the high God and sinful people, a gap that cannot be crossed by creation, even with the help of grace and union with Christ.⁵⁸ J. Todd Billings agrees

57. Mannermaa, "Justification and Theosis," 38.

58. For example, Wendel assures, "The author of the *Institutes* had already shown himself too hostile to any glorification or deification of man, and of earthly and sinful man above all. . ." Wendel, *Calvin*, 235, 259. Tamburello claims that Calvin rejected essential union for the sake of spiritual one. Tamburello, *Union with Christ*, 105. Norris, not being an antagonist of deification himself, concludes, "John Calvin seems to have avoided teaching deification or not known of it." Norris, "Deification," 420. A similar objection is raised by a representative of Radical Orthodoxy, John Milbank, who argues that Calvin, being a product of medieval nominalism, insisted on the imputation of righteousness, so that he became blind in respect to patristic teaching on deification. Milbank, "Alternative Protestantism," 27–30. I am indebted for this note to Billings, *Calvin, Participation, and the Gift*, 10. Slater finds no ground in arguing for deification in Calvin, because believers participate in Christ's humanity, not divinity. Slater, "Salvation as Participation." Another critical voice against "The New Perspective on Calvin" is Wenger, who discards as anachronistic an attempt to define the central or controlling idea (e.g., union with Christ) in Calvin's thought. Wenger, "New Perspective on Calvin." McCormack uses an argument from silence to reject the idea of deification, finding no

that when taking Gregory Palamas's definition of deification with his essence-energy distinction as the standard, the idea of deification scarcely appears in Western theologies.[59] Billings, nonetheless, suggests that Calvin taught a distinctive idea of deification, "Drawing upon the language of participation, ingrafting, and adoption in select Pauline and Johannine passages, Calvin teaches the participation of humanity in the Triune God, affirming the differentiated union of humanity with God in creation and redemption."[60] Calvin believed that the final goal of humankind is participation in God by becoming one with Christ. Unlike the Greek fathers, in the Reformer's mind, it is possible only through the imputation of Christ's righteousness without any human effort or synergism. This imputation of external righteousness, nonetheless, is not an external act, because Christ himself is present in believers and endows them with all his attributes.

One should consider Calvin's apparently "negative" anthropology as negative in relation to the accidental sinful humanity, rather than the original good Adamic humanity that was in union with God before the fall. The Swiss Reformer claimed that in regeneration corrupted humankind lose everything of their own. Billings explains that, in reality, it meant everything "sinful" or humanity "from the flesh," not humanity in general as created beings (*Inst.* 2.3.6).[61] Humanity at its best before the fall is understood as good and in union with God (*Inst.* 2.1.5).[62] To be created in God's image is, for Calvin, "participation in God" (*Inst.* 2.2.1). Thus, the sinfulness of people is *accidental* (an Aristotelian category) to humanity's good nature. However, this accidental feature is temporal as good human nature will attain final redemption.

---

ground for *perichoresis* in the Reformer's theology (in fact, Calvin did not discuss it at all, whether positively or negatively), "*But he has dispensed completely with that which made divinization theories possible: the idea of an interpenetration of the natures.*" McCormack, "Union with Christ," 516 (emphasis original). Similarly, McClean argues that Calvin did not utilize perichoresis at all and preferred to talk about "Spirit-mediated" union of God and believers. McClean, "Perichoresis, Theosis and Union," 130–41. Seifrid finds the term perichoresis in divine-human relations "entirely unobjectionable," but still lacking necessary distinction between human and divine persons. Seifrid, "Paul, Luther, and Justification," 228–29. Butin assures that perichoresis of the natures in Christ is the ground for the restoration of the image of God in believers through the agency of the Spirit. Butin, *Revelation, Redemption, and Response*, 68–69.

59. Billings, "United to God."

60. Billings, "United to God," 316–17. Billings suggests a middle ground for understanding Calvin's soteriology as both forensic and transformational, "Calvin's theology of union with Christ is articulated with reference to participation, adoption, imputation, and the wondrous exchange. It is a multifaceted doctrine, utilizing both legal and transformative images." Billings, *Calvin, Participation, and Gift*, 23.

61. Calvin, *Calvin*. See also Calvin, *Bondage and Liberation*, 212.

62. Billings, "United to God," 320.

Powerless sinful humanity needs to be obliterated in death with Christ before the Spirit vivifies it in Christ's resurrection. Moreover, the death of corrupted humanity with Christ does not mean the death of good humanity, but of sinful desires. For Calvin, participation in Christ's death is dying to the "old self" so that the "new self" can live through the Spirit, fulfilling the *telos* of God's original creation (*Inst.* 3.3.5–9). Furthermore, God replaces with good gifts sin's negative consequences. Believers appropriate divine favor only in Christ, who lives within them. Calvin stated,

> How do we receive those benefits which the Father bestowed upon his only-begotten Son—not for Christ's own private use, but that he might enrich poor and needy men? First, we must understand that as long as Christ remains outside of us, and we are separated from him, all that he has suffered and done for the salvation of the human race remains useless and of no value to us (*Inst.* 3.1.1).

Thus, the author of the *Institutes* developed his soteriology not merely as the transfer of Christ's benefits, such as righteousness, but as the transfer of Christ himself into believers.

Romans 6, 8, and 11 served as a basis for Calvin's theology of participation with Christ in his death and resurrection, adoption by God with access to the Father in the Spirit, and the ingrafting of believers into Christ and God's people by grace. The Reformer followed the famous patristic formula of divine-human exchange, wherein the Son of God became what we are so that we become what he is by grace (*Inst.* 2.12.2). As a result of ingrafting into Christ, believers partake in the person of Christ, including his righteousness, "For in what way does true faith justify, save when it binds us to Christ so that, made one with him, we may enjoy participation in his righteousness?" (*Inst.* 3.17.11). The image of ingrafting became instrumental for Calvin to illustrate participation in the person of Christ and his achievements *pro nobis*, "For we await salvation from him not because he appears to us afar off, but because he makes us, ingrafted into his body, participants not only in all his benefits but also in himself" (*Inst.* 3.2.24). It is only when a person receives God himself that he or she receives the abundance of God's gifts.

In his commentary on Rom 6, Calvin tied a cluster of ideas, such as participation, adoption, and ingrafting, to express the transformation not only of human life but also of nature, "in the former [the ingrafting of trees] the graft draws its aliment from the root, but retains its own nature in the fruit; but in the latter [in spiritual ingrafting] not only we derive the vigor and nourishment of life from Christ, but we also pass from our own to his nature" (*Comm.* Rom 6:5; *CR* 49:107). This statement espouses ontological change that originates from the real union between human and divine. Faith saves not because it has value in and of itself or intellectually recognizes Christ's achievements on the cross, but because, as an empty "vessel," it embraces Christ, welcomes him inside one's heart, joins with and ingrafts the believer into the body of Christ (*Inst.* 3.2.30; 3.11.7). Calvin asserted, "In a word, faith is not a distant view, but a warm embrace, of Christ, by which he dwells in us, and we are filled with the Divine Spirit" (*Comm.* Eph 3:17; *CR* 51:187).

Billings traces some similarities between Calvin's and Osiander's views on participation, growth in sanctification and grace.[63] Nevertheless, they disagreed on the issue of forensic justification. Osiander rejected the idea, arguing for infusion of Christ's divine righteousness into believers:

> If the question be asked according to what nature Christ, His whole undivided person, is our Righteousness, then, just as when one asks according to what nature He is the Creator of heaven and earth, the clear, correct, and plain answer is that He is our Righteousness according to His divine, and not according to His human nature, although we are unable to find, obtain, or apprehend such divine righteousness apart from His humanity.[64]

As is apparent from this quote, strong accent on Christ's divinity, for Osiander, is not a reason to exclude Christ's humanity altogether. In contrast to Osiander, Calvin viewed forensic and transformational justification, pardon and indwelling as inseparably different. The righteousness of Christ, who is both divine and human, is imputed, infused and possessed by the Christian, who participates in undivided Christ. In Calvin's words,

> For even though Christ if he had not been true God could not cleanse our souls by his blood, nor appease his Father by his sacrifice, nor absolve us from guilt, nor, in sum, fulfill the office of priest, because the power of the flesh is unequal to so great a burden, yet it is certain that he carried out all these acts according to his human nature (*Inst.* 3.11.9).

Osiander's opponent affirmed that justification is a legal notion, but it should not be detached from the grace of regeneration, albeit they are distinct concepts (*Inst.* 3.11.11). Being distinct matters, both forensic justification and personal sanctification inseparably depend on the person of

---

63. Billings, "United to God," 326.

64. Bente and Dau, *Concordia Triglotta*, 156. Cited in Weis, "Calvin versus Osiander," 356–57.

Christ. Calvin responded to Osiander's claims, saying, "As Christ cannot be divided into parts, so the two things, justification and sanctification, which we perceive to be united together in him, are inseparable. Whomsoever, therefore, God receives into his favour, he presents with the Spirit of adoption, whose agency forms them anew into his image" (*Inst.* 3.11.6; cf., *Comm.* 1 Cor 1:30). These two soteriological concepts should not be divorced because they indivisibly exist in Christ (*Inst.* 3.16.1).[65] Calvin wrote,

> Therefore, that joining together of Head and members, that indwelling of Christ in our hearts—in short, that mystical union—are accorded by us the highest degree of importance, so that Christ, having been made ours, makes us sharers with him in the gifts with which he has been endowed. We do not, therefore, contemplate him outside ourselves from afar in order that his righteousness may be imputed to us but because we put on Christ and are engrafted into his body—in short, because he deigns to make us one with him. For this reason, we glory that we have fellowship of righteousness with him (*Inst.* 3.11.10).[66]

Forensic justification is necessary to release a Christian from the anxiety of conscience and uncertainty in salvation, as well as to establish the graciousness of God's gift and genuine gratitude of obedient God's child. All of these things, however, are the result of the personal union, wherein adopted children are enclothed with the divine Son incarnate.

Calvin disagreed with Osiander about the infusion of Christ's divinity into the Christian, preferring to talk about the Holy Spirit, who enables personal communion with the Savior but not in his essences. A believer participates in the whole person of Christ and the whole Trinity while remaining distinct (*Inst.* 3.11.5–8).[67] Calvin was eager to preserve

---

65. Carpenter, "Question of Union?," 375–76. In fact, one should note that Calvin, in his *Institutes*, treated the teaching on sanctification prior to justification to show that, although a sinner is justified by faith alone, saving faith is never devoid of good works. The French teacher assured that "a man is justified freely by faith alone, and yet that holiness of life, *real* holiness, as it is called, is inseparable from the free imputation of righteousness" (emphasis original) (*Inst.* 3.3.1; cf., 3.11.1).

66. Johnson expresses well Calvin's distinction without separation of justification and regeneration, "Justification does not include or cause sanctification, nor can sanctification ever include or cause justification. Christ gives both, inseparably, in himself.... There is no justification without sanctification because there is no faith without the possession of Christ and *all* his benefits." Johnson, "Luther and Calvin," 73–74; Johnson, "New or Nuanced?," 556.

67. Vanhoozer calls this participation in Christ's "personal history." He argues that union with Christ includes not just justification and sanctification as immediate fruits thereof, but also election and glorification, which all together constitute Paul's

the metaphysical distinction between God and the deified, in commenting on 2 Pet 1:4, "But such a delirium as this [that God's nature swallows up our nature] never entered the minds of the holy Apostles; they only intended to say that when divested of all the vices of the flesh, we shall be partakers of divine and blessed immortality and glory, so as to be as it were one with God as far as our capacities will allow" (*Comm.* 2 Pet 1:4; CR 55:446). Participation in the triune God does not mean, for Calvin, any fusion of humanity into Godhead, but merely an accommodation to the life of God.[68] More precisely, the distinction of identities in the mystical union allows for the ever-growing union, not its dissolution, "Christ is not outside us but dwells within us. Not only does he cleave to us by an indivisible bond of fellowship, but with a wonderful communion, day by day, he grows more and more into one body with us, until he becomes completely one with us" (*Inst.* 3.2.24). Osiander's emphasis on the deifying divinity of Christ de-emphasized Christ's humanity, his saving work on the cross, his mediatory role, and the work of the Spirit in salvation.

This point led Slater to argue that, for Calvin, believers receive the human righteousness of Christ that he achieved by obedience.[69] Citing *Institutes* 2.12.2, Slater interprets the phrase "*to transfer to us what is his [Christ's], making that which is his by nature to become ours by grace*" as "extending to us what is his according to his human nature."[70] It is unclear, however, what Christ's human nature apart from divine nature could contribute to believers. It seems that Slater, perhaps unwittingly, sided with Stancaro, another Calvin's opponent, who contended against Osiander that Christ could be our Mediator only as a human.[71] According to Stancaro, to claim that Christ is a Mediator between God and human in his divinity would surmise that the Son's divinity is lower than the Father's and would lead to Arianism.[72] Calvin himself openly opposed Stancaro's idea of Christ's mediation solely in his humanity:

and Calvin's *ordo salutis*, "Union with Christ arguably spans the whole of redemptive history, from eternal election to heavenly session." Vanhoozer, "From 'Blessed in Christ,'" 8, 11, 19.

68. Wendel is quick to underline that participants of the union preserve their respective characteristics, "There is no question, when Calvin is speaking about union or communion with Christ, of any absorption into Christ, or any mystical identification that would diminish human personality in the slightest degree, or draw Christ down to us." Wendel, *Calvin*, 235, 237; Canlis, *Calvin's Ladder*, 141–42.

69. Slater, "Salvation as Participation," 41, 45, 52.

70. Slater, "Salvation as Participation," 44 (emphasis original).

71. Lee, "Calvin on Deification."

72. Stancaro, and by inference Slater, fell into a sort of Nestorianism by ascribing Christ's righteousness only to his humanity. Edmondson, *Calvin's Christology*, 14.

[Christ] could not fulfill other aspects of the office unless by his divine power: it was not within man's capacity to overcome death and the devil, nor could man alone win righteousness, give life, or grant all the benefits which we receive from him . . . It is also true to say that all the actions which Christ performed to reconcile God and man refer to the whole person, and are not to be separately restricted to only one nature.[73]

The hypostatic union of Christ's humanity and divinity guaranteed his righteousness. When the Genevan Reformer asserted Christ's human righteousness, he often modified it by the affirmation of Christ's divine identity (*Inst.* 3.11.8-9). Thus, it is more suitable to read Calvin here in a patristic way, i.e., Christ's attributes as a theandric person are by grace conveyed to believers. Further, the Reformer did not assign Christ's righteousness to one of his natures, but to his person as Mediator (e.g., *Inst.* 2.1.6; 3.2.24).[74] In fact, Calvin stated that Christ could not have achieved righteousness as a human, was he also not God. Otherwise, Christ would be a perfect legalist, who fulfilled the law without divine agency, which would be unthinkable to the Reformer. Instead, Christ's obedience to the Father, with the assisting role of the Spirit, is a clear manifestation of the Son's "triune identity" and the intratrinitarian community in the divine economy.[75]

Joseph McLelland thinks that forensic justification is a later development of Calvin's students.[76] However, this is not the case. Calvin perceived both mystical union with Christ and forensic justification as complementary soteriological categories. Justification precedes sanctification—albeit logically, not chronologically—and ultimately justification and sanctification are indispensable and inseparable from each other.[77] It was precisely the point of Calvin's disagreement with the Council of Trent, whereby Rome erased the distinction between justification and sanctification. The Genevan Reformer insisted that, although both are the inseparable gifts of Christ, they are, nonetheless, distinct:

73. Cited in Tylenda, "Christ the Mediator," 169-71.

74. See also Tylenda, "Calvin's Understanding," 153; Canlis, *Calvin's Ladder*, 96.

75. Canlis, *Calvin's Ladder*, 121. It is only through the interrelationship of Christ with the Father that Christ's human obedience is released from moralism. "Yet if Christ's primary expression of righteousness on earth is maintained (as Calvin elsewhere does) as his unswerving communion with the Father, then human salvation is both by this obedient communion and for communion. Only when this is brought to the fore can a moralistic account of Christ's life diminish and, with it, a corresponding moralistic account of the Christian life." Canlis, *Calvin's Ladder*, 112.

76. McLelland, "Sailing to Byzantium."

77. Billings states that "there is no temporal gap between the gifts—for they are inseparable, yet distinguishable." Billings, "John Calvin's Soteriology," 428.

It is not to be denied, however, that these two things, Justification and Sanctification, are constantly conjoined and cohere; but from this it is erroneously inferred that they are one and the same. For example: The light of the sun, though never unaccompanied with heat, is not to be considered heat. Where is the man so undiscerning as not to distinguish one from the other? We acknowledge, then, that as soon as any one is justified, renewal also necessarily follows: and there is no dispute as to whether or not Christ sanctifies all whom he justifies. It were to rend the gospel, and divide Christ himself, to attempt to separate the righteousness we obtain by faith from repentance (*TT* 3:115–6).[78]

Thus, Calvin maintained that the double operation of grace in believers occurs in *distinctio sed non separatio*. Wendel highlights this point well when he states that Calvin never imagined a causal or chronological link between justification and regeneration, one is impossible without the other, and "placed them side by side upon the same level."[79]

Union with Christ, however, precedes justification, because justification is one of the benefits the Christian receives, becoming one with the source of justification. This is not to deny imputed righteousness, which is transferred to believers, because Christians are not righteous by nature or achievement, but only in union with Christ. In Calvin's words, "You see that our righteousness is not in us but in Christ, that we possess it only because we are partakers in Christ; indeed, with him we possess all its riches" (*Inst.* 3.11.23). Likewise, in the discussion of the Lord's Supper, Calvin returns to the crucial point that union with Christ by faith is a prerequisite for the appropriation of his righteousness and other benefits, "And indeed, I do not see how anyone can trust that he has redemption and righteousness in the cross of Christ, and life in his death, unless he relies chiefly upon a true participation in Christ himself. For those benefits would not come to us unless Christ first made himself ours" (*Inst.* 4.17.11). This union and participation in Christ are not a human achievement, but the result of the Spirit's work, bridging the gulf between Christ and the people of faith, "the Holy Spirit is the bond by which Christ effectually binds us to himself" (*Inst.* 3.1.1; 3.1.4; 3.2.5). Billings highlights the contemporaneity

78. Cited in Johnson, "New or Nuanced?," 556.

79. Wendel, *Calvin*, 233–34, 256–58. "One must also avoid making one the final aim of the other. Sanctification is not the purpose of justification. It proceeds from the same source but remains independent, or, more correctly, is logically distinct from justification." Wendel, however, maintains that union with Christ is not the cause of imputation, but that both are two distinct aspects of the same saving event. Wendel, *Calvin*, 258. This position, I think, disregards the fact that justification and sanctification are some of the benefits one receives by becoming one with Christ.

of the juridical and practical sides of salvation in the Reformer, "In Calvin, the 'forensic' imputation of Christ's righteousness and the mystical union with Christ are held in the closest possible relationship—one is unthinkable without the other."[80] In Calvin's words,

> Why, then, are we justified by faith? Because by faith we grasp Christ's righteousness, by which alone we are reconciled to God. Yet you could not grasp this without at the same time grasping sanctification also. For he "is given unto us for righteousness, wisdom, sanctification, and redemption" [1 Cor. 1:30]. Therefore Christ justifies no one whom he does not at the same time sanctify. These benefits are joined together by an *indissoluble bond*, so that those whom he illumines by his wisdom, he redeems, those whom he redeems, he justifies, those whom he justifies, he sanctifies.
> . . . Although we may distinguish them, Christ contains them both *inseparably* in himself. Do you wish, then, to attain to righteousness? You must first possess Christ, but you cannot possess him without being made partaker in his sanctification, because *he cannot be divided into pieces* [1 Cor. 1:13]. Since, therefore, it is solely by expending himself that the Lord gives us these benefits to enjoy. *He bestows both of them at the same time, the one never without the other.* Thus it is clear how true it is that we are justified not without works yet not through works, since in our sharing in Christ, which justifies us, *sanctification is just as much included as righteousness.* (*Inst.* 3.16.1, emphasis added).

To separate justification from sanctification means to bring division into Christ, who contains both of these benefits as one gift, namely himself.[81] The centrality of union with Christ for Calvin's soteriology is supported by Marcus P. Johnson's research, who considers that "[i]t is no exaggeration to say that Calvin's soteriology is grounded in the fundamental reality of the believer's incorporation into the salvific person of Jesus Christ."[82]

Are Christians passive in receiving the gift of external righteousness or are they somehow active? Calvin approached this issue synthesizing the twofold operation of grace.[83] Having discussed the nature of saving faith, which is not "devoid of good works," the Reformer concluded:

80. Billings, "United to God," 329.
81. Niesel astutely summarizes the unity and diversity of the two doctrines, "[t]he two things—justification and sanctification—are one in Him but only in Him." Niesel, *Theology of Calvin*, 138.
82. Johnson, "Luther and Calvin," 59.
83. Billings, *Calvin, Participation, and Gift*, chap. 4; Billings, "John Calvin's

Christ was given to us by God's generosity, to be grasped and possessed by us in faith. By partaking of him, we principally receive a double grace: namely, that being reconciled to God through Christ's blamelessness, we may have in heaven instead of a Judge a gracious Father; and secondly, that sanctified by Christ's spirit we may cultivate blamelessness and purity of life (*Inst.* 3.11.1).

The idea of *duplex gratia* implies that the one part of grace is forensic justification, which is acquired in the union and ingrafting into Christ. Thus, justification comes not from outside, but from Christ, who is present within believers. The other part of grace is regeneration and sanctification through adoption and participation in Christ by faith. This participation occurs not through works, albeit not without works, "since in our sharing in Christ, which justifies us, sanctification is just as much included as righteousness" (*Inst.* 3.16.1). Talking about the logical priority of personal justification, Calvin inferred, "Therefore, it is necessary that the righteousness of faith alone so precede in order, and be so pre-eminent in degree, that nothing can go before it or obscure it" (*Acts of the Council of Trent with the Antidote*; *TT* 3:128). To avoid the unwarranted chronological priority of one over the other, Johnson correctly recaps that justification and sanctification in Calvin are a "twofold grace" or a "double grace" (*duplex gratia*), not "double graces."[84] Justification and sanctification occur hand-in-hand as the dual effect of one gracious event. The two effects of the same grace are distinct but inseparable (like the two natures of Christ) and simultaneous; one is impossible without the other. "In this first grace," according to Billings, "Calvin is speaking not simply about a legal decree, but about an entrance into a new way of being and acting through union with Christ. Moreover, the inseparable second grace—as living out the implications of this first grace in a trinitarian context of adoption—is highly active."[85] Likewise, faith has a twofold character: it is a gift of the Spirit and a human response, which can grow and mature by means of the Word and the Spirit. In the same way, Calvin presented a sort of double justification, whereby God justifies sinners without works, but also God accepts good works produced by the Spirit in the justified (*Inst.* 3.17.4–5).

Further, for Calvin, participation in Christ is not mere imitation, but substantial union (*Comm. Rom* 6:4–5; *CR* 49:105–6). Billings traces the development of Calvin's sacramental theology in the early and later versions

---

Soteriology," 435.

84. Johnson, "New or Nuanced?," 553.

85. Billings, *Calvin, Participation, and Gift*, 114–15.

of the *Institutes*, concluding that the intensification of the participation language is clearly evident in his work, rather than a symbolic interpretation of the sacraments.[86] Calvin went beyond the language of the symbolic union when he elaborated on Eph 5:30–31, "Such is the union between us and Christ, who in some sort makes us partakers of his substance" (*Comm.* Eph 5:30–31; *CR* 51:225-6). As Eve was naturally from the flesh and bones of Adam, so the members of the church constitute Christ's one body. Calvin recalled the famous patristic dictum, stating that partaking in the Eucharist implies partaking in Christ's vivifying substance, "being made a sharer in our human mortality, he [Christ] made us partakers in his divine immortality" (*Inst.* 4.17.4). Unlike Bullinger and other Zwinglians, Calvin supported the substantial presence and reception of Christ in the Eucharist, not mere memorial participation. The Genevan Reformer blatantly claimed substantial partaking of Christ, saying, "our souls are truly fed by the substance of Christ's flesh," and "by the secret virtue of the Holy Spirit, life is infused into us from the substance of his flesh" (*TT* 2:277).

Similarly, in baptism, one participates in Christ's body and the church. Participation in God's substance is possible not because of the transfusion of the divine nature (Osiander), but because of the indwelling Spirit and union between Christ and the church. Therefore, Billings convincingly argues that Calvin's sacramental theology demonstrated essential participation in Christ, "Thus, through the sacraments believers truly participate in Christ; they do not simply imitate Christ or partake of his benefits. In baptism and the Lord's Supper, believers participate in the person of Christ, ingrafted into his body."[87]

The sacramental sign, albeit united, is different from the substance (i.e., Christ) of the sacrament, lest the elements receive idolatrous glory due to God alone. Since Christ has a real human body that has spatial limitations, Calvin, unlike Lutherans and Roman Catholics, rejected Christ's bodily presence in the elements but taught the believer's ascension into heaven to partake of Christ (*Inst.* 4.17.30). This ascension into heaven in the Eucharist does not mean spatial change, because, for the Spirit, who

---

86. Billings, *Calvin, Participation, and Gift*, chap. 3. In the 1536 edition of the *Institutes*, Calvin upheld the belief in participation in Christ's death and resurrection through baptism, but it was not clearly expressed as ontological participation, because of the controversy over the Catholic Mass. In the 1539 edition, in which he incorporated his studies on Romans, Calvin expanded the idea of participation, claiming participation not only in eternal life, but also in God through Christ and by the Spirit. This position was even clearer in the final 1559 edition. In contrast, see Raith's surprising conclusion that Calvin, unlike Aquinas, discarded participatory framework in his commentary on Romans. Raith II, *Aquinas and Calvin*, 207.

87. Billings, "United to God," 323–24.

makes this participation in Christ possible, space is an improper category. Although Christ's body has spatial circumscription, it does not mean that he dwells only in heaven. Heaven's "distance" is not spatial, but transcendental in nature and can be bridged only by the Spirit. Likewise, baptism is a manifestation of the trinitarian double grace. In Calvin's words, through baptism "the free pardon of sins and the imputation of righteousness are first promised us, and then the grace of the Holy Spirit to reform us to newness of life" (*Inst.* 4.15.5). Baptism is an outward sign of forgiveness and adoption by the Father, as well as participation in Christ through the Spirit.

Although the language of *substance* was much debated among the Reformers, Calvin, following Cyril, persisted on human participation in the life-giving substance of Christ present in the Lord's Supper.[88] Thus, Billings is correct when he calls this participation "ontological and objective,"[89] because the divine Christ is really and fully present in the Eucharist, as well as in the church, by faith through the Spirit. Calvin's teaching on participation in Christ preserved the orthodox position on incommunicable divine nature by employing the concept of union with Christ's divine person and mediation of the Holy Spirit. Partaking of the body of Christ in the Eucharist is not a Nestorian division of Christ's natures because the church partakes in Christ's person through the Spirit. The church, being the body of Christ, exists in inseparable union with the Son of God, remaining distinct in nature. This idea is the heart of the patristic doctrine of deification.

Participation in Christ also leads to a beatific vision of God, "when as partakers in heavenly glory we shall see God as he is" (*Inst.* 2.14.3). In glorifying Christ, the godly, in their turn, will be glorified by God, who wants them to reflect his glory. Calvin wrote, "If the Lord will share his glory, power, and righteousness with the elect—nay, will give himself to be enjoyed by them and, what is more excellent, will somehow make them to become one with himself, let us remember that every sort of happiness is included under this benefit" (*Inst.* 3.25.10; cf., *Comm.* 2 Thess. 1:12).[90] Christ's

---

88. Billings, "United to God," 331–32. McCormack correctly supposes that, for Calvin, participation in Christ means participation in the "compound person" of Christ. He is, however, wrong to assume that deification is impossible because, for Calvin, there is no interpenetration of natures in Christ and believers participate only in the human nature of the Mediator. McCormack, "Union with Christ," 514–16. Arguably, this statement is close to what Calvin called the "pulling of the two natures of Christ apart" (*Inst.* 2.14.5). Deification is possible precisely because human persons participate in the divine person of the Son.

89. Billings, *Calvin, Participation, and Gift*, 65.

90. Cited in Mosser, "Greatest Possible Blessing," 46. Contrary to Slater, who thinks that saints will regain their original glory, Calvin defines this glory as "divine" and "his [Lord's]" glory. Slater, "Salvation as Participation," 42.

ascension into heaven is the ground for believers to follow their Mediator. As Calvin taught in his commentary on John, "we have an entrance into heaven in common with him who clothed himself with our flesh, that he might make us partakers of all blessings" (*Comm.* John 3:13). By sharing in God's glory by grace, believers partake in the divine attribute that exceeds their natural capacity. The distinction between God and saints in eternity notwithstanding, Christians will "be partakers of the divine glory," while their nature will become "spiritual, and endued with a heavenly and blessed immortality" (*Comm.* 1 John 3:2).

I consent to Billings's claim that Calvin's soteriology was both Christocentric and trinitarian because the Father adopts believers, who receive the Spirit in the context of union with Christ.[91] Calvin's version of deification has trinitarian feature and is based on a union between the Father and the Son. The life and love that the Son shares with the Father become accessible to saints through the union with Christ, "Hence, too, we infer that we are one with the Son of God; not because he conveys his substance to us, but because, by the power of his Spirit, he imparts to us his life and all the blessings which he has received from the Father" (*Comm.* John 17:21). The incarnation and redemption of the Son is the ground for human access to God himself, not only to the incarnate Christ:

> By this we are taught not only that by the Son's intercession do those things which the Heavenly Father bestows come to us but that by mutual participation in power the Son himself is the author of them. This practical knowledge is doubtless more certain and firmer than any idle speculation. There, indeed, does the pious mind perceive the very presence of God, and almost touches him, when it feels itself quickened, illumined, preserved, justified, and sanctified (*Inst.* 1.13.13).

Calvin adamantly stated that Christ's redemptive death on the cross is only a half-achievement without ultimate union and ascent of the faithful to God the Father. In the Reformer's words, the Son's descent

> was that he might unite us to God; for until we have reached that point, we are, as it were, in the middle of the course. We too

91. Billings, "John Calvin's Soteriology," 428–29. See also cogent thesis on Calvin's trinitarian theology in Butin, *Revelation, Redemption, and Response*. Butin thinks that the lack of scholarly treatments of Calvin's view on the Trinity was caused by predominantly dialectical approaches to the divine-human relationships. Muller suggests that the Reformers gradually shifted from the critique of tradition to openly patristic trinitarian language after 1540s due to emergent antitrinitarian Protestant groups. Muller, *Post-Reformation Reformed Dogmatics*, 4:60–62. This observation is in line with my aim to demonstrate continuity between the patristic and Protestant trinitarian theology.

imagine to ourselves but a half-Christ, and a mutilated Christ, if
he do not lead us to God . . .

Let us therefore learn to behold Christ humbled in the
flesh, so that he may conduct us to the fountain of a blessed
immortality; for he was not appointed to be our guide, merely
to raise us to the sphere of the moon or of the sun, but to make
us one with God the Father (*Comm.* John 14:28).

This ascent, however, is not merely an imitation of Christ's moral qualities, but participation and communion with the triune God.[92]

Likewise, the Holy Spirit is the one, who "breathes divine life into us" (*Inst.* 3.1.3). In fact, Christ is of no avail unless the Spirit brings the saved into union, "By the grace and power of the same Spirit we are made his members, to keep us under himself and in turn to possess him" (*Inst.* 3.1.3). The instrumentality of the Spirit allows for the mystical union of human beings with the Trinity, without the mixture of their essences, "that man is made to conform to God, not by an inflowing of substance, but by the grace and power of the Spirit . . . who surely works in us without rendering us consubstantial with God" (*Inst.* 1.15.5).[93] Commenting on the dominant role that the Spirit plays in Calvin's soteriology, Wendel even suggests:

In a good many passages, indeed, the Holy Spirit plays the part
of an obligatory mediator between Christ and man, just as the
Christ is mediator between God and man. And in the same
way that Jesus Christ is the necessary instrument of redemption, so is the Holy Spirit the no less necessary instrument by
means of which this redemption reaches us, in justification
and regeneration.[94]

It should be noted that the doctrine of union with Christ in Calvin in recent scholarship, unfortunately, gives the less prominent role to the Holy Spirit, who is a personal agent in salvation, and not simply a "bridge" or "means" of incorporation in Christ.[95] Only a thoroughly pneumatological presentation of Calvin's soteriology can do justice to his Christology and anthropology. Consequently, the author of the *Institutes* deduced that

92. Canlis, *Calvin's Ladder*, 129. She finds the notion of adoption through the Spirit a safe way of presenting participation of human persons in the life of the divine persons without losing ontological distinction between God and human and trivializing atonement. Canlis, *Calvin's Ladder*, 136–39.

93. Thus, Niesel rightly concludes, "That union of the faithful with Christ which Calvin teaches has nothing whatever to do with the absorption of the pious mystic into the sphere of the divine being." Niesel, *Theology of Calvin*, 126.

94. Wendel, *Calvin*, 239–40.

95. Canlis, *Calvin's Ladder*, 154.

salvation is a trinitarian achievement, "I do not deny that Christ, as he is God and man, justifies us; and also that this work is the common task of the Father and the Holy Spirit; finally, that righteousness of which Christ makes us partakers with himself is the eternal righteousness of the eternal God" (*Inst.* 3.11.9). Hence, Torrance confirms that the Spirit is equally the "Author and Source of our justification and sanctification, of truth, grace, and every good thing."[96]

Calvin confessed the traditional trinitarianism of Gregory of Nazianzus, whereby the unity of Godhead was indivisibly connected with distinct divine persons. Calvin quoted Gregory, "I cannot think on the one without quickly being encircled by the splendor of the three; nor can I discern the three without being straightway carried back to the one" (*Inst.* 1.13.17; Gregory of Nazianzus, *On Holy Baptism*, Or. 40.41). Calvin's understanding of trinitarian relations, including the monarchy of the Father, is in full concord with church fathers, when he stated:

> [W]hen we profess to believe in one God, under the name of God is understood a single, simple essence, in which we comprehend three persons, or hypostases. Therefore, whenever the name of God is mentioned without particularization, there are designated no less the Son and the Spirit than the Father; but where the Son is joined to the Father, then the relation of the two enters in; and so we distinguish among the persons. But because the peculiar qualities in the persons carry an order within them, e.g., in the Father is the beginning and the source, so often as mention is made of the Father and the Son together, or the Spirit, the name of God is peculiarly applied to the Father. In this way, unity of essence is retained, and a reasoned order is kept, which yet takes nothing away from the deity of the Son and the Spirit (*Inst.* 1.13.20).

As with Luther, for the Genevan Reformer, the doctrine of the Trinity is not a scholastic exercise in reasoning about incomprehensible divine nature, but the knowledge of God revealed in his works, the Bible, and the person of Christ (*Inst.* 1.5.9; 1.2.2).[97] Commenting on Ephesians, Calvin wrote, "The Son of God became man in such a manner, that God was his God as well as ours . . . for God's glory, as a Father, consists in subjecting

---

96. Torrance, "Calvin's Doctrine," 174. A brilliant article on the patristic background of Calvin's understanding of the Trinity.

97. Powell, "Rethinking Trinitarian Theology," 48. Murphy, arguing for a Reformed version of *theosis*, asserts its trinitarian characteristic, "Our entire person—mind, body, soul—is designed to be in communion with the Trinity, to be totally embraced by God and enveloped by the glory of the Lord." Murphy, "Reformed Theosis?," 200.

his Son to our condition, that, through him, he might be our God" (*Comm. Eph* 1:17). On another occasion, he expressed the *perichoretic* nature of the Father-Son relationships in connection to human beings:

> The Father, therefore, was in the Son, in accordance with that statement—I am in the Father, and the Father in me (John 10:38). Therefore he that hath the Son, hath the Father also. For Paul has made use of this expression with this view—that we may learn to be satisfied with Christ alone, because in him we find also God the Father, as he truly communicates himself to us by him (*Comm.* 2 Cor 5:19).

Not surprising then is Billings's inference, "Relying upon interpretations of John and Paul as well as Irenaeus and Augustine, Calvin teaches that the final end and goal for humanity is a trinitarian union of humanity with God. The oneness and unity of the Trinity extend to incorporate the believer: 'Just as he [Christ] is one with the Father, let us become one with him'" (Sermon on 1 Sam 2:27–36; CR 29:353).[98] Christ becomes completely one with us, so that "day by day, he grows more and more into one body with us, until he becomes completely one with us" (*Inst.* 3.2.24; 2.16.3). Union with Christ is not final in itself because the ultimate goal is to unite believers to the triune God, "[the Word] took upon himself the person and office of Mediator, that he might join us to God" (*Inst.* 1.13.24; cf., 2.15.5). It is through the Spirit that one is united with the Son and with the Father so that oneness that exists between the Father and the Son is the same that is made between Christ and his body through the mediation of the Spirit (*Inst.* 3.1.2; 1.13.14; 1.13.26). The anointing and empowering work of the Spirit in the Son's earthly ministry has the same effect on believers, who experience communion with the Father and the Son through the spiritual bond of the Spirit (*Inst.* 3.1.1; 3.2.5; 3.2.10; *Comm.* John 14:20; *Comm.* Rom 8:4, 9; *Comm.* Gal 4:6). Calvin consistently presented christological and pneumatological dynamics in the restoration of God's image in human beings (*Comm.* Rom 13:14; *Comm.* 2 Cor 3:17).[99]

---

98. Billings, "United to God," 324. Similarly, Canlis argues that, for the Reformer, the scope of divine operation in salvation extends to the whole Trinity, rather than Christ's substitution on the cross. "His mission is not that of rescue or appeasement (though it has components of those), but can only be understood as part of this larger Trinitarian movement of divine love descending to the lost and bringing them back into this same love." Canlis, *Calvin's Ladder*, 92. Tamburello also acknowledges a "trinitarian element" in Calvin's view of union. Tamburello, *Union with Christ*, 106.

99. These aspects are discussed in detail by Butin, *Revelation, Redemption, and Response*, chaps. 5–6. Butin considers that a trinitarian approach to Calvin's theology better reflects its complexity than a christological, "We regard a perichoretically trinitarian

Billings takes heed from Gösta Hallonsten in drawing a difference between the *theme* of deification and the *doctrine* of deification.[100] Hence, Billings correctly disagrees with McLelland that Calvin espoused a notion of *theosis* similar to Gregory Palamas on the basis that Calvin taught about mystical union with Christ.[101] Billings concludes that, depending on a definition of deification—whether it is of Athanasius, Augustine, Gregory of Nyssa or Gregory Palamas—Calvin's understanding of deification may or may not qualify. Calvin would agree with a metaphorical type of deification, being cautious of the term, rather than espousing the literal understanding that predominated in the late Byzantine theologies of *theosis*. He tended to use biblical terms with extra-biblical content, remaining distinct from theologians that elaborated on essence-energies terminology. Billings summarizes Calvin's distinctive view of deification:

> The genuinely catholic elements of Calvin's doctrine of deification should not blind us to Calvin's distinctive claims: participation in Christ is impossible without imputation; participation in the life-giving *substantia* of Christ in the sacraments is inseparably linked with ecclesial unity and love; full humanity as humanity united with God means that partitive, synergistic understandings of grace and the Spirit must be rejected.[102]

In other words, Calvin heavily drew from the patristic well of deification, remaining committed to the biblical ideas and language. Given the fact that the Trinity is a part of the mystical union between human and divine persons, I propose to read the Reformer in the context of *triadosis*,[103] rather

---

perspective as more comprehensively adequate than a more narrowly Christological one for describing the complexity of Calvin's understanding of the divine-human relationship, primarily because it does greater justice to the immense significance that Calvin constantly places on the close relationship of the Father and the Spirit to the work of Christ on behalf of humanity." Butin, *Revelation, Redemption, and Response*, 127.

100. Hallonsten, "Theosis in Recent Research." Mosser, who acknowledges the *theme*, not the *doctrine* of *theosis* in Calvin, suggests that Calvin's hesitancy to more openly express the patristic doctrine of *theosis* is due to his desire to disassociate himself from "false deification" (false apotheosis) practiced by pagans (*Inst.* 2.8.26). Mosser, "Greatest Possible Blessing," 53. In like manner, Canlis finds some resemblance with the doctrine of *theosis* in Calvin, but not "pagan divinization." Canlis, *Calvin's Ladder*, 125. Collins agrees that Calvin's teaching "contain[s] something of the architecture of the metaphor of deification," but not the doctrine per se. Collins, *Partaking in Divine Nature*, 150.

101. McLelland, "Sailing to Byzantium."

102. Billings, "United to God," 334.

103. Or as Beilby names it, "trinification." Beilby, "Lecture on Doctrine." Cited in Murphy, "Reformed Theosis?," 206.

than *theosis* or Palamite *energeosis*. I suggest that Calvin's soteriology could be appropriated as *christosis* that ultimately leads to *triadosis*.

Conclusion

If Mannermaa's assertion that "the doctrine of the participation of the believer in the divine life of Christ is the core of the doctrine of *theosis*, or divinization"[104] is correct, then the two Reformers are in agreement with the early church fathers. If it is a fair statement about the main Reformers, then the truncated reading of Paul's soteriology in terms of justification by faith alone with sanctification and union with Christ as a by-product thereof must be blamed on subsequent Lutheranism and Calvinism. The Finnish Lutheran researchers

> found that for Luther faith is a real participation in Christ, that in faith a believer receives the righteousness of God in Christ, not only in a nominal and external way, but really and inwardly. According to the forensic model of justification, it is *as though* we are righteous, while in reality we are not. But if through faith we really participate in Christ, we participate in the whole Christ, who in his divine person communicates the righteousness of God. Here lies the bridge to the Orthodox idea of salvation as deification or *theosis*.[105]

Johnson properly observes that the subsequent generations of Lutherans and Calvinists shifted away from expressing the central and unifying role of union with Christ in the Reformers's soteriologies to emphasizing the priority of justification by faith and downplaying sanctification as subsequent to it.[106]

Scholars disagree about whether the nature of union with Christ is a metaphorical or real-ontic expression for the Reformers. Dennis Bielfeldt objects to the ontological reading of a mystical union with Christ.[107] He claims that Luther's expressions, such as "Christ gives himself to us," should not be read as "we participate in Christ's being," as if a finite being could partake in the nature of an infinite. While it may be correct to say

104. Mannermaa, "Justification and Theosis," 26.
105. Braaten and Jenson, *Union with Christ*, viii.
106. Johnson, "Luther and Calvin," 76. "[J]ustification rather than union with Christ often became the focal point of Protestant reflection on the *ordo salutis* . . . [in the Formula of Concord or the Heidelberg Catechism] union with Christ ceases to function, determinatively, in the same way as it did for Luther and Calvin."
107. Bielfeldt, "Response to Sammeli Juntunen," 165–66.

that Luther hesitated to claim an absolute union of natures between Christ and the church, still the marriage metaphor, employed by Luther, pointed to an understanding deeper than a mere declaration-statement. He espoused an intimate spiritual and mystical union of the two in one flesh. Here is how Luther supported personal exchange through the imagery of marriage between Christ and the church, "If he gives her his body and very self, how shall he not give her all that is his? And if he takes the body of the bride, how shall he not take all that is hers?" (LW 31:351; WA 7:54). Accordingly, Christ shares with the church his person and physical body.

I want to argue that Luther believed in personal participation in Christ, whereby the essential divine-human exchange of some kind happens. Since the exchange of essential attributes is not absolute, Luther believed that the language of *communion* manifested deification, but not essential change into divine. This communion occurs on the level of persons, divine and human, due to the indwelling of the Spirit, not on the level of substances. His divine nature cannot be shared with the church, lest she loses her human identity. Luther, in his lectures on Gal 2:20, clearly identified participation in Christ's person with participation in his being to the extent that it is possible for human beings enabled by the Spirit:

> But faith must be taught correctly, namely, that by it you are so cemented to Christ that He and you are as one person, which cannot be separated but remains attached to Him forever and declares: "I am as Christ." And Christ, in turn, says: "I am as the sinner who is attached to me and I to him. For by faith we are joined together into one flesh and bone." Thus Eph. 5:30 says: "We are members of the body of Christ, of his flesh and bones," in such a way that faith couples Christ and me more intimately than a husband is coupled to his wife (LW 26:168; WA 40.1:285-6).[108]

Again, the author is not claiming that he is "one nature with Christ," but "as one person." Furthermore, the diversity of persons in the union is preserved by the fact of likeness ("I am as Christ") and attachment, not absolute identification ("I am Christ"). Nevertheless, the closeness of participants in the divine-human spiritual marriage is more intimate than the relationships of "one flesh and bones" between husband and wife.

Further, Metzger thinks that the transformation of human beings and the exchange of attributes with Christ opened the door for people to become really human, rather than divine.[109] Communion with the divine

---

108. Cited in Johnson, "Luther and Calvin," 65.
109. Metzger, "Luther and Finnish School," 207.

persons and participation in their divine attributes does presuppose a kind of *perichoresis*, whereby mutual interpenetration allows transformation of humanity into the likeness of the divine beings. This is not to eliminate human nature, but to reach its original and final goal, to be the image- and likeness-bearers of God, to be children of God, to be partakers of the divine nature (2 Pet 1:4) in communion with the Trinity. Salvation is an act of the whole Trinity. Thus, to be saved is to experience the grace and love, justification and sanctification, deliverance from sin and immortality in union with Christ and participation in the life of the three divine persons.

Noticeable is the degree of consistency between the Reformers and the church fathers. Calvin drew heavily on Irenaeus and Athanasius particularly regarding the fact that participation is about personal communication, rather than essential fusion. Hence, the maintenance of the ontological distinction between God and humanity that the fathers affirmed continued in the writings of Luther and Calvin. Consequently, also the need for a mediator who shares in the ontology of both parties facilitates their discussion of Christology. This necessity becomes evident in Billings's account of the indispensability of prayer for Calvin: prayer is important precisely because this is a matter of interpersonal communication. All of that helps to expose how radically different Litwa's account of the Mediator is when we come to it in chapter 5.

In contrast to the Palamite definition of deification, Calvin affirmed that some of the divine attributes are "incommunicable." Believers participate in the person of Christ, not in a Nestorian way, i.e., in Christ's humanity only. As it was for Irenaeus and Athanasius, for the Genevan Reformer, the term "deification" is an essentialistic category, albeit not without certain reservation. Calvin affirmed that the *telos* of the gospel is "to render us eventually conformable to God, and, if we may so speak, to deify us" (*Comm.* 2 Pet 1:4; *CR* 55:446).[110] Billings concludes, "In a similar way, 'deification' can be an appropriate term for Calvin's theology of union with God through Christ, if understood as a soteriology that affirms the unity of humanity and divinity, such that redemption involves the transformation of believers to be incorporated into the Triune life of God, while remaining creatures."[111] Billings is puzzled by Julie Canlis's statement that Calvin espoused non-substantial participation in Christ.[112] Indeed, Calvin distanced his thinking

---

110. Lee translates "quasi deificari" as "a kind of deification," arguing that "[w]e will be partakers of the divine kind, but not of the divine essence." Lee, "Calvin on Deification," 278–79.

111. Billings, *Calvin, Participation, and Gift*, 54.

112. Canlis, "Calvin, Osiander and Participation," 184; Billings, *Calvin, Participation, and Gift*, 62. This is perhaps due to the fact that Canlis's work reflects the views of her

from Osiander's fusion of human and divine natures. Nevertheless, it did not preclude the Reformer from employing the metaphysical language of substance to disclaim the superficiality of symbolic participation in Christ. Thus, despite the rare usage of deification language by Luther and Calvin and distinctive emphases on forensic justification, their theologies are in essential agreement with the patristic vision of participation in the life of the Trinity by means of incorporation into Christ through the Spirit.

Finally, one should note how important the sacraments, notably the Lord's Supper, are to the discussion in the Reformers. Their debates (and their agreements) about the nature of participation were centered on a particular and extensive Pauline text (1 Cor 11, in its broader context from 10–12). Baptism is important too, though, and it is crucial that it is the Pauline deployment of the imagery (burial and resurrection) that is so influential for their understanding of transformation into the personal God.

---

supervisor, Alan Torrance, who minimizes the place of active participation. Torrance emphasizes the views of Irenaeus and Athanasius that participation is incarnational, but this something in which all humanity participates passively. Hence the non-substantialist emphasis in Canlis. I am indebted to Grant Macaskill for this point.

Chapter 4

Contemporary Eastern Orthodox Retrieval of Triadosis

Introduction

IN THIS CHAPTER, I will discuss deification as it is elaborated by an influential Eastern Orthodox theologian, the Metropolitan of Pergamon, John Zizioulas. He finds deficiencies in the theological constructs of the Alexandrian and Evagrian *apotheosis* and Palamite *energeosis*. The way John Zizioulas resolves the dilemma of human participation in the imparticipable nature of God (2 Pet 1:4) is through the application of his understanding of personhood to the divine and human beings. Zizioulas stands in the long Cappadocian tradition of trinitarian theology that, unlike Western tradition, does not give primacy to nature over persons in the Godhead. In the following pages, I will present Zizioulas's understanding of personhood in his trinitarian theology that makes a foundational imprint on his anthropology, soteriology, ecclesiology, and eschatology. Before expounding Zizioulas's approach, I will present his critiques of alternative approaches to deification.

Zizioulas's Critiques of *Apotheosis* and *Energeosis*

According to Origen and Evagrius, salvation is a process of gradual ascension to God through the contemplation of the divine *logoi*, the ascetic purification of the mind from passions, which leads to a cognitive union with God and a change from mere human nature into divine-like nature. Being heavily influenced by Platonism, Origen concentrated more on the eternal Logos as the ideal contemplative subject, rather than Christ incarnate, who deified the human nature in himself. Zizioulas identifies a problem with this approach in that this contemplative union leaves no place for otherness between the divine Object and the subject of contemplation, and thus deprives creation of its human existence.[1] Further, the deification of people for Clement, Origen, and Evagrius meant that humans lose their initial corporeality and transcend to a superior state of being—they become *pneumatikoi*, "Through participation in God they have ceased to be men; having ascended to the supreme God, they have been transformed from men into angels or gods."[2] Since Origen's *theosis* is mainly intellectual perfection toward the ideal, it precludes some humans and especially those with mental incapacities to achieve the divine likeness. If the goal of creation were to participate in the divine nature, that would imply minimization of created particularity and even obliteration of particular human corporeality in eternity.

According to Zizioulas, the Cappadocian and Maximian *personalistic* approach to the communion of creation with the person of Christ is preferable to the Palamite *energistic* participation, because in the latter the incarnation of the Logos is not necessary while the divine energies are accessible to the world since its creation.[3] Moreover, salvation by participation in the divine energies would minimize the soteriological activities of the divine persons. Zizioulas states,

> The divine energies *qua* energies never express God's *personal* presence, since they belong to the level of *nature* and to *all three persons* of the Trinity. If the world and God were to be united through the divine energies *qua* energies, the unity would have been one with *all three persons* simultaneously, and not via the Son—it would not have been a *hypostatic* union.[4]

Since energies, first of all, are the essential manifestations of God, union with the divine energies would imply union with the anhypostatic divine essence. Precisely, how a person can unite with an impersonal quality of God is an unresolved difficulty introduced by Palamas. In an attempt to preserve

1. Zizioulas, *Communion and Otherness*, 21–22.
2. Russell, *Doctrine of Deification*, 146.
3. Zizioulas, *Communion and Otherness*, 28.
4. Zizioulas, *Communion and Otherness*, 29 (emphasis original). Polkinghorne is correct in writing that some forms of the discourse on divine energies in Orthodox theology "may seem to be in danger of verging on a form of emanationism." Polkinghorne, *Science and Trinity*, 98n15. Zizioulas clarifies Orthodox doxology and iconology in the context of persons and energies in the following way: "In the Orthodox Church, we venerate *persons*, not natures or energies. Even in venerating and kissing the icons we do so only because they *explicitly* carry with them the representation of a person or persons." Zizioulas, *Communion and Otherness*, 30n50 (emphasis original).

God's essence intact, *energeosis*, ironically, allows for some approximation to the essence and leaves hypostases out of view as a less fruitful possibility for the union. In response, by marginalizing the divine essence, Zizioulas, in Harrison's words, marginalizes the divine energies.[5]

Vladimir Lossky (1903–1958) was an influential Russian Orthodox theologian and one of the leaders of neo-Palamism, who advocated for the appropriateness of divine energy as a category in the discussion of divine-human relationships. A fair critique of Lossky's soteriology by Aristotle Papanikolaou corresponds to Zizioulas's argument against Palamas. Papanikolaou notices that Lossky's Christ is not the archetype for human deification: what deified the human nature of Christ was not the divine energies, but the divine nature while human beings unite with the divine energies. Unlike in saints, there is no progression in Christ toward *theosis*. Papanikolaou says, "Though the divine persons communicate the divine energies, the issue is whether participation in the divine energies is something less than participation in the triune personal existence of God, especially since divine personhood is itself something more than a participation in the divine energies."[6] In a similar vein, Rowan Williams suspects Palamas of overstating God's essence above persons, which would be illogical since essence does not exist in an abstract, personless condition.[7] Indeed, if divine-human communion occurs on the level of energies, pertinent to nature, there is no point in the personal revelation and salvific acts of the three divine persons, but only of one God. Moreover, if energies are uncreated constant means of communication of God to another, it presupposes an eternal pantheistic coexistence of the created world, toward whom these energies are directed.[8]

Zizioulas's View of Personhood

In contrast to the Western tradition, the Cappadocian fathers, according to Zizioulas, located the ultimate ontological principle of God not in *essence*,

---

5. Harrison, "Zizioulas on Communion," 281. Harrison contends for maximization of divine energy, because she thinks energy is a manifestation of the interpersonal relations of God to the world. She, however, does not make clear how a common energy can be one and many to express multiple persons in the same revelatory event.

6. Papanikolaou, "Divine Energies," 377. Papanikolaou raises question about Lossky's application of apophatic theology to the Trinity—the critique is applicable to Palamas as well—and finds it wanting: "How can one know that God exists as trinitarian persons as freedom and love if God in Godself is shrouded in the apophaticism of the *hyper*-essence?" Papanikolaou, "Divine Energies," 376.

7. Williams, "Philosophical Structures."

8. Williams, "Philosophical Structures," 37.

but in *person*, i.e., God's personal trinitarian existence.[9] For the Cappadocians, God was one and the many at the same time, because there is no space and time between the distinct persons of the Trinity, which exists as one God in three persons from the "start."[10] Zizioulas considers that a true being is necessarily a personal being that possesses freedom and love in being "for" the other, "True being comes only from the free person, from the person who loves freely—that is, who freely affirms his being, his identity, by means of an event of communion with other persons."[11] Since a personal being is constituted in communion with other persons, its identity is inconceivable in isolation from other personal subjects. The concept of divine personhood is *"not* a 'collection of properties' of either a natural or a moral kind. It is only a 'mode of being' comprising relations (σχέσις) of ontological constitutiveness."[12] To live means to freely love and be loved, that is, to exist in unique and unrepeatable relationships with the other. Being a person simultaneously implies the existence of another person and relationships with her. Without otherness, there is no person, because a person is known only in relations with other free persons. "Otherness," writes Zizioulas, "is not secondary to unity; it is primary and constitutive of the very idea of being. Respect for otherness is a matter not of ethics, but of ontology: if otherness disappears, beings simply cease to be."[13] The ontological otherness of beings allows them to exist freely and be the way they are. Hence, God exists because he is a person, not the other way around. This is because, in St. Basil's view, substance never exists in a "naked" form, but always in *hypostasis*.[14] According to Zizioulas, in patristic thought, the ontology of being is postulated by two theses:

> (1) There is no true being without communion. Nothing exists as an "individual," conceivable in itself. Communion is an ontological category.
>
> (2) Communion which does not come from a "hypostasis," that is, a concrete and free person, and which does not lead to

---

9. Zizioulas, *Being as Communion*, 40. Zizioulas states, "Among the Greek Fathers the unity of God, the one God, and the ontological 'principle' or 'cause' of the being and life of God does not consist in the one substance of God but in the *hypostasis*, that is, *the person of the Father*." For an excellent overview of appraisals and critiques of Zizioulas's theology see Grenz, *Rediscovering Triune God*, 131–47.

10. Zizioulas, "Doctrine of Holy Trinity," 49.

11. Zizioulas, *Being as Communion*, 18.

12. Zizioulas, *Communion and Otherness*, 173.

13. Zizioulas, *Communion and Otherness*, 11.

14. Letter 38.2, PG 32:325. Basil of Caesarea, *Letters 1–185*.

"hypostases," that is concrete and free persons, is not an "image" of the being of God. The person cannot exist without communion; but every form of communion, which denies or suppresses the person, is inadmissible.[15]

This leads Zizioulas to the conclusion of the concurrency of divine personhood and divine nature, "Outside of Trinity there is no God, that is, no divine substance, because the ontological 'principle' of God is the Father."[16] In the Cappadocian formulation, God exists as hypostatic essence and essential hypostases. The concomitance of the divine persons and nature is an ontological and theological principle of Zizioulas's theology, in contrast to Western essentialism and "social trinitarianism" of his Orthodox contenders.[17] The Metropolitan dismisses any attempts to ascribe certain characteristics to a person, because, for him, it would place a person into a category, thus destroying her uniqueness and irreplaceability. It should be noted, in response to Gunton's protest against Zizioulas's refusal to assign qualities to a person,[18] that one has to deal with the immanent and economic Trinity differently. The only differentiating qualities that can be assigned to the divine persons in the immanent Trinity based on revelation are that of Father, Son and Spirit. But even these names do not perfectly correspond to descriptions known to us from our human experience. As to the economic Trinity, I do not think that either Cappadocians or Zizioulas refused to assign certain functions to the divine persons, such as sending Father, crucified Son and sanctifying Spirit. The Metropolitan disapproves the application of the term "individual" to God, as it brings the Western notion of self-conscious isolated subjects into the Trinity. Hence, it is incorrect to reduce the idea of a person to a set of essential accidents or a mere existential individualism.[19]

15. Zizioulas, *Being as Communion*, 18.

16. Zizioulas, *Being as Communion*, 41; *Communion and Otherness*, 106.

17. Brown mentions three contenders such as Lucian Turcescu, Andrew Louth, and John Behr. They claim that the Greek fathers did not prioritize *person* over *substance* and did not differentiate *person* from *individual*; thus, Eastern fathers are not different from Western trinitarian theologians. Brown, "On the Criticism of Being," 35. Gunton laments the subordination of personhood to nature in Western theology: "In our tradition the particularity of the persons tends everywhere to be so subordinated to a relentless stress on the unity of God that theology is often unable to follow Scripture in ascribing particular actions to particular persons of the Trinity, the result being that all is attributed to 'God' in such an undifferentiated way that his actions cease to be trinitarianly construed." Gunton, "Persons and Particularity," 103.

18. Gunton, "Persons and Particularity," 106.

19. Thus, according to Damascene, "ὑπόστασις-πρόσωπον" and "οὐσία" create single indivisible ontology, because hypostasis is essential and essence is enhypostatic

The issue is whether the concept of "personhood as communion" advocated by the Metropolitan leads to tritheism (i.e., three independent self-conscious centers in God) or mere "relations" without a clear identity. In this regard, Zizioulas reiterates that St. Basil preferred to talk about the unity of the Trinity in terms of the communion of persons (κοινωνία ὑποστάσεων), rather than substantial sameness:

> Instead of speaking of the unity of God in terms of His one nature, he [Basil] prefers to speak of it in terms of the *communion of persons*: communion is for Basil an ontological category. The *nature* of God is communion. This does not mean that the persons have an ontological priority over the one substance of God, but that the one substance of God coincides with the communion of the three persons.[20]

From this teaching on the Trinity, one learns that "otherness is *constitutive* of unity, and not consequent upon it. God is not first one and then three, but simultaneously one and three."[21] The relationship of trinitarian persons presupposes their distinctiveness not in psychological or moral terms, but in personal terms because there is no real communion but self-contemplation without the ontological otherness of persons. None of the persons of the Trinity is conceivable at any moment independently from the other persons, while at the same time each of them preserves personal non-transferable uniqueness. The Father is inconceivable without inter-relationships with the fully divine Son and Spirit at the same time. The differences between the divine hypostases are recognizable only through their respective *tropos* of being (τρόπος ὑπάρξεως).[22] Thus, Zizioulas claims, "otherness is inconceivable apart from *relationship*. Father, Son and Spirit are all names indicating relationship. No person can be different unless he is related. Communion does not threaten otherness; it generates it."[23] Here, according to Zinkovskiy, Zizioulas makes a mistake

---

(*Contra Jacobitas*, PG 94:1441d). Zinkovskiy, *Patristic Categories*, 179.

20. Zizioulas, *Being as Communion*, 134 (emphasis original); Zizioulas, *Communion and Otherness*, 159; Volf, *After Our Likeness*, 202.

21. Zizioulas, *Communion and Otherness*, 5 (emphasis original). "[God's oneness] is also expressed through the unbreakable *koinonia* that exists between the three persons, which means that otherness is not a threat to unity but a *sine qua non* condition of it."

22. Zinkovskiy, *Patristic Categories*, 114. Zinkovskiy convincingly argues that the *tropos* of being, or a mode of existence, should not be identified with a hypostasis, but relates to and logically follows the essence and hypostasis. Thus, a person may have several *tropes* of being. Zinkovskiy, *Patristic Categories*, 117–23.

23. Zizioulas, *Communion and Otherness*, 5, 140 (emphasis original).

by identifying a person with the relationship, as if relatedness (σχέσις) is ontologically prior to the notion of *hypostasis*.[24]

The patristic tradition attests to continuous attempts to express the biblical truth that God is one and that God is personal. As was shown above, the Cappadocians were among those fathers who employed the notion of the Father's monarchy to explain scriptural teaching on the oneness of God in light of the Son's incarnation. The Metropolitan of Pergamon claims to follow this tradition. Although Zizioulas confirms the Father as the source of the Son and the Spirit, his own identity as the Father depends on communion with the Son and the Spirit. In other words, how could God be the Father if there are no the Son and the Spirit? For Zizioulas, the mutuality and interdependence of persons in the Trinity are asymmetrical and do not exclude the monarchy of the Father. Although the Father's identity and existence are conditioned on the Son and the Spirit, the Father is not constituted or caused as the Son and the Spirit are caused by the Father.[25] This approach allowed the Greek fathers, according to Zizioulas, to maintain personhood as the ontological principle of God.[26] Zizioulas, contrary to Athanasius, argues that it is the person of the Father who causes the being of the Son and the Spirit, not the Father's substance.

Several commentators object to the idea of the Father's monarchy, stating that the intratrinitarian *perichoresis* and the equality of divine persons, which constitute one God, contradict to the hierarchical model of the Father's monarchy.[27] In response, Zizioulas claims that the Cappadocians,

24. Zinkovskiy, *Patristic Categories*, 187. For a critique of Zizioulas's interpretation of the Trinity as "three personal relations," rather than "three relational persons," see Awad, "Personhood as Particularity."

25. Zizioulas, *Communion and Otherness*, 119, 129–30; Volf, *After Our Likeness*, 79.

26. Zizioulas, *Being as Communion*, 40–41.

27. Alan Torrance, following Thomas F. Torrance, is critical of Zizioulas's understanding of the Father's *monarchia* as the source of Godhead and the hypostases of the Son and the Spirit. Rather, he is in favor of the intra-divine co-equality of persons. Torrance thinks that the ontological precedence of the Father is inconsistent with Zizioulas's claim that communion is a primordial ontological concept. It also comes close to the subordinationism of the Son and the Spirit. Torrance, *Persons in Communion*, 290–93; Torrance, *Trinitarian Faith*, 238. Volf states that the begetting of the Son does not imply personhood of the Father, but his fatherhood. Thus, the Father had to be a person before begetting the Son, therefore, a person precedes communion. Volf suggests that Zizioulas reads his hierarchical ecclesiology into his construal of the Trinity. Volf, *After Our Likeness*, 79. I partially agree with Volf, because the Father's fatherhood is a *tropos* of the Father's being that follows his person. However, if a person precedes communion, the Father would not be a person, but would become a person with begetting of the Son, according to Zizioulas. I propose to think that the communion of persons does not follow their being, but coincides and constitutes them as persons. Thus, the Father is a person because he exists in communion with the Son

and indeed the Orthodox East, rejected the *Filioque* because it would introduce two ontological sources within the Godhead and hence, two Gods.[28] The Son and the Spirit are "economically although not ontologically subordinate" to the Father, because, according to the Scriptures, the Son and the Spirit are *"obedient to and sent into the world* by the Father."[29] Both the Son and the Spirit proclaimed and established the kingdom of the Father on earth. The distinction and unity of the Trinity are expressed through the willing obedience of the Son to the Father and in glorifying the Son and the Father by the Spirit.[30] For Zizioulas, the name "Father" is inherently a

---

and the Spirit. The fatherhood, sonship, and spiration are the names or descriptions of that communion. Wilks, mistakenly in my view, argues that Zizioulas overemphasized the role of Father's monarchy in the Cappadocians, for whom the principle of unity, in Wilks's understanding, was based on the *ousia*, not the monarchy. Wilks, "Trinitarian Ontology," 77–78. As I have shown earlier, Basil and Gregory of Nazianzus, and to a lesser degree Gregory of Nyssa, indeed used the monarchy of the Father as the principle of unity. See also Zinkovskiy's treatment of the topic, who maintains that all three Cappadocians espoused the idea of the Father's monarchy. Moreover, he states that the Father is the personal source in the Trinity, not ontological. Zinkovskiy, *Patristic Categories*, 57–73, 180. Papanikolaou comes to a similar conclusion in his article Papanikolaou, "Is John Zizioulas an Existentialist?" Even if Rostock is correct—and I think he is not—that for the Cappadocians the unity of nature is the basis of oneness of God, it does not follow that nature precedes the person of the Father as the cause of the Son and the Spirit. Rostock, "Two Different Gods?," 329. In contrast to Rostock, LaCugna aptly summarizes that nature by itself cannot be a point of reference for the unity of God, because *"it is impossible to think of the divine essence in itself or by itself,"* but only in its enhypostatic existence. Hence, these Greek fathers held in tension the monarchy of the Father and common essence. LaCugna, *God for Us*, 70–72, 246 (emphasis original). Turner explains why the idea of Father's *monarchia* should not be charged with subordinationism: "The Father as the ontological principle of God does not create a subordinationism because the divine persons share the same substance, and because, considered in isolation from the Son and Spirit, the Father alone is not a personal *hypostasis*, or personal mode of existence. Father and divine substance would be synonymous because Father would not express a particular personal mode of existence." Turner, "Eschatology and Truth," 18. I also disagree with Loudovikos, who argues that Zizioulas introduces the "dictated otherness" by rejecting the reciprocal offer of otherness from the Son and the Spirit back to the Father. Loudovikos, "Person Instead of Grace," 692. Zizioulas highlights that the Father's identity is, in fact, depends and exists in relations with the Son and the Spirit. Perhaps the contended *monarchia* of the Father can be helpfully modified by Weinandy's proposal that the begetting of the Son and procession of the Spirit are simultaneous and constitutive for the person of the Father as Father. Weinandy, *Father's Spirit*, 17, 29.

28. Zizioulas, *Lectures in Christian Dogmatics*, 78–79.

29. Gunton, "Persons and Particularity," 98. Gunton, however, disapproves the absolute monarchy of the Father and argues for reciprocal constitution within the Trinity, "all three persons are together the cause of the communion in which they exist in relations of mutual and reciprocal constitution." Gunton, *Promise of Trinitarian Theology*, 196.

30. Pannenberg, "Divine Economy and Eternal Trinity," 81–82. Pannenberg himself

relational term. Thus, the origination of the Son and the Spirit is not linear, but interdependent. Gunton supports Zizioulas, saying that communion and *perichoresis* are secondary to the person because they are a result of personal relations, not their cause and, thus, should be kept secondary.[31] I side with Zinkovskiy, who considers that the *perichoretic* quality of the divine persons is not primary or secondary to their unity, but simultaneous to their unity in one nature.[32] One cannot do away with the notion of the Father's *monarchia*, because of the nature of personal names, which assume their unique relations: the "Father" implies unbegottenness, the "Son" implies begottenness, and the "Spirit" implies spiration. These are incommunicable personal modes of existence, which reveal the uniqueness, differentiation, and the order of trinitarian relationships between the persons.[33] As John stated in his gospel, "the Father has life in himself" and he "has granted the Son to have life in himself" (John 5:26, NIV). To have life in himself means to have non-contingent existence, which, according to Jesus, the Father gave to the Son. Such a claim presupposes an ontological "order" within the Trinity that expresses relations and roles, not necessarily essential inequality.[34] Zizioulas also thinks that the idea of monarchy frees the Trinity from ontological necessity. The existence of God is freely willed or "caused" by the Father, who freely wills the existence of the Son with the Spirit as well as his own existence. Without the monarchy, the being of all three persons is an ontological necessity.[35]

---

adopts the trinitarian model of reciprocal relationships among the divine persons in order to avoid the modalist tendencies of the West. Whapham, *Term "Person,"* 148.

31. Gunton, "Persons and Particularity," 100.

32. Zinkovskiy, *Patristic Categories*, 182–83.

33. This is why I disagree with McCall, who thinks that the Father's uncausedness (or *being unthrown*, as he calls it) cannot be his personal property. McCall, "Holy Love and Divine Aseity," 202. McCall raises a fair question, however: Is the Father a person before he wills the Son and Spirit, i.e., before communion? Perhaps, the willing of the other by the Father constitutes his ek-static personhood.

34. I am indebted to Dr. Donald Fairbairn for this point. From personal e-mail correspondence, June 29, 2015.

35. Zizioulas, "Doctrine of Holy Trinity," 51–55. Zinkovskiy, who correctly, in my view, indicates the problem of overemphasizing personhood over nature, however, questions this statement. This approach leads Zizioulas to an unnecessary double and asymmetrical ontology (personal vs. natural) instead of preserving a single person-nature ontology. The scholastic prevalence of natural oneness over personal triness should not cause an opposite extreme. Zinkovskiy, *Theology of Person*, 163–65. Harrison points in the same direction when she writes that "essence cannot be emptied of content," because the divine persons "are also related to each other through the divine essence." Harrison, "Zizioulas on Communion," 279.

God's *ek-static* love does not mean going beyond his nature; thus, the eternal begetting of the Son and pouring of the Holy Spirit bring the free communion of equally divine persons. These mutual interrelationships of the divine persons, described by the term *perichoresis*, mean that every divine person represents the whole of God, as well as the other two persons. Volf defines it in the following sentences,

> Perichoresis refers to the reciprocal *interiority of the* trinitarian persons. In every divine person as a subject, the other persons also indwell; all mutually permeate one another, though in so doing they do not cease to be distinct persons. In fact, the distinctions between them are precisely the presupposition of that interiority, since persons who have dissolved into one another cannot exist in one another. Perichoresis is "co-inherence in one another without any coalescence or commixture."[36]

Karen Kilby is skeptical about the usefulness of the term *perichoresis*, which social trinitarians take by analogy from the human relationship and use for something we do not understand (i.e., how three persons are one). Then they circularly project it on God and from God on human relationships. Instead, she resorts to a simple apophatism, stating the doctrine of the Trinity without due explanation.[37] Even if Kilby's critical observation of projection in social trinitarianism is correct, I contend that her analysis is not entirely right in the case of Zizioulas in areas of theology and anthropology. First, he assumes the idea of Father's monarchy, which allows him to uphold a willing and self-conscious subject in the Trinity that wills the existence of others. But his self-understanding is constituted by the existence of others, who share the same substance and being as one God. In addition, relations presuppose self-awareness, because relations cannot relate; only self-conscious subjects can relate. Second, a fundamental difference between human and divine communion is that mutual indwelling is a prerogative of exclusively divine interrelationship and not a divine-human or human-human ones. Unlike the divine nature, the human nature is divisible and created in space and time. Thus, people cannot completely interpenetrate each other without the loss of their identity.[38] The human subjects do not act in and through the Spirit as the Spirit acts in humans. Thus, the

---

36. Volf, *After Our Likeness*, 209; Prestige, *God in Patristic Thought*, 298.

37. Kilby, "Perichoresis and Projection," 442.

38. Zizioulas, *Lectures in Christian Dogmatics*, 63. On the asymmetrical nature of divine-human co-inherence Tanner states, "God cannot give Godself, in imitation of trinitarian relations of perfect divine communion, to what is not God, simply as such." Tanner, *Jesus, Humanity and Trinity*, 42.

reciprocal indwelling of divine and human participants within each other is asymmetrical (Rom. 8:9; cf., John 6:56; 14:20; 17:21). It means that the social trinitarian model, even when applied to people, has its limitations and cannot be projected on humanity without some alteration.

Brown is correct in his defense of Zizioulas's version of social trinitarianism. Since each of the persons of the Trinity is the bearer of the totality of Godhead, there are not three gods, but one. The divine persons are not self-conscious individuals because their identities are not conceived in isolation from each other. Zizioulas resolves the problems of individualism and "mere relations" in the Trinity by assigning a causal role to the Father, but at the same time, stressing that the Father is never conceived alone without the Son and the Spirit. Each of the divine persons encompasses the whole God; hence, the charge of tritheism is avoided. The person is not pure relations either because the mode of existence is not the same as the existent being even though it is constituted by its relations. Zizioulas's teaching on the Trinity is not "communitarian," because the Trinity exists consubstantially as *one* God and not a communion of three gods united by some ordering principle.[39] If the proper way to talk about God is to identify, first and foremost, the persons of the Trinity, then the participation of a human being in the divine being should occur on the level of persons and not on the level of natures or energies.

Zizioulas's anthropological ontology of the person is based on the theological ideas of *corporate personality* (i.e., Adam, who as a bearer of "the *totality* of human nature" represented the many and vice versa) and the *personal source of the Trinity* (i.e., God the Father).[40] Since only God is a person *par excellence*, people are persons as far as they participate God's personhood. The Metropolitan defines personhood in the following words, "The person is an identity that emerges through relationship (*schesis*, in the terminology of the Greek fathers); it is an 'I' that can exist only as long as it relates to a 'thou' which affirms its existence and its otherness."[41] The two

39. Brown, "On the Criticism," 65.

40. Zizioulas, "On Being a Person," 39–40.

41. Zizioulas, *Communion and Otherness*, 9. To be a real person, one needs to have the other and be free from the other, "and yet because, as we have already observed, one person is no person, this freedom is not freedom *from* the other but freedom *for* the other. Freedom thus becomes identical with *love*. God is love because he is Trinity. We can love only if we are persons, that is, if we allow the other to be truly other, and yet to be in communion with us. If we love the other not only in spite of his or her being different from us but *because* he or she is different from us, or rather *other* than ourselves, we live in freedom as love and in love as freedom." Zizioulas, *Communion and Otherness*, 9–10 (emphasis original). A critique of Zizioulas's relational anthropology and over-realized eschatology is the focus of Russell, "Reconsidering Relational

features of a human person are an ek-static movement toward communion and the *enhypostasization* of the human nature in its totality. A person is characterized by "absolute ontological freedom," freedom from circumscribability, "being irreplaceable within community," and by being a *hypostasis* of the human nature.[42] Existentialists claim that it is impossible for a human being to attain the total ontological freedom of personhood because it depends on many social "givens" and can be expressed only by suicide. Moreover, they assume that absolute freedom would imply the destruction of the other because others will always constitute a threat to one's egocentrism.[43] Zizioulas agrees with these existentialists's claims but calls such an existence the "biological existence" of a "biological *hypostasis*" after the fall. To become a person, an individual needs to transcend his or her biological mode of existence.

As was indicated earlier, Zizioulas, following Greek fathers, does not supply a positive definition of *hypostasis* because, by ascribing to it certain qualities, it would place *hypostasis* in categories shared by others, like a category of nature. Such a categorization would destroy the uniqueness of the *hypostasis*. Therefore, it is proper to assert that the *hypostasis* is something that other is not. Although the *hypostasis* is by definition a relational entity, it preserves its absolute uniqueness, particularity, and irreplaceability in relation to others, "This hypostatic fulness as otherness can emerge only through a relationship so constitutive ontologically that relating is not consequent upon being but is being itself."[44] The human being is a "person" only when she reflects the image of the tripersonal God, that is, when she exists as "being as communion." Since God's personhood ontologically coincides with his nature, to be a being, created in the image of God, means to be a "person," whose existence is constituted

---

Anthropology." It should be noted, however, that Zizioulas does not reject the imperfect state of the church in history, when he writes, "The Church in history is clearly not identical with the kingdom of God. The trauma of history means that along with the rest of the world, Christians struggle with evil, and the way of the cross is this struggle. The Church is not the society of those who have overcome evil but of those who are struggling against evil. The holy Church is full of sinners, being made holy. Therefore, we must say that the kingdom of God is *depicted* in the Church." Zizioulas, *Lectures in Christian Dogmatics*, 136 (emphasis original). LaCugna expresses well Zizioulas's intention, when she states that ecclesial persons point to the future beyond themselves, but now they live in tension between the existential necessities of individualism and their call for the universal communion of persons. LaCugna, *God for Us*, 264.

42. Volf, *After Our Likeness*, 83; Zizioulas, *Communion and Otherness*, 43; Zizioulas, "Human Capacity," 415, 441 nn. 1, 3.

43. Brown, "On the Criticism," 61.

44. Zizioulas, "Communion and Otherness," 112, 166–67.

by her relationships of love and freedom with the other. If the nature of a personal "I" manifests itself through movement to communion with others, then an "I" can represent the "many" and vice versa. Papanikolaou finds Zizioulas's employment of *hypostasis* as a reasonable way out of the conundrum between complete apophatism in divine-human relationship and the mingling of natures in pantheism:

> Zizioulas is correct in thinking that *hypostasis* is the category through which to think divine-human communion, especially if such a communion is to be trinitarian, i.e., *in* Christ. The language of *hypostasis* allows for a conceptualization of the realism of such a divine-human communion in a way not open to language of essence or of *hyper-essence*.[45]

Contrary to the Western definition of a human being as a self-conscious and self-enclosed individual that possesses human nature, Zizioulas defines a person as a relational being. The others represent a threat to the individual because they encroach on one's resources, value, and happiness by their mere presence. The individual, who strives to deal with the "enemy" by imposing her own image on the other or distancing from the other, considers difference and otherness inimical.[46] On the contrary, a person, in Zizioulas's understanding, realizes herself only outside herself in a movement toward the other:

> Thus, personhood implies the "openness of being," and even more than that, the *ek-stasis* of being, that is, a movement towards communion which leads to a transcendence of the boundaries of the "self" and thus to *freedom*. At the same time, and in contrast to the partiality of the individual which is subject to addition and combination, the person in its ekstatic character reveals its being in a *catholic*, that is, integral and undivided, way, and thus in its being ekstatic it becomes *hypostatic*, that is, the bearer of its nature in its totality.[47]

A person, unlike an individual, cannot exist without a relationship with the other, while remaining unique and free from the other. A person loses her very being in isolation from her counterparts, or when she acquires sameness with the other. Otherness is constitutive in defining human identity. This otherness in respect to God and the rest of creation is expressed in freedom to love and creativity, i.e., the image of God. "Death

---

45. Papanikolaou, "Divine Energies," 378 (emphasis original).
46. Zizioulas, "Communion and Otherness," 349–50.
47. Zizioulas, *Communion and Otherness*, 212–13 (emphasis original).

is the worst enemy of otherness,"[48] as Zizioulas accurately put it, because it reduces the uniqueness of a participant-in-communion to a set of physical characteristics. Knight explicates that, for Zizioulas, becoming a particular person means to become like Christ, a genuinely human person, and involves relationships with other humans:

> [B]ecoming human is about becoming better able to concede the otherness of other people. We come to be ourselves by properly seeing people for who they are and attributing to them the distinctiveness that God intends for them. Our ability properly to respect others, giving them neither too little nor too much recognition, is itself given to us by God.[49]

The real freedom of a human being is realized at the moment of baptism in Christ's body when a *hypostasis* changes her "biological existence" to "ecclesial existence."[50]

The individualization of human beings is a postlapsarian state. Consequently, according to Zizioulas, the original sin and fall, in essence, are self-assertion over against God, separation from and rejection of the other. The human being was created mortal with a capability and vocation to commune with the immortal God. The problem of the fall is the rupture of communion, whereby the realization of a person became impossible. Death is not a result of sin as such, but an ontological necessity due to personal estrangement from the personal God. A sinner is an individual—in contrast to being a person—who strives to be self-conscious, different and distanced from others.[51] The fear of the other as a threat to individual freedom is a consequence of the fall. Zizioulas ascertains, "The fact that the fear of the other is pathologically inherent in our existence results in the fear not only of the other but of *all otherness*."[52] The inward movement of an individualized self, i.e., idolatry, replaced the outward movement of a person. Otherness, from being a constitutive part of being because it allows a particular being to survive the generalization of nature, began to antagonize those who previously

---

48. Zizioulas, *Communion and Otherness*, 41.
49. Knight, "Spirit and Persons," 184.
50. Schroeder, "Suffering towards Personhood," 250. Zinkovskiy reminds that the idea of new ecclesial hypostasis in Zizioulas reflects the biblical language of "birth from the Spirit" (John 1:13) and "I became your father through the gospel" (1 Cor 4:15). Zinkovskiy, *Patristic Categories*, 200.
51. Zizioulas, *Communion and Otherness*, 3. "Different beings become distant beings: because difference becomes division, distinction becomes distance. . . . Hell, eternal death, is nothing but isolation from the other, as the desert Fathers put it." This division is not resolved by ethics, but only through a new birth.
52. Zizioulas, *Communion and Otherness*, 2 (emphasis original).

existed in a community. The problem of humankind is not simply a moral, but an ontological one. Since death is not a penalty that can be removed by a substitutionary death of a sacrifice, an ontological change of a person should happen to secure her eternal survival. Thus sin and death, according to Zizioulas, should be viewed not as much in juridical terms as a legal offense and punishment, but more in terms of existential disintegration.[53] I concur with Russell and Gunton to some extent, who are disappointed with "an inadequate doctrine of sin" and redemption in Zizioulas.[54] Similarly, Ables argues that Zizioulas's pessimistic anthropology cannot present a fair picture of intrinsic goodness and fallenness of humanity.[55] Also, Zinkovskiy correctly criticizes hamartiology that accepts sin only as an ontological problem and ignores the essence-hypostasis ontological unity of human beings, whereby personhood is impacted by sin as much as nature.[56]

Since the union of people with the divine energies is questionable, it is more appropriate to assume that the union on the level of *hypostases* represents the essence of Zizioulas's soteriology.[57] It is only in Christ, in

53. Zizioulas thinks that a proper balance between juridical notions of salvation and vocational restoration needs to be observed. "There are, therefore, two aspects of Christology, one negative (redemption from the fallen state) and another positive (fulfilment of man's full communion with God; what the Greek Fathers have called *theosis*). Only if the two are taken together, can Christology reveal human destiny in its fulness." Zizioulas, *Communion and Otherness*, 237. Awad accurately summarizes that salvation for Zizioulas is in becoming a relational being after breaking individualistic isolation, "Salvation is not a deliverance of the individual from submission to sin and slavery by gaining chaotic freedom. Rather, salvation is being in the image of God by participating in God's relational personality." Awad, "Personhood as Particularity," 5.

54. Russell, "Reconsidering Relational Anthropology," 178–81; Gunton, "Persons and Particularity," 104. To be fair, Russell and Gunton assess Zizioulas's hamartiology from a Reformed view, while the Metropolitan speaks within his Orthodox tradition and—as it is natural to all traditions—emphasizes one aspect of a doctrine over the other.

55. Ables, "Being Church," 119–20. Ables also finds a contradiction in Zizioulas, when the latter identifies freedom with natural capacity to become a hypostasis and freedom as a capacity/product of a hypostasis. Ables, "On the Very Idea," 674–75.

56. Zinkovskiy, *Patristic Categories*, 209.

57. Aristotle Papanikolaou points out that, in contrast to Zizioulas but following Palamas, Lossky rejected the idea of human participation in the divine nature as well as in hypostasis. "Even though we share the same human nature as Christ and receive in Him the name of Sons of God, we do not ourselves become the divine hypostasis of the Son by the fact of the Incarnation. We are unable, therefore, to participate in either the essence or the hypostasis of the Holy Trinity." Lossky, *Mystical Theology*, 70. Papanikolaou, "Divine Energies," 370. I side with Tanner, who ascribes the salvific efficacy to the person of Christ, not to his humanity common to all human beings. Hence, the union between Christ and believers occurs not on the level of natures, but persons. Tanner, *Jesus, Humanity and Trinity*, 54–55. Wesche, although correctly understanding

whom all creation is *hypostasized*, through his death and resurrection that believers receive their new particularity and identity. Death, which threatened the uniqueness and otherness of persons, was overcome through Christ.[58] Christ has restored the union and movement of human nature toward God, recapitulating humanity in his person. Christ, being the person *par excellence* due to his filial relations with the Father, made the personalization of human beings a historical reality. This restored human personhood is similar to divine personhood by virtue of union with the person of Christ, thus "becoming 'Christ' on the basis of the same filial relationship constituting Christ himself."[59] The human personhood is reconstituted "in communion with true personhood in Christ."[60] Since true human personhood cannot exist in isolation from relationships with God, this personhood finds its fulfillment in Christ:

> In Christ, therefore, every man acquires *his* particularity, *his* hypostasis, *his* personhood, precisely because, by being constituted as a being in and through the same relationship which constitutes Christ's being, he is as unique and unrepeatable and worthy of eternal survival as Christ is by virtue of his being constituted as a being through his filial relationship with the Father, which makes him so unique and so eternally loved as to be an eternally living being.[61]

Zizioulas continues by saying that Christ in his relationships with the Father is "one" and "many" at the same time because human *hypostases* now constitute the Son's being. Christ's relationships with the Father received a new dimension in that all those who are "in Christ" constitute the being of the Second person of the Trinity. Hence, the person of Christ is constituted by his trinitarian and ecclesiological relationships. Christ is not a representative on behalf of separate human individuals, but became "the ontological ground

---

the problem of individualization, still prefers to resolve it through participation in the divine uncreated energies, rather than persons. Wesche, "Doctrine of Deification." Olson suggests that only those who espouse Palamite *energeosis* could properly adopt the term "deification," while other forms of participation in God should be called "divinization." Olson, "Deification in Contemporary Theology." I contend that the term "deification" was appropriate to the early church fathers even before essence-energy distinction came into play. In this regard see Nispel, "Christian Deification"; Mosser, "Earliest Patristic Interpretations."

58. Zizioulas, *Communion and Otherness*, 75.
59. Volf, *After Our Likeness*, 86.
60. Turner, "Eschatology and Truth," 20.
61. Zizioulas, *Communion and Otherness*, 240 (emphasis original).

of every man."[62] Jesus Christ died on the cross not as an individual but as a person who constituted the whole of humankind, so that humanity might be restored as the community of persons in relationships with God and the rest of creation. Christ is a "corporate personality" and those persons, who participate in him by baptism, become "corporate personality" as well. Through the "new birth" in baptism, a person receives a new *hypostasis*, "the hypostasis of ecclesial existence."[63] To "put on Christ" means that a believer experiences the restoration of nature in its catholicity, i.e., "in its ekstatic movement of communion" through the hypostatic union of Christ.[64] Ciraulo, however, is right when he states that the logical conclusion of Zizioulas's concept of ecclesial *hypostasis* is that non-baptized are not persons and that there is no person outside the church.[65] Since it is hard to ignore that there is some sense of community outside the church, it would be helpful to state that the image of God, true personhood, in the society is not completely lost, but fractured and deformed, as the Greek fathers taught.

The salvation of the human being, its true identity and personhood, comes through union with God in the person of Christ. Since for Zizioulas, the predicament of humanity is not merely a legal offense against God, but estrangement from God and the loss of personhood. Salvation is the restoration of personal relationships with the personal God, attaining to the likeness of divine personhood. Soteriology is the transformation of human personhood by means of participation in Christ by grace, not the transformation of human nature into the likeness of divine nature. Therefore, Zizioulas defines the Orthodox view of salvation or *theosis* as the transformation of the mortal individual into the eternal person:

62. Zizioulas, *Communion and Otherness*, 243.

63. Zizioulas, *Being as Communion*, 53. Torrance objects to Zizioulas's notion of salvation as transferring from biological to ecclesial hypostasis, whereby an individual becomes a person. 1) How such salvation is possible for cognitively incapable people? 2) The vicarious death of Christ and the cross are minimized and limited to those in the eucharistic communion only, "the vicarious life and work of Christ risks being reduced, in terms of this kind of ontology, to its ek-static effect, that is, its creating and sustaining a dynamic of ecclesial communion, where its significance is limited to the ecclesial hypostases of those in whom the conditions of 'personhood' are thus realised." Torrance, *Persons in Communion*, 302. I think that the first objection is not fair, because cognitive abilities are the characteristics of the Western image of an individual, while, for Zizioulas, a person is primarily—but not exclusively—characterized by relations. As to the second objection, Zizioulas points out that the Eastern Church as an eschatological community directs its focus, especially during the liturgy, not simply to the cross, but also to the resurrection and final restoration of the whole creation and communion with the Trinity. Zizioulas, *Lectures in Christian Dogmatics*, 67–68, 135.

64. Zizioulas, *Communion and Otherness*, 245.

65. Ciraulo, "Sacraments and Personhood," 994–95.

The eternal survival of the person as a unique, unrepeatable and free "hypostasis," as loving and being loved, constitutes the quintessence of salvation, the bringing of the Gospel to man. In the language of the Fathers this is called "divinization" (*theosis*), which means participation not in the nature or substance of God, but in His personal existence. The goal of salvation is that the personal life which is realised [sic] in God should also be realized on the level of human existence. Consequently salvation is identified with the realization of personhood in man.[66]

Theosis, for the Cappadocians, meant that a human being should live not according to her nature (isolation) that will ultimately lead to death, but according to her person, like God himself lives. Zizioulas writes, "Living, on the other hand, according to the image of God means living in the way God exists, that is, as an image of God's personhood, and this would amount to 'becoming God.'"[67] Since people's original destiny was to live in relationships with the personal God, they were created in the image of the Trinity:

> The highest form of capacity for man is to be found in the notion *of imago Dei*. Yet, if this notion is put in the light of personhood rather than nature, it has to be modified, for what it in fact means is not that man can become God in his "nature," but can be in communion with God. The word *Dei* in this expression implies not a Deistic view of God but a Trinitarian one: man can himself live the event of communion which is realized in divine life and he can do this with and for the entire creation; he is in fact made as *imago Trinitatis*, and this is possible for him only because of his ability to be *a person*.[68]

---

66. Zizioulas, *Being as Communion*, 49–50. Volf notices that faith plays a limited role in Zizioulas's theology, because it contains a grain of a cognitive knowledge of God. For the Metropolitan, God does not enter into communion with a person by means of cognitive knowledge, but by means of free love. Faith is an eschatological reality and ends where knowledge begins. Zizioulas, *Lectures in Christian Dogmatics*, 34–39. Hence, Volf objects, "Even though the Christian faith cannot be reduced to cognitive content, it is nevertheless inconceivable without this cognitive content; in order to believe, one must at the very least be able to distinguish God, as the person in whom one believes, from idols, something possible only cognitively. Yet if faith is essentially a cognitive act (albeit not only such), then according to Zizioulas it cannot lead to communion, since it must be an individual act." Volf, *After Our Likeness*, 95. I concur to Volf that faith with a cognitive aspect is indispensable for salvation as the sphere, in which the divine communion with God occurs, not as "accompanying phenomenon." Volf, *After Our Likeness*, 171.

67. Zizioulas, *Communion and Otherness*, 165–66.

68. Zizioulas, *Communion and Otherness*, 249 (emphasis original); Zizioulas, *Lectures in Christian Dogmatics*, 69. On a similar idea of the tripersonal image of God in

The image of God's personhood is the Trinity. Thus, transformation into the likeness of God is a transformation into the likeness of the Trinity or, as I chose to call it, *triadosis*. Deification, for Zizioulas, however, is not direct with all three persons, but mediated through the Son, "The deification (*theosis*) of human nature, which is to say of humanity in general, is *not* attributed to man's union with 'God' in general, but only because man becomes united with the Son. In other words, *theosis* is union *in Christ*. All humanity exists in Christ."[69] Consequently, *triadosis* occurs in Christ or through *christosis*.

This transformation of an individual into a person is possible only by new birth, through incorporation in the only authentic image of the Father, in Christ. *Triadosis* is not an imitation of divine impersonal attributes or energies shared by Father, Son, and Spirit, but God's gracious adoption of believers through personal integration into the body of Christ. The principle of hypostatic identity presumes its uniqueness and inimitableness. The particularities of persons are not eradicated but assumed in the very idea of communion, which otherwise would become sameness without differentiation of identities. The identity of a person is constituted by the Trinity and other human persons and not diminished because only in communion she truly understands her difference. Salvation implies the restoration of communion with the other, following Christ's example in *kenotic* movement to his creation through the cross, "Since the Son of God moved to meet the other, his creation, by emptying himself through the *kenosis* of the Incarnation, the 'kenotic' way is the only one that befits the Christian in his or her communion with the other—be it God or one's 'neighbour.'"[70]

The trinitarian dimension of *theosis* presupposes an involvement of the Holy Spirit, who baptizes believers in Christ. Since God is a relational being, and otherness of Father, Son and Spirit constitutes God's ontology, the Holy Spirit brings communion and otherness in the life of believers united with God. The role of the Holy Spirit in creating a personal identity of the Christian is of an ontological nature:

> When the Holy Spirit blows, he creates not good individual Christians, individual "saints," but an event of communion, which transforms everything the Spirit touches into a *relational* being. In that case, the other becomes an ontological part of

Maximus the Confessor see Thunberg, *Man and Cosmos*, 47.

69. Zizioulas, *Lectures in Christian Dogmatics*, 116 (emphasis original). Zinkovskiy, following Iustin Popovich, calls hypostatic-ontological harmony of the human person *"christosis"* (*okhristovlenie*) and *"triadosis"* (*otroichenie*), which are possible only in church as the body of Christ. Zinkovskiy, *Patristic Categories*, 220.

70. Zizioulas, *Communion and Otherness*, 5–6.

one's own identity. The Spirit de-individualizes and personalizes beings wherever he operates.[71]

The Spirit guarantees the particularity of persons *hypostasized* in Christ and prevents the absorption of many members of Christ's body into an undistinguished whole. The otherness of persons in communion also precludes the absorption of human persons into the person of the Son. Hence, Volf is incorrect, when he thinks that for Zizioulas persons are "constituted into an undifferentiated multiplicity through the christological event,"[72] precisely because the Spirit constitutes their otherness and unity within the church. Relations with others define the uniqueness of other:

> In a relational ontology there is no Other without Others, for every being obtains its identity through its relations and not through separation. Therefore, since the unique being, the object *of eros*, receives its identity from its relationship with other beings, in loving this being uniquely one also loves whatever relates to it and constitutes its identity.[73]

Thus, to be in communion with the Son means to be in communion with the Father and the Spirit; to know the Father means to know the Son and the Spirit; to have the Spirit means to have the Father and the Son. To be like God means to be like the persons of the Trinity, to be created in the image of God means to be created in the image of the Trinity. Moreover, the Spirit's transformational role has an eschatological dimension, so that a person needs to be viewed not on the basis of his or her past and present, but from a future perspective.

Consequently, Zizioulas argues that the salvation of a person is not an isolated reality but always occurs in the context of ecclesial relationships.[74] For him, the church is not a group of individuals united ideologically by the same doctrines, but ontologically through a personal union with Christ as a community or *koinonia* of persons. Hence, the church, in essence, should reflect the nature of the intratrinitarian relations within one Godhead. This unity, however, is not sameness or uniformity that

---

71. Zizioulas, *Communion and Otherness*, 6 (emphasis original).
72. Volf, *After Our Likeness*, 182, 189.
73. Zizioulas, *Communion and Otherness*, 73 (emphasis original).
74. Zizioulas, "Church as Communion." Volf appropriately encapsulates this thought: "The concrete locus of deindividualization and personalization is the church. The church can be so, however, only because it is the pneumatologically constituted body of Christ. For this reason, it is in the church that human beings can become persons through baptism and can live as persons through the Eucharist." Volf, *After Our Likeness*, 83–84.

eradicates all diversity. Instead, racial, gender and social diversities are welcomed, because they create a context for a *kenotic* movement between church members. The ministry of a bishop, who, being one, represents the many, while a local "catholic" church represents all churches. For the Metropolitan of Pergamon, the ministry of the bishop is necessary for the constitution of church's unity, which makes ecclesiastical hierarchy indispensable.[75] The ecclesiastical order of the bishop, however, is constituted by the order of laity. Thus, one is indispensable without the other. Both orders represent equal significance for the church. The Eucharist represents the climax of church's communion, whereby the otherness is not suppressed but reconciled on vertical and horizontal levels. Knight expresses the eschatological dimension of the Eucharist well, "Each eucharist is an event of the transformation and perfection of creation, or rather a moment in which the finished creation makes itself felt within the present, unfinished and partial, creation."[76] Thus, the church is the eucharistic and eschatological community, which unites people of different strands of society in a given location and the whole world.[77]

Taking into account Zizioulas's view on the transformation of a biological *hypostasis* into ecclesial *hypostasis*, Farrow provides a comprehensive definition of human personhood, "For him [Zizioulas] personhood is a vocation, a process, a destiny. It is ecclesial in nature, liturgically accessed, and eschatologically consummated. Personhood, properly speaking, is the result of deification."[78] Contra Zizioulas, Farrow rejects the dialectic between creaturely necessities that need to be overcome and the freedom of personhood, as if the human person ceases to be a creature by overcoming necessities. Indeed, as several commentators complained, if the creatureliness of human nature is identified with the fallen necessities of human beings, it will necessitate a corrupted creation from the beginning.[79] In my view, however, Zizioulas

75. Bathrellos argues that the overemphasized structure of the church contradicts Zizioulas's idea of overcoming human nature by way of personhood in communion with others in freedom and love, "This ecclesiology runs the risk of leaving little room for proper particularity, development and differentiation in place and time." Bathrellos, "Church, Eucharist, Bishop," 140. Zizioulas recognizes the need for diversity and particularity, but not at the expense of unity. For him, the role of the bishop is to guard both unity and diversity in the church, "Equally, this one minister should be part of the community, and not stand above it as an authority in itself. All pyramidal notions of Church structure vanish in the ecclesiology of communion. There is *perichoresis* of ministries, and this applies also to the ministry of unity." Zizioulas, "Church as Communion," 10.

76. Knight, "Spirit and Persons," 193.

77. Zizioulas, "Local Church."

78. Farrow, "Person and Nature," 111.

79. Loudovikos, "Person Instead of Grace," 686; Ciraulo, "Sacraments and

identifies fallenness not with human nature as such, but with human nature particularized in the isolated individual. Salvation is not God's triumph over human nature for the sake of personhood, but the realization of the human nature's vocation to become truly personal. Farrow claims,

> For the function of the God-man is not to introduce personhood (a divine reality) into the impersonal (the creaturely), so that the latter might attain authentic existence. His function is rather to perfect, together with the Spirit, a human *analogy* to divine personhood; that is, to secure for human personhood its essential openness to God and to the other...[80]

For Farrow, the ultimate threat to personhood is not created necessity, but sin that makes an authentic communion of persons impossible. Deification as freedom from natural necessity should not mean the end of creaturely necessity, but freedom *in* necessity because the human being remains a creature and does not become God. Thus, in church, an individual overcomes her existential isolation, becoming a free person through deifying communion with Christ and other persons. Such an ecclesial person is called *catholic* and bears human nature in its entirety as a microcosm.

Harrison rightly assumes that Zizioulas's ecclesiology is built primarily on his Christology, whereby "an intrinsic ontological inequality" of Christ and his members is applied to the bishop and his congregation. His ecclesiology would perhaps benefit from developing the implications of trinitarian ontology, with the figure of a bishop taking up the monarchical role of the Father,[81] but still remaining equal with each church member, which actively—not merely in receptive form—represents the whole community as a free person.[82] Several writers identified a problem in Zizioulas's complete identi-

---

Personhood," 995. Zizioulas is not so anti-nature, as Loudovikos seems to suggest, because, for the Metropolitan, nature is simultaneous with person, not primary to it. Zinkovskiy correctly affirms that in baptism the biological hypostasis does not die, but begins the transformation of the mode of human existence, including biological. Zinkovskiy, *Theology of Person*, 181–82.

80. Farrow, "Person and Nature," 122.

81. Zizioulas, *Lectures in Christian Dogmatics*, 129. Zizioulas's identification of the bishop with Christ or the Father is not consistent as was seen from the previous reference. Zizioulas, *Lectures in Christian Dogmatics*, 146.

82. Harrison, "Zizioulas on Communion," 289–90. Loudovikos goes further, stating that the idea of "one and the many" is applicable to the Father and the Trinity, but not to Christ and the church, even less to a bishop and a church because a bishop is one of many in relation to Christ. Loudovikos, "Christian Life and Institutional Church," 130. I contend that the idea of one representing the many is valid, but on a different level, so that Christ as one of human beings represents all believers to the Father and a bishop as one of believers represents a local community to the Trinity.

fication of Christ with the church, so that the personal identity, the "I," of the church is the "I" of Christ. Therefore, when during the Eucharist the church is praying to the Father, the Son is praying to the Father.[83] According to the New Testament, it is not Christ who prays through us, but we pray *through* Christ *in* the Spirit and also the Spirit prays *in* us (Rom 1:8; 8:15, 26; 16:27; Gal 4:6; 1 Cor 14:15).[84] A problem with such an identification, according to Volf, is the absorption of the church into Christ, "Yet just as in the constituting of a person the particularity of that person is lost and the individual is absorbed into Christ, so also the church itself is threatened with being absorbed into Christ."[85] While accepting a legitimate language of the *imago Trinitatis* of ecclesial humanity, Farrow disapproves the equation of ecclesial humanity with divine *perichoresis*.[86] The human person is not a person in the same way as a divine person is a person. Therefore, even if it is proper to say that the divine persons are co-inherent in each other, it is not the same with human persons. It does not mean that with and in each human person the whole church is. It is not the divine type of *perichoresis*. For Zizioulas, a local church represents the fullness of the church, because the fullness of Christ is indivisibly present in each Eucharist, "Each of the Churches that celebrate the Eucharist has the whole presence of Christ, indeed each of them is the whole presence of Christ, for that place."[87] That is why the Eastern Church, unlike the Western Church, gives precedence to local churches over the universal church, as it does in relation to persons over nature. Volf, however, thinks that the "universal church vs. local churches" formula should not be equated with the "divine nature vs. divine persons" formula, because in the *eschaton* the distinction between the universal and local church will be removed, unlike the distinction between divine nature and persons.[88] Human beings, acquiring true freedom as the image-bearers of God, have a goal to be the agents of communication between creation and Creator. Since salvation relates not only to humankind but also to all creation, the historical event of salvation has a transformative ontological significance, not only moral.

83. Zizioulas, *Lectures in Christian Dogmatics*, 117.
84. Volf, *After Our Likeness*, 100n151.
85. Volf, *After Our Likeness*, 100. Gunton accurately points that Zizioulas identifies the church with Christ, so that the humanity of Christ is diminished. Gunton, "Persons and Particularity," 105. Likewise, Farrow objects to the personal equation of the church and Christ, so that it becomes problematic to substitute the title "Christ" for Jesus. Farrow, "Person and Nature," 117.
86. Farrow, "Person and Nature," 118.
87. Zizioulas, *Lectures in Christian Dogmatics*, 141.
88. Volf, *After Our Likeness*, 203.

It is appropriate to conclude the study of Zizioulas's theology with an extended quote, wherein the Metropolitan expresses the essence of personal identification with the tripersonal God and presumably shortcomings of alternative views:

> This divine movement is one of divine *persons*, not of divine substance and energy as such. God is not a physical object radiating loving energy. It is as persons that he "emigrates" with his ἔρως and fills the gulf of otherness with his love. A non-personalist theology would turn God into a natural object and would have nothing to do with the living God of the Bible and the worshipping Church.
>
> God and the world are united without losing their otherness only in the person of the divine Logos, that is, only in Christ. It is a person that makes this possible, because it is only a person that can express communion and otherness simultaneously, thanks to its being a mode of being, that is, an identity which, unlike substance or energy, is capable of "modifying" its being without losing its ontological uniqueness and otherness. All other, that is, non-personalist, ways of uniting God and the world, while safeguarding otherness, involve either a non-ontological relationship between God and the world (e.g., ethics, psychology, religiosity, etc.) or an undermining of the Incarnation, that is, of the "hypostatic (= personal) union" between created and uncreated being.[89]

The Metropolitan Zizioulas presented a greatly stimulating and provocative retrieval of the traditional doctrines of Christian theology, such as trinitarian ontology, personalistic anthropology, and participationist soteriology in the context of *ecclesia* of hypostases. Virtually all aspects of his approach are met with appraisals as well as critical scrutiny. Zizioulas represents a helpful bridge between the modern East and West, in a way that is not attested in Lossky or Staniloae. His account of *theosis* is in dialogue with Western theology and deliberately seeks to recover a pre-Palamite way of thinking. It is also developed with an eye to the New Testament, particularly to the Pauline material on communion and *ecclesia*. Also, his account of *theosis* is one that has been prominent in Western attempts to recover notions of deification, as Knight's engagement with it attests.

In his reaction against a methodological mistake of the West in prioritizing the nature over the person, Zizioulas, arguably, overemphasizes person and relationships over nature, instead of upholding a balanced person-nature ontology. I think such a symmetrical ontology would have

---

89. Zizioulas, *Communion and Otherness*, 29 (emphasis original).

saved him from many rejoinders. The dubious overcoming of natural human necessities notwithstanding, Zizioulas developed a very helpful distinction between the notions of isolated individual and person in communion. His inadequate hamartiology does not prevent the Metropolitan from outlining an elegant soteriology as the establishment of a human person in restored communion with a personal God and other human persons through the Son in the Spirit. Even though Zizioulas is less articulate about the role of faith in salvation, he is on the right path in identifying salvation with *triadosis*, the participation of divine image-bearers in the life of trinitarian and ecclesial communities. His ecclesiology welcomes particularity and diversity alongside unity and hierarchy. His over-realized eschatology does not ignore present human frailty and imperfection. It would be fair to conclude that he espoused, what I call, a paradigm of *triadosis* via *christosis*, i.e., a communion with the whole Trinity through the incorporation of believers into the Son in the Spirit.

Conclusion

In comparing the theologies of the two Reformers and John Zizioulas, one can conclude that they agree, at least thematically, that Christian salvation is more than the declarative statement of justification. It involves union with Christ and transformation of an individual sinner into a corporate person that exists in a community with her Savior and the church. As in the case of the Reformers, the subsequent generations of Christians after the Cappadocian fathers, especially in the West, had lost the proper understanding of personhood and its meaning for the doctrine of God and human beings. The all-pervasive dominance of "nature" distorted their view of the Trinity, just as the "fallen nature" of Adam eclipsed the problem of human depersonalization and estrangement from personal relations with the Trinity and other persons.

Undoubtedly, the Reformers placed a greater emphasis on the doctrine of sin, faith, and forensic justification, than their Orthodox partner does. Being Protestant Reformers, Luther and Calvin made a clear distinction between the human identity of the church and the divine identity of Christ; the two cannot coincide in the body of Christ. The Reformers, as people of the West, operated within the categories of an individual self, turned to herself, but they did not break the mold of personhood, by envisioning the transformation of isolated beings into an ek-static communion of persons.

Both Zizioulas and the Reformers discarded the idea of participation between humans and Christ on the level of natures, preferring to talk about intimate personal relationships and indwelling of the person of Christ in believers. In union with Christ, believers receive access to all his spiritual gifts, but, most importantly, to communion with divine persons. This communion transforms estranged biological creatures into spiritual persons, who realize their potential and ultimate goal in the life of the church and the Trinity. The Son becomes one of us so that we may enter into communion with the Trinity by the Spirit. The identity of human participants, as well as their createdness, is preserved in this divine-human union. Nevertheless, the mutual indwelling and spiritual *perichoresis* of believers and Christ transform Christians into a type of persons that live in the likeness of divine existence (2 Pet 1:4). God the Savior is a triune God. One should not consider the saving role of Christ in isolation from the saving functions of the Father and the Spirit. Hence, *theosis* is, in essence, *triadosis* and the accommodation of human life to the life of the Trinity. Having concluded that *theosis* with a particular trinitarian feature is a suitable category for expounding both Protestant and Eastern Orthodox theologies, I will analyze recent attempts among New Testament scholars to retrieve the doctrine for Pauline study.

Chapter 5

Recent Retrievals of *Theosis* in Paul

Introduction

IN THIS CHAPTER, I will engage three recent attempts to interpret Paul's theology in light of *theosis*. These are M. David Litwa's, Ben C. Blackwell's, and Michael J. Gorman's approaches.[1] The input of these studies for promoting a holistic reading of Paul with respect to the ancient concept of deification is appreciated. Litwa provides a historical background of deification antecedent to Paul, which helps to understand the apostle's religious setting. Blackwell applies a retrospective reading of deification from patristic era to Paul's theology. Gorman focuses on the exegetical side of the discussion about the appropriateness of *theosis* in Paul. Each scholar has contributed to a better understanding of *theosis*. The value of different approaches notwithstanding, each study has its limitations, which will be assessed below.

M. David Litwa

M. David Litwa, in a brilliant and well-informed study, questions the traditional patristic understanding of deification and focuses on deification's roots in Jewish and Greco-Roman traditions.[2] Litwa criticizes Russell and Blackwell for inconsistency in calling their versions of deification "realistic," while allowing no change in the human nature of the deified. Litwa complains that the "participationist" understanding of deification in metaphorical terms is a later patristic monotheistic influence. It is, therefore, anachronistic to read it into Paul, whose view of deification was probably closer to his Jewish and Hellenistic contemporaries, whereby humans actually become divine or

---

1. Litwa, *We Are Being Transformed*; Blackwell, *Christosis*; Gorman, *Inhabiting Cruciform God*.

2. Litwa, *We Are Being Transformed*.

gods.³ Against Russell's objection that there was no clear understanding of Christ as God by the first-century Christians, Litwa points to texts like John 1:1 and concurs with Larry Hurtado that it is very likely that Paul and early Christians considered Jesus to be God. Against Blackwell, Litwa argues that Blackwell limited his approach by using later patristic metaphysical categories that were designed to combat gnostic ideas and read them back into Paul. The biggest problem with using church fathers is that it reads the later Christian versions of deification into Paul's first-century background. These later concepts include triune divine relations, the distinction between divine essence and attributes, creator-creature gap, and *creatio ex nihilo*.⁴ Likewise, Litwa claims that some scholars grounded the previous rejections of deification in Paul on a false presupposition that Hellenistic deification always meant fusion with a deity. Since neither mystery religions nor Paul believed in a fusion with a deity or the loss of personal identity, deification—properly understood—is a valid soteriological category.

Litwa points that "likeness" is an inadequate term to describe the content and degree of deification. He prefers to talk about the participation of humans with a divine being, sharing the divine attributes that constitute divine identity without fusing into one identity. The participation of the Son in the Father beyond likeness does not mean the loss of the Son's identity.⁵ Since *theosis* is a later Christian version of deification, while *apotheosis* is a non-Christian version, Litwa preferred the term "deification" to avoid an anachronistic and ahistorical reading. For Litwa, "mysticism" does not fit Paul's idea of deification either, because of its individualistic sense: "In my reading, Pauline deification is (1) not an experience limited to a few, (2) is mostly worked out in community, (3) can be explained using concepts, and (4) does not involve a confused mixing with divinity."⁶

Although the term deification is absent in the Pauline writings, a few concepts indicate its presence in Paul, such as attaining deathlessness, incorruption through bodily resurrection, immortality, glorification, superangelic existence, and possession of the whole world (1 Cor 15:35-53; Rom 8:29-32; Phil 3:21; 2 Cor 3:18; 1 Cor 6:2-3; Rom 16:20; 1 Cor 3:21-23). Litwa sums up the concept of deification in Paul with the following points:

---

3. Litwa, *We Are Being Transformed*, 9-10, n. 20.

4. Litwa, *We Are Being Transformed*, 29n110. Litwa questions Blackwell's distinction between participation in the divine essence and divine attributes, such as immortality and power. How can attributes be divine if they are not part of that essence? Litwa, *We Are Being Transformed*, 293.

5. Litwa, *We Are Being Transformed*, 32.

6. Litwa, *We Are Being Transformed*, 34.

It is thus primarily three factors, all closely intertwined, that
suggest a form of deification in Paul, namely: (1) ruling over "all
things" (including superhuman beings), together with (2) the
expectation of existing in a superhuman, immortal and incorruptible corporeality. Both of these factors are viewed as functions of (3) assimilation to Christ, a divine being.[7]

Litwa's historical approach, however, is deficient in four premises.

The Invalidity of Subsequent Theological Approach

The first deficient premise relates to the danger of reception history. According to Litwa, the patristic accounts of Christian deification are an evolution
of Greco-Roman ideas of deification. From a historical point of view, it is
logically appropriate to situate Paul's vision of human transformation into
the image of a God Christ in his surrounding culture, rather than to bring
later ecclesiastic developments formulated in a different context. Litwa argues that a historian needs to trace the prior beliefs of deification and not to
impose subsequent interpolations into Paul's thought.

One of Litwa's premises is that the first-century Greco-Roman and
Jewish thinkers were less concerned with the ontological diversification
of gods as a class. Instead, they espoused a Platonic ontology of essence,
whereby spiritual beings belong to the same class of divinity, in as much
as they participated in the true Primal Being. Moreover, non-divine-class
beings, such as humans, could gradually assimilate to a divine being. Non-
human beings that acquired immortality, superhuman power and virtues
were considered divine and a part of a "God" category. Hence, there is no
need for later Nicaean metaphysical explanations to appreciate deification
as Paul's soteriological ideal. Also, Litwa presumes that a strict ontological
divide between the transcendent God and created beings was a Christian response to unorthodox competitors, rather than something that constituted
Paul's worldview. There was no need for the apostle to claim the ontological
equality of the Son with the Father because he could easily accommodate
Christ on the vertical axis of divine beings, even if his divinity was less than
that of the High God. In this regard, the acknowledgment of Christ's pre-
existence in Phil 2, for Litwa, does not flow out of the patristic category of
homoousios with the Father, but merely a statement about his status in the
realm of divine beings.[8]

---

7. Litwa, *We Are Being Transformed*, 13.
8. Litwa, *We Are Being Transformed*, 4–5n9.

Litwa contends that a more rigid ontological distinction between the later developed doctrine of the Trinity and spiritual beings, including deified humans, was introduced at the ecumenical councils of Nicaea and Constantinople (325–381 CE). In particular, Litwa considers Blackwell's choice of Irenaeus and Cyril of Alexandria as Paul's interpreters "a tragic decision," because "[t]hese two heresiologists are prone to make totalizing, metaphysical distinctions between God and creation as well as Christ and believer that are simply not present in Paul's letters."[9] Instead, Litwa suggests it would be better to interact with Clement of Alexandria and Origen because they represent a way of thinking that is prior to, and outside the box of, later Orthodox theologizing.[10] He overlooks, however, the fact that these church fathers also combated different heresies and fought against subordination among the divine persons. Besides, they employed metaphysical concepts foreign to Paul as was shown in chapter 2. Moreover, Irenaeus chronologically precedes both Alexandrians. Hence, the issue is not merely historical proximity to Paul. Litwa's assessment of the Alexandrians is problematic in light of the recent studies of their theologies. Hence, his alliance with Clement and Origen is, at the least, overoptimistic to his program, or misguided at worst.

Since Litwa relies on the Alexandrians, who, according to his presumption, exemplify his way of reasoning, I will address these church fathers briefly here, specifically their view of divine ontology and taxonomy. It should be stressed that early Christian writers were not uncritical in their appropriation of philosophical ideas, albeit utilizing Platonic categories for the service of theology. For these church fathers, the "genetic" assimilation of human beings with God always had ontological limitations. The saints become gods by grace as far as it is possible for created beings. In the second book of the *Stromateis* 16, Clement as a Christian heresiologist stated that participation in the transcendent God

> has no natural relation to us, as the authors of the heresies will have it; neither on the supposition of His having made us of nothing, nor on that of having formed us from matter; since the former did not exist at all, and the latter is totally distinct from God unless we shall dare to say that we are a part of Him, and of the same essence as God.[11]

---

9. Litwa, *We Are Being Transformed*, 28–29.

10. Litwa, *We Are Being Transformed*, 29. Clement and Origen argued for deification as a goal for a Christian "gnostic."

11. Clement of Alexandria, *Clement of Alexandria*.

As evident from this quote, Clement employs the metaphysical language of "essence" and strongly objects to any notion of essential human participation in God, being "by nature wholly estranged" from him. Instead, to express the relationship between God and Christians Clement refers to Paul's language of adoption, which he calls "the greatest advancement of all." Similarly, in the next chapter, Clement states that our desire to be like the Lord is impossible by "essence (for it is impossible for that, which is by adoption, to be equal in substance to that, which is by nature); but [we are like Him] only in our having been made immortal, and our being conversant with the contemplation of realities, and beholding the Father through what belongs to Him" (*Strom.* 2.17). Moreover, the Alexandrian ascribes to a heretic Basilides, not to an orthodox view, the essential likeness of creatures with God—"a creation worthy of the essence of the Creator"—and the knowledge of God by nature (*Strom.* 5.1). Even in the context of interpreting the fifth commandment, where Clement calls those who know God "His sons and gods," he writes, "The Creator of the universe is their Lord and Father; and the mother is not, as some say, the essence from which we sprang, nor, as others teach, the Church, but the divine knowledge and wisdom . . ." (*Strom.* 6.16). For Clement, there is no essential divine protology or teleology of humans called "gods," because God's essence remains outside human knowledge (*Strom.* 6.18), not least participation. The only way they can be called gods is because they can imitate the incarnate God, the Logos, in a dynamic and gradual process. As was pointed in chapter 2, Clement considered that the Scripture functions in a deifying way by transforming its readers to the likeness of God. It seems fair to conclude that Clement, like other church fathers, operated within clear ontological distinction between God and creation, contrary to Litwa's assumption.

Further, in contrast to Litwa's claim that Clement's theology reflects a subordinate Christology, it is worth considering Henny Fiskå Hägg's critical study of the father's theology.[12] There she argues that in *Excerpta ex Theodoto* the full divinity and consubstantiality of the Son and the Father are affirmed. For instance, in *Exc.* 8.1, Clement wrote, "We [as opposed to the Valentinians] maintain that the essential Logos is God in God (τὸν ἐν ταὐτότητι λόγον θεὸν ἐν θεῷ), who is also said to be 'in the bosom of the Father,' without separation or division, one God."[13] Later he stated that the Logos's sonship is not a result of acquired later connaturality with the Father, rather "the essential Logos became a son, by delimitation and not in essence" (κατὰ περιγραφὴν οὐ κατ' οὐσίαν γενόμενος [ὁ] υἱός, *Exc.* 19.1–2).

---

12. Hägg, *Clement of Alexandria*.
13. Cited in Hägg, *Clement of Alexandria*, 200–201.

The individuation of the Son did not sever him essentially from the Father. Further, the term "Logos" for Clement is not a designation of a subordinate being because the Father himself is called "the essential Logos" (*Exc.* 19.4). Hägg affirmatively summarizes, "For Clement, then, immanence and incarnation did not mean severing the Son from the Father; their unity of substance and thus also their unity in divinity is upheld."[14] Moreover, it seems that the church father espoused a form of consubstantial trinitarianism, defending the divinity of the Spirit, "But they do not know that the Paraclete, who now works continuously in the Church, is of the same substance and power as he who worked continuously according to the Old Testament" (τῆς αὐτῆσοὐσίας ἐστὶ καὶ δυνάμεως τῷ προσεχῶς ἐνεργήσαντι κατὰ τὴν παλαιὰν διαθήκην, *Exc.* 24.2).[15] Even if Clement's Christology and trinitarianism were underdeveloped, there is no sure ground to consider him advocating for full-blown christological subordination, as Litwa seems to assume. In addition, as current debates around eternal subordination of the Son show, the Son's submission to the Father does not necessarily mean a gradation of divinity, which Litwa advocates, but rather can reflect the issues of contingency and voluntary submission.

Similarly, Litwa perceives Origen's presumably subordinate Christology as an early patristic exemplification of his own historical interpretation of Paul's theology and soteriology. It should be noted, however, that this characterization of the father's theology is questionable, as Ilaria Ramelli has pointed out recently.[16] In particular, in his *Commentary on Romans*, Origen expressed the full equality and connaturality of the Father and the Son. On Rom 9:1–5, he comments that Paul was ready to be accursed and separated from the love of Christ, which is, in reality, impossible, just as Christ "who is by nature inseparable from the Father and immortal" (*Comm. Rom.* 7.13.5).[17] Origen's trinitarian interpretation of 1 Cor 8:6 is worth an extended citation in light of this text's importance for Litwa's argument:

> What amazes me is how certain persons who read what this same Apostle says elsewhere, "There is one God, the Father, from whom are all things, and one Lord, Jesus Christ, through whom are all things," should deny that the Son of God ought to be confessed to be God, lest they should appear to speak of

---

14. Hägg, *Clement of Alexandria*, 201.

15. Cited in Hägg, *Clement of Alexandria*, 201.

16. I am indebted for the following exposition of Origen to Ramelli, "Origen's Anti-Subordinationism"; Ramelli, "Origen, Greek Philosophy, and Birth."

17. Origen of Alexandria, *Commentary on Epistle*.

two gods. What will they do about this passage of the Apostle in which Christ is explicitly recorded to be "God over all"? But, those who interpret these things this way fail to observe that he has not called the Lord Jesus Christ "one Lord" in such a way that therefore God the Father may not be called Lord. Likewise, he has not called God the Father "one God" in a sense in which the Son would not be believed to be God. For that Scripture is true that says, "Know that the Lord himself is God [Ps 100:3]." But both are one God, since there is no other source of deity for the Son than the Father; but of that one paternal fountain, as wisdom says, the Son is "the purest emanation [Wis 7:25]." Christ, therefore, is "God over all . . ." He who is over all has no one over himself. For he himself is not later than the Father, but from the Father. But the wisdom of God has granted that this same thing be understood of the Holy Spirit as well, where it says, "The Spirit of the Lord filled the earth, and he who contains all things, has knowledge of his voice [Wis 1:7]." If, therefore, the Son is called "God over all" and the Holy Spirit is recorded to contain all things, but God is the Father "from whom are all things," then clearly the nature and essence of the Trinity, which is over all things, are shown to be one (*Comm. Rom.* 7.13.9).

Here Origen, as a forerunner of later Cappadocian formulations, expressed the equality of the Son and the Father, sharing one essence. Likewise, he acknowledged not only their personal distinction—which later will be expressed by means of Father's *monarchia* and the eternal generation of the Son—but also the essential unity of the Trinity. It is hard to imagine that such an interpretation could fuel later Arianism. Equally, prayers, petitions, thanksgiving, and honor have to be offered to Christ as to the Father, who are one in essence, "while they are two, considered as persons or subsistences [δύο τῇ ὑποστάσει πράγματα], are one in unity of thought, in harmony and in identity of will" (*Comm. Rom.* 8.5.2; *Cels.* 8.12; *ANF* 4:644).[18] The Alexandrian laid the ground for the future definition of ὑπόστασις in contrast to οὐσία, as well as expressing the substantial unity of the Father with the Son through a common will. Further, Origen disparages heretics who separate or confuse the persons of the Trinity, which exist in one essence:

There are, for example, all the heretics who certainly announce the Father and the Son and the Holy Spirit; but they do not announce well or faithfully. For either they wrongly separate the Son from the Father, when they say that the Father is of one nature and the Son is of another nature, or they wrongly confuse

18. Roberts and Donaldson, *Ante-Nicene Fathers*.

them, when they imagine either that God is composed of three or that he is merely referred to by three names. But whoever announces the good news well will bestow upon each one, the Father, the Son, and the Holy Spirit, his own unique characteristics; but he will not confess that there is any difference in essence or nature (*Comm. Rom.* 8.5.9).

Here the Alexandrian refuted Sabellianism with its confusion of personal distinctions within Godhead, as well as pre-Arian subordinationists with their essential distinction between the Father and the Son. He pointed in the direction of unique personal subsistence that later Cappadocians will ascribe to *hypostasis*. The Father, the Son, and the Holy Spirit share the same essence, having their own unique properties.

Origen's anti-subordinationist expressions are not limited to his exegetical works, but also are evident in *Prin.* 4.1.28, "For we do not say, as the heretics suppose, that some part of the *substance* of God was converted into the Son, or that the Son was procreated by the Father out of things non-existent [ἐξ οὐκ ὄντων], i.e., *beyond His own substance*, so that there once was a time when He did not exist [ἦν ποτε ὅτε οὐκ ἦν]" (*ANF* 4:376 (emphasis added)). The father continued by accentuating that any notions of temporality are inappropriate to the divine persons, "whereas the statements made regarding Father, Son, and Holy Spirit are to be understood as transcending all time, all ages, and all eternity. For it is the Trinity alone which exceeds the comprehension not only of temporal but even of eternal intelligence." Origen made clear the distinction between creation and the Son, who, unlike creation, was not made of nothing (a later Arian slogan), but was from the very essence of the Father. At the same time, the Father's essence suffered no change. In his *Scholia in Matthaeum*, Origen employs the traditional trinitarian formula μία οὐσία, τρεῖς ὑποστάσεις, as well as the term ὁμοούσιος in relation to the Son's co-essentiality with the Father (PG 17:309c–d).[19]

All this evidence leaves one to conclude that Origen's heritage cannot be placed easily in a box of an "orthodox" or "heretical" teacher. Irenaeus, Athanasius, and the Cappadocians used the philosophical categories of their predecessors to preserve the ontological unity and personal distinction within the Trinity. It seems, however, that Clement and Origen were

19. Ramelli points to other texts in Origen, where he expressed the oneness of the divine essence (ἕν οὐσίᾳ) and the belief that the Son is God, being born κατ' οὐσίαν. Nonetheless, the Son is hypostatically distinct from the Father (*Comm. Jo.* 2.10.74; 10.37.246; 23.149; *Fr. Jo.* 1; *Comm. Matt.* 17.14). Ramelli, "Origen's Anti-Subordinationism," 27. Ramelli maintains that the Cappadocians closely depended on Origen's terminology and concepts, just as Pamphilus, Athanasius, and Rufinus.

at some points closer to their Greco-Roman philosophical contemporaries than to Paul in their taxonomy and theological construal. Although Litwa uses Clement and Origen to show that the patristic interpreters closest to Paul taught a sort of Christ-subordination and the ontological participation of human beings in the Logos, he ignores the complexity and problematic features of their philosophical models of God, the salvific imitation of Christ, the pre-existence of souls, and *apokatastasis* that rendered Paul's teachings inadequately narrow. As we have seen above, Clement's and Origen's versions of *apotheosis* were considered deviations, rather than the rule accepted by the majority of orthodox believers. An attentive study of Paul's texts made later fathers uneasy about Clement's and Origen's anthropological, christological, and soteriological propositions and caused them to reject some of these as unorthodox. Thus, the later fathers were much more in line with Irenaeus's, than with the Alexandrians's interpretation of Paul. All these comments about the Alexandrians are not to minimize some of the texts that could be read in subordinationists terms, but to show the complexity and, perhaps, the contradictory elements of their theology (as, arguably, with many church fathers) that ought to be accounted before claiming their support.

Also, Litwa is very eclectic concerning patristic teachings. While openly disavowing an anachronistic input of the fathers, in particular, the Athanasian trinitarian ontology, he applauds the Athanasian formula of exchange.[20] Quoting Gregory of Nazianzus's funeral oration, where he claims that he is "bidden to be a God" (*Or. Bas.* 48), Litwa fails to note that, in such contexts, the Cappadocians always presumed a specific condition: as much as it is possible for people.[21]

Another argument advanced by Litwa in support of the essential transformation of humans into divine beings is his rejection of God's absolute transcendence grounded on the *ex nihilo* doctrine.[22] This teaching is supposedly a later move in Christian apologetics against gnostics and possibly a version of Platonism. Accordingly, Paul could not have had the view of God's wholly otherness, because the Son of God already crossed the ontological gap in his incarnation and made possible the reverse transit of humans into divine status. As was shown above, Clement and Origen utilized the *ex nihilo* doctrine in their argumentation, witnessing to its early origin. There is no place here to argue for Paul's view of creation from noth-

20. Litwa, *We Are Being Transformed*, 261.
21. Litwa, *We Are Being Transformed*, 270. In n. 30, Litwa recognizes that Gregory operated during a theological revolution and in another oration stated that "created cannot be God" (*Or.* 29.4). This makes Litwa's unfair eclecticism more apparent.
22. Litwa, *We Are Being Transformed*, chap. 9.

ing, but perhaps Rom 4:17 (καλοῦντος τὰ μὴ ὄντα ὡς ὄντα) can indicate his familiarity with the idea. In my opinion, Litwa's treatment of later patristic writers is flawed, which makes his rejection of subsequent theological developments unsubstantiated. Now we can look at his major concern, i.e., Paul's religious background, to see whether Litwa's historical account of deification is entirely attainable.

The Supremacy of Antecedent Historical Approach

The second deficient premise relates to overrating of the historical quest. Litwa claims that he pursues an exclusively historical approach to discover similarities and distinctions between the ancient concepts of deification and Paul's soteriology. Therefore, from his perspective, the later trinitarian categories such as the essential equality of the divine persons, the hypostatic union of natures in Christ, and other similar notions should be avoided as an anachronistic distortion of Paul. Instead, Litwa focuses on studying the previous notions of divinity that circulated in Jewish and Greco-Roman cultures to illuminate the apostle's soteriological teaching. The historical background of deification in application to Paul should take precedence over any theological or ecumenical concerns. Inherently, such approach assumes that Paul's more obscure teaching on the union of believers with Christ will become apparent and meaningful when Greco-Roman and Jewish concepts of divinity are applied to an interpretation of the apostle.

This presupposition, however, begs the questions. Why other religious writings and cultural mores should shed light on Paul and not vice versa. Further, as Litwa himself acknowledges if Paul "adapt[s] and transform[s] certain elements of Greco-Roman forms of deification to his own soteriology,"[23] how do we assess the degree of such an adaptation? What criteria are there to judge whether Paul operates within a graded scheme of divinity or assumes an essential divide between Creator and created? Ultimately, if Paul was thinking in the categories of Greco-Roman deification, why did he never adopt the term? It is not to suggest that he was intrinsically inimical to the idea of deification. It only raises the question about the level of similarity between Paul and those outside the Jesus-movement, which Litwa so confidently promotes, and the apostle's desire to disassociate from the dubious beliefs and practices in surrounding culture.

The limitations of a historical analysis of Paul is evident when one considers the broad range of cultural, religious, and philosophical ideas in the ancient Mediterranean basin. The only thing that one can conclude

23. Litwa, *We Are Being Transformed*, 288.

from a historical excavation of the period is a possible influence on the apostle, who undoubtedly adapted any such ideas in light of his experience of Christ. How do we know and to what degree Paul, who often produced counter-cultural statements, assimilated to ancient ideas and beliefs? The level of such an adaptation would ever remain at a level of hypothesis and interpretation among scholars, rather than that of sufficient historical certainty. Leander E. Keck points to the nature of historical accounts, which usually are abridged versions of certain beliefs. Such tendency is characteristic of not only biblical authors but also non-biblical.[24] Thus, historical criteria to assess Paul's version of deification, to which Litwa strives, are not fully historically attainable. Further, the search for analogies between Paul and surrounding culture risks the over-emphasis of similarities and the dismissal of distinctions, depending on the historian's preferences or agenda. For instance, Litwa agrees that Paul discarded the Roman emperor cult, but, nonetheless, shared its logic.[25] While acknowledging distinctions between Paul and ancient beliefs concerning deification, much of Litwa's concerns are focused on the continuity between the apostle and his non-Jewish contemporaries. Paul operated in the domain of the first-century Jesus-followers. It would be more natural to consider his views concerning deification in his canonical background, rather than trying to fit his statements in the extra-biblical milieu and maximize their convergence.[26] The issue of judgment is also pertinent: how many analogies and/or distinctions are enough to constitute the presence or absence of an idea in Paul. All this shows that Pauline theology is not a static affair, "Rather, its patterns and dynamics may be newly illumined and realized within new contexts and by means of later conceptualities, which are to some degree 'foreign' to the texts themselves."[27]

Hill helpfully summarizes reasons for the neglect of later dogmatic interpretations in the historical reconstructions of Paul's theology in contemporary scholarship.[28] First, he points to Gabler's and Wrede's programs

---

24. Keck makes a comment about how NT texts reveal only a part of what specific persons and/or a community knew about Christ and made another part of their Christology unknown to the reader. Keck, "Toward Renewal," 371. Keck points to the necessity of systematic theology in the help of NT exegesis to define the identity of Jesus due to the diversity of Christologies pertinent to NT texts themselves.

25. Litwa, *We Are Being Transformed*, 31.

26. Bockmuehl suggests, "[T]he polyphonous diversity of voices in the Bible . . . nevertheless entail[s] a canonical 'impulse,'" which, obviously, is lacking in the extra-canonical material. Bockmuehl, *Seeing the Word*, 22.

27. Hill, *Paul and Trinity*, 46.

28. Hill, *Paul and Trinity*, chap. 1.

of the separation of biblical studies from dogmatic theology.[29] Second, he points to the growing interest in "low" or "high" Christology in light of early Jewish monotheism as a subject in its own right, which caused a shift from a broadly trinitarian theology to christocentrism. John Webster also notes an "expansion" of economic Christology and a corresponding "contraction" of immanent theology proper in the following statement:

> [I]t is not Christology per se but a doctrine of God's triune being and his inner and outer works (including the Godhead of the Son and his works in time) which occupies the pre-eminent and commanding place in Christian teaching . . . In much modern (and notably, but not exclusively, Protestant) systematic theology these matters [a stance on the function and scope of Christology] have acquired a special prominence, because discrete teaching about the person and work of Christ has often annexed the fundamental role which earlier theologies more naturally recognized in teaching about the Trinity, and so has come to serve as the hallmark of the genuineness, purity, and distinctiveness of Christian doctrine.[30]

Litwa's depiction of Jesus is similar to what Webster identified as "christological nominalism,"

> Christological nominalism presupposes an ontological separation of Jesus and God, with the result that the content of the term "God" is filled out by appeal to all manner of resources which are not Christologically shaped: "theos" and "Christos" are not mutually determinative. Once this bifurcation is allowed, then the doctrine of the incarnation is immediately unworkable, for that doctrine claims an ontological unity between God and the human career of the man Jesus, a unity not conceivable within the terms of the metaphysics of theism.[31]

Therefore, Webster suggests that systematic theology should preserve the right balance between Christology and theology proper, without fragmentation or diminution of either of them.[32]

---

29. Sandys-Wunsch and Eldredge, "J. P. Gabler and Distinction"; Wrede, "Task and Methods."

30. Webster, "Place of Christology," 612.

31. Webster, *Word and Church*, 130.

32. Thus, "systematic Christology connects teaching about Incarnation [and reconciliation] to the doctrine of the immanent Trinity." Webster, "Place of Christology," 616, 620.

In chapter 1, I highlighted a number of reasons why later theological concepts can become either an obstruction or a useful tool to unlock the inner logic of Paul's texts that is not evident from a merely historical inquiry. There is no need to repeat them here; suffice only to say that, studying Paul through a historical lens, the historian should not evacuate all subsequent knowledge and interpretation to make sense of Paul. According to Bockmuehl, New Testament scholarship needs to engage "effective history." He writes:

> [A] more historically embedded understanding of not just the background but also the foreground (so to speak) of the New Testament, including its reception and understanding in the patristic period and beyond. Instead of perpetually going behind the text, the whole battery of historical-critical and synchronic tools could usefully be applied to approaching the New Testament from its meaning and function "in front of the text," where it was in fact heard and heeded (or ignored).[33]

Contemporary theologians should utilize the best tools and theories of the day to reopen Pauline theology anew. What is the point of applying old erroneous interpretations to Paul expecting new results? Against a "naturalized" historicism of the post-Reformation period, which views the church's dogma as stagnation in ecclesial politics, Webster advises considering the church as "the Spirit-enlivened community," in which doctrine is a manifestation of the living gospel. He concludes, "To say that is—emphatically—*not* to remove dogma from history or immunize it from criticism; it is simply to identify that, *in* its historicity and contingency, dogma is a definitive showing of the gospel's truth and a presentation of the gospel's claim."[34]

With this in mind, two constructive studies will be consulted in analyzing Litwa's attempts to describe Paul's theology in categories of deification. In the first, Wesley Hill undertakes an exegetical reading of Paul with the aid of "trinitarian theologies[, which] will be employed as hermeneutical *resources* and, thus, mined for conceptualities which may better *enable* a genuinely historical exegesis to articulate what other equally 'historical' approaches may have (unwittingly or not) obscured."[35] In the second, Chris Tilling addresses the issue of Paul's monotheism and Christology by exegeting the whole of Pauline corpus. He then assesses some intertestamental

---

33. Bockmuehl, *Seeing the Word*, 65, chap. 6.
34. Webster, *Word and Church*, 142–43 (emphasis original).
35. Hill, *Paul and Trinity*, 45 (emphasis original).

passages that are often used to claim the flexibility of Jewish monotheism and are treated as the antecedents of subordinate Christology.[36]

The Use of Terminology

The third deficient premise relates to underdetermined taxonomy. Litwa's use of some key terminology seems problematic. First, his understanding of "divinity" and "God" is unhelpfully broad, so that it is difficult to draw a clear essential distinction between the High God, the whole range of divine beings, and the deified creatures. "The basis of deification," Litwa affirms, "is sharing in *a* or *the* divine identity—that is, sharing in those distinctive qualities which make (a) God (a) God."[37] This statement is problematic on two accounts.

1. The way many scholars define the term "identity" is misleading because it assumes, according to C. Kavin Rowe, a "static entity," which can be easily circumscribed, approximated as to a certain status. In this sense, the divine identity is a sign of nature, rather than personal entity. In reality, the biblical text presents God as a part of the narrative, in which he is an actor and relates to all other things in dynamic interaction and is unknown otherwise.[38] Hill similarly thinks that such static understanding of identity produces Christologies that are characterized by "vertical axis"—how high or low is Christ's divinity in respect to God. Instead, Paul's narrative defines God as the one who is identified by his relationship with Christ, the Holy Spirit, and his people.[39]

36. Tilling, *Paul's Divine Christology*.

37. Litwa, *We Are Being Transformed*, 32 (emphasis original). Litwa considers "likeness" a too vague term, because the degree of likeness is not specified by this term. Ironically, when he talks about believers becoming divine, he faces the same problem: to what degree or extent believer's divinity is different from Christ's and the Father's divinity.

38. Rowe, *Early Narrative Christology*, 17. Rowe notices this problem in relation to Lukan studies, "In previous investigations of Luke's use of κύριος, scholars have operated (if unwittingly) with a rather simple, if not simplistic, concept of identity in which the assumption that governs the thought about the identity of Jesus or God (or any other character) is what we may call static—as opposed to narrative and dynamic—in its structure. Identity in this sense is conceptualized as a static entity which can, in turn, be related to other static entities (with, for example, an = or ≈ or ≠ sign)." Rowe, following Ricoeur, opted for "narrative identity."

39. Hill, *Paul and Trinity*, 24–25, 44. Contemporary trinitarian theologies emphasize "the mutual involvement of the trinitarian persons in the identities of the other persons: *each person is only identifiable by means of reference to the others*" (emphasis original).

2. Litwa's statement also presumes that there are universally distinctive divine qualities. However, this is hardly the case given the enormous variety of deities in the ancient world, which not necessarily were considered gods in some cultures. It appears that the meaning of "the divine identity," for Litwa, is very broad and can encompass the High God and all stripes of created divine beings equally. If one takes, for example, a god of sky or sea, there is a slim possibility of drawing any analogies that would amount to deifying assimilation with such deities. Hence, this definition has to be qualified at least by mentioning that a God should exhibit qualities of a person. For Richard Bauckham, the "identity" of God corresponds to the question *who* God is in contrast to "nature" that corresponds to *what* God is.[40] Similarly, Hill contends that sharing in the title of God, i.e., κύριος, places Christ on the same level with Yahweh, not in terms of natural approximation, "Jesus is not placed on the same level with YHWH in terms of *association* but is depicted as a participant in the unique designation and activity by which God is distinguished from all other reality."[41] For Litwa, the distinction between God and gods consists not in essence, but only in the extent of possessed divinity and power. In other words, what distinguishes God the Father from other created gods is not the difference in nature or the gift of grace as church fathers assumed, but the degree of possessed divinity: Christ more, his followers less. Thus, Litwa states, "Paul's converts can participate in the divinity of the God Christ. He is the God whom Paul imitates (1 Cor 11:1). He is the God who lives in Paul (Gal 2:19-20). He is the God whom Paul follows in the pattern of death and resurrection." At this point, the binitarians or trinitarians should not yet applaud, because he adds "Pauline deification occurs through the mediate God, Christ."[42]

Second, Litwa is inconsistent in his use of essentialist language. On the one hand, he renounces essentialist language as an introduction of anachronistic patristic categories to Pauline framework of thought that knew no such distinctions as "nature," "person," and "energies." On the other hand, in the introduction, he criticizes both Russell and Blackwell for watering down the "realistic" deification by equating it with a "metaphorical" or "relational

---

40. Bauckham, *Jesus and God of Israel*, 6–7. Nonetheless, a strict separation between identity and nature is not advisable, because personhood is not reducible to and indivisible from nature, as we have seen in chapter 4.
41. Hill, *Paul and Trinity*, 106.
42. Litwa, *We Are Being Transformed*, 265.

participation."[43] Litwa contends that realistic deification should resemble a real ontological change of human nature into divine, "I want to remain open to the idea, in other words, that Christian deification was not simply metaphorical (or nominal or analogical), but that it involved a realistic transformation into deity such that humans truly transcended their (human) nature and became Gods or divine."[44]

Indeed, the essentialist language seems unavoidable, when he says, "Those conformed to the pneumatic Christ—who are made incorruptible, immortal, and pneumatic—share in Christ's *divinity*" and "Being physically 'one pneuma' with Christ—thus '*connatural*'—was how Paul envisioned the union of the Christian self with a divine self (Christ)."[45] Later Litwa discusses a form of a connaturality of humans and divine Christ in 1 Cor 6:17. Admittedly, he rejects the fusion of identities, but, nonetheless, makes a bold ontologically inappropriate conclusion, "A fuller identification comes at death or the parousia, when believers will receive bodies fully made up of the *substance* of this life-giving divinity."[46] Again, when Litwa distinguishes between an unknowable essence of the primal God and Christ's identity, he uses them interchangeably, "The pattern that emerges is this: if one cannot share in the essence of primal divinity, one can share the identity of Paul's Prime *Mediate* divinity."[47] As to immortality, that Litwa considers as a distinctly divine quality, one might object that spiritual principalities and powers (cf., Eph 3:10; 6:12; Col 1:16; 2:15), although immortal, are not necessarily divine or share in the divinity of God, but are, in fact, demonic. Litwa's misunderstanding of early Alexandrians's Christology together with the underdetermined usage of essentialist language become evident in his treatment of Paul's christological texts.

An Inadequate Account of Pauline Christology

The fourth deficient premise relates to questionably Pauline hierarchy of deities. Litwa depicts Paul's Christ as a divine being akin to a multitude of other ancient deities. According to Litwa, the idea of created gods was not foreign to Judaism, as well as to some early Christian circles, such as Origenists and Arians.[48] Although Christ shares in God's creative power, they are

43. Russell, *Doctrine of Deification*, 1; Blackwell, *Christosis*, 106.
44. Litwa, *We Are Being Transformed*, 9n20.
45. Litwa, *We Are Being Transformed*, 166, 169 (emphasis added).
46. Litwa, *We Are Being Transformed*, 169 (emphasis added).
47. Litwa, *We Are Being Transformed*, 265 (emphasis original).
48. Litwa, *We Are Being Transformed*, 267–70.

not equal, "Thus he [Christ] shares in the deity of the primal God to a much greater degree than humans. But the Father's deity was not threatened by Christ, who remained in subordination (1 Cor 15:28)."[49] In fact, for Litwa, Christ is not God by nature or origin, but by participation,[50] the idea that is reminiscent of the Christian adoptionism.

Litwa claims that a theory of summodeism can reconcile Jewish and Christian monotheism on the one hand, and the divinization of humans into lesser deities on the other hand.[51] Summodeism assumes the existence of the High God, as well as a stratified hierarchy of subordinate gods. By participating in the sovereign power of the High God, the subordinate gods do not compromise the supremacy of the High God. According to Litwa, Paul espoused a form of summodeism:

> Paul's picture of the divine world, I would argue, is another variant of the graded divinity paradigm. He acknowledges a transcendent deity "from whom" everything exists and a mediate deity "through whom" everything exists (1 Cor 8:6). He envisions, in other words, a Prime Mediate demiurgic deity—Christ—and a primal God called "the Father." Below Christ is a whole range of angels and archangels (e.g., 1 Cor 6:3; 1 Thess 4:16) . . . Immortalized and pneumatified (i.e., deified) Christians are destined to enter the divine world at some point above these daimonic powers (1 Cor 6:2–3; Rom 16:20).[52]

Not surprisingly, the summodeistic Christ, although God, is nonetheless lower than the Father. Worshipping to the subordinate deity, i.e., Christ, the Philippians increase the glory of the High God (Phil 2:10–11).[53] In a footnote, Litwa disclaims, "Christ is not just a 'heavenly being,' he is (a) God. I fully recognize that he is not an independent God, but God only in relation to the one (i.e., Almighty high) God, the Father. The same understanding, I am arguing, applies to deified Christians."[54] Since Litwa's Christ

---

49. Litwa, *We Are Being Transformed*, 273. Bauckham already in 1998 noticed that those approaches that look for the Jewish antecedents of intermediary gods as an argument for the divinity of Christ, neglect the broad and clear evidence of God's uniqueness and, in result, produce an Arian-like Christ. Bauckham, *Jesus and God of Israel*, 4–5.

50. Litwa, *We Are Being Transformed*, 274.

51. Litwa, *We Are Being Transformed*, 239–40. Litwa is following Voegelin, *Israel and Revelation*.

52. Litwa, *We Are Being Transformed*, 242.

53. Litwa, *We Are Being Transformed*, 243.

54. Litwa, *We Are Being Transformed*, 246n48. Hence, Litwa lists Christ in the same category with Michael (Dan 7:11–12), Philo's Logos (QG 2.62), and Melchizedek (11Q

is a lesser deity than the Father, the ontological leap of humans to the same image as Christ does not make them divine like the Father, so there is no essential infringement on the Father's divine uniqueness. Further, he states that since Christ is a divine being, transformation into the image of Christ is "a participation in Christ's divinity."[55] He recognizes that the deified are not "*naturally* divine," because deification involves a reflective character of cognitive and physical transformation.[56] This relationality should presume some limitations so that Christ never becomes equal to God and the deified equal to Christ. Litwa, however, never clearly states that deification can mean a potential blurring of the borders. Obviously, Litwa advocates for a version of "low" Christology.

In contrast, Bauckham contends that one need not wait until Nicaea to appreciate a fully developed "high" Christology, but on a different ground, because for him

> the New Testament writers are already, in a deliberate and sophisticated way, expressing a fully divine Christology by including Jesus in the unique identity of God as defined by Second Temple Judaism. Once we recognize the theological categories with which they are working, it is clear that there is nothing embryonic or tentative about this. In its own terms, it is an adequate expression of a fully divine Christology. It is, as I have called it, a Christology of divine identity.[57]

Obviously, Litwa and Bauckham understand "the divine identity" differently. Whereas for Litwa, to be identified with the High God does not make Christ equally divine with the Father, for Bauckham, it means sharing in the unique divine status equal with the Father, Creator, and Sovereign Ruler of all things. Contrary to Litwa, Bauckham contends that it is precisely "Greek philosophical—Platonic—definitions of divine substance or nature and Platonic understanding of the relationship of God to the world [that] made it extremely difficult to see Jesus as more than a semi-divine being, neither truly God nor truly human."[58] That is precisely what one encounters in Litwa's account of Christ.

Litwa's historical survey of the Jewish and Greco-Roman background of intermediate divine beings seems to be aimed at the rebuttal

---

Melch).
    55. Litwa, *We Are Being Transformed*, 220.
    56. Litwa, *We Are Being Transformed*, 222.
    57. Bauckham, *Jesus and God of Israel*, 58.
    58. Bauckham, *Jesus and God of Israel*, 58.

of Bauckham's and Hurtado's "high" Christology.⁵⁹ Their arguments for the divine Christology are vulnerable to historical reconstructions such as Litwa's that explore—however exceptional in comparison to the dominant pattern—instances of a breach in the "ontological and devotional divide" between human and divine.⁶⁰ Tilling and Hill employ the concept of "relationality" that is called to provide internal exegetical support to Bauckham's and Hurtado's conclusions, reinterpreting the historical evidence in light of a new pattern. Tilling's central thesis is that the relationships between believers and Christ in Paul's letters operate according to the pattern of Israel's relationships with God in the Hebrew Bible. Hill's concern is to show that the identities of divine persons in Godhead are mutually dependent and yet asymmetrical.

In response to the reading of Phil 2:11b in terms of subordinate Christology, Hill distinguishes the elements that indicate the unity of God and Jesus (such as ἐν μορφῇ θεοῦ, ἴσα θεῷ, sharing the title κύριος, alluding to Isa 45) and their distinction (Jesus's obedience to God, receiving exaltation and the name from God).⁶¹ This twofold interpretation of the passage allows Hill to uphold both the oneness of God with Jesus and at the same time their distinction. He calls these relations *asymmetrical mutuality*, because the identity of Jesus as κύριος depends on God's bestowal of this title, but also the identity of God is dependent on his relationship with Jesus, who shares the same title. In Paul, God is known as the Father of the Lord Jesus Christ, which means that the Father's identity is indivisibly connected and determined by his relation to Jesus. In other words, God cannot be known as the Father without a Son. This mutual constitution of identity is, nevertheless, asymmetrical, because there is a certain order of relations from God to Jesus. Such mode of relations, however, does not suggest any form of subordination between God and Jesus but shows that the incarnate Logos assumed a position of an obedient servant in the economy of salvation.⁶²

As an example of Litwa's questionable interpretation of Paul's Christology, we can now turn to Paul's interpretation of the Shema in light of his

59. Mainly, but not exclusively, represented in Bauckham, "Worship of Jesus"; Bauckham, *Jesus and God of Israel*; Hurtado, *One God, One Lord*; Hurtado, *At the Origins*; Hurtado, *Lord Jesus Christ*.

60. See Douglas Campbell's foreword to Tilling, *Paul's Divine Christology*, xviii.

61. Hill, *Paul and Trinity*, chap. 3.

62. Crisp, *Divinity and Humanity*, chap. 3. In this chapter, Crisp discusses the idea promulgated by Karl Barth, i.e., an *anhypostatic* (impersonal) human nature was *enhypostasized* (personalized) in union with the Logos. By taking a human nature, he assumed a constrained and subordinate position, freely and voluntarily, remaining fully divine. For a definition of *anhypostasis-enhypostasis* see also Davidson, "Theologizing Human Jesus," 135.

monotheistic reading of Deut 6:4–5. Litwa comments on Paul's appropriation of the Jewish confession in 1 Cor 8:4–6, "There is one primal God, Paul says, from whom we exist, and one mediate—and arguably subordinate (1 Cor 15:24–28)—God (Christ), through whom we exist (1 Cor 8:6)."[63] What is striking in this paraphrase is that it transmutes the divine mediator into a mediate being. Litwa introduced a subordinate deity, Jesus, into the divine identity of κύριος. Such rewording disrupts Paul's logic whereby the mediator shares the ontological nature of the divine and human parties and performs communication between them. Instead, Litwa's mediate being is neither of those but ontologically in-between. Litwa confuses a theandric mediator with an ontologically subordinate medium. It seems that Litwa is more concerned with the coherence of his grade schema, rather than remaining attentive to the wording of Paul's interpretation.

Bauckham interprets this passage as the inclusion of the Lord Jesus Christ into the unique identity of Yahweh. Jesus is neither a subordinate God, who in a blasphemous way appropriates the name of Israel's God nor an equal rival in ditheism.[64] Bauckham maintains that the traditional Jewish monotheism ascribed to God both the causal and instrumental aspects of creation while Paul ascribed the instrumental διά to Jesus. Hence, the God of Israel shares his identity as Creator with Jesus. Similarly, Moberly upholds that the apostle includes Jesus into both the taxonomy and reality of Israel's God because in encountering the Messiah, one encounters the Creator God. Moberly's conclusion expresses the point well:

> For present purposes the significant point is that the God who is "one" and who is to be loved without reserve and to the exclusion of idolatrous alternatives—the Jewish confession—becomes inseparable from Jesus Christ—the Christian confession. If the Christian confession of Jesus is not to succumb to a renewed suspicion of idolatry—that it confuses the creature with the Creator—a robustly trinitarian theology may need to be restored to accounts of Christian interpretation of Scripture.[65]

Hill observes the elements of oneness and distinction between God and Jesus in Paul's reference to Deut 6:4 (Ἄκουε, Ισραηλ· κύριος ὁ θεὸς ἡμῶν κύριος εἷς ἐστιν, LXX). The one divine agent in the OT (κύριος ὁ θεὸς) becomes two distinct agents in Paul's interpretation (θεὸς ὁ πατὴρ and κύριος

---

63. Litwa, *We Are Being Transformed*, 248.

64. Bauckham, *Jesus and God of Israel*, 27–30. McGrath interprets 1 Cor 8:6 as an addition of the Jesus-element to the traditional oneness of God. Thus, the one God in heaven has one earthly viceroy, the Lord Jesus Christ. McGrath, *Only True God*, 40–41.

65. Moberly, "Toward an Interpretation," 142.

Ἰησοῦς Χριστός, 1 Cor 8:6). Paul is not adding a new agent to the Shema; he is reinterpreting the one agent of the Shema, "the Lord our God," being two divine persons and co-bearers of the name κύριος, "God the Father" and the "Lord Jesus Christ."[66] When compared with Rom 11:36, wherein God is the sole source, instrument, and goal of all being, 1 Cor 8:6 splits these functions between God and Jesus, who share one identity of κύριος.

Further, the contrast between "one God" and "many gods and many lords" (1 Cor 8:4–6) is not between the High God and lower deities, but between God and idols/demons as is evident in 1 Cor 10:14–22. Paul allows for the existence of the so-called gods only because he acknowledges the existence of demons. God's uniqueness to Jesus-followers consists in relational terms: in v. 5 the apostle recognizes the existence of spiritual beings, in v. 6 he begins with ἀλλ' ἡμῖν εἷς θεός, showing that the oneness of God has a relational character in respect to believers.[67] Thus, MacDonald rightly states, "There are indeed many gods that exist, but *for us* (ἡμῖν) there is only one God. The absolute terms are confessional, not ontological."[68] Unlike MacDonald, I would not stress a sharp distinction between confession and ontology, because confession is based on and reveals the ontology behind a confession, as MacDonald himself recognizes.[69] Paul's confession, in my view, reveals his ontology vis-à-vis his non-Jewish contemporaries, i.e., any spiritual beings that exercise superhuman power are considered gods by human standards, but they are no-gods by his Judeo-messianic standards. These "gods" do not live up to the God, whom he identifies as the Father and the Lord Jesus Christ, from whom, for whom, and through whom everything exists. The power to create for Paul distinguishes clearly "our" God from those so-called gods. The apostle's cosmology allows only one creator

66. Hill, *Paul and Trinity*, 114. Wright calls Paul's redefinition of the Shema "a sort of christological monotheism." Wright concludes, "Here, as there [Phil 2 and Col 1], we find a statement of the highest possible christology—that is, of Jesus placed within the very monotheistic confession itself—set within an argument which is itself precisely and profoundly monotheistic." Wright, *Climax of Covenant*, 129, 132.

67. In this context, "relational uniqueness" should not be confused with the statements of those who urge compatibility of Christian beliefs with other religions, as Webster points. The lordship of God for Israel and Christ for his followers is indeed exclusive. Webster, *Word and Church*, 134.

68. MacDonald, *Deuteronomy*, 96 (emphasis original). Litwa also recognizes this "openly subjective side" of the Jewish confession. Litwa, *We Are Being Transformed*, 251–52.

69. "Thus, YHWH is seen to be unique through the relationship he has with Israel and, by implication, does not have with other nations. Thus, in both cases something is said about the nature of YHWH, an ontological statement, so to speak, but a statement that cannot be divorced from the personal claim on Israel." MacDonald, *Deuteronomy*, 207.

God, who manifests his power in creating everything, including spiritual beings (cf., Col 1:15-17). This single source of being is what distinguishes Paul's monotheism from surrounding hierarchies of divinities. According to Paul's ontology, nothing can threaten the supremacy of the Creator in the cosmic realm, but other gods can threaten his supremacy in human minds, diverting human allegiance elsewhere.

The Shema reflects the personal nature of Israel's relationship with Yahweh, whereby "our" God's uniqueness vis-à-vis other gods ought to be manifested in all-consuming love toward God (Deut 6:5). 1 Corinthians 8:4-6 is a continuation of Paul's statement in 8:3,[70] wherein Israel's covenantal relations with Yahweh in love and knowledge are mutually defining and are the ground for the monotheistic confession of the Shema. Thus, the two parts of Deut 6:4-5 (the confession of one God and the love of God) are present in Paul's interpretation, albeit in reverse order. Tilling correctly advances Hurtado's emphasis on cultic worship as a criterion for Jewish monotheism by stressing that Israel's love of God and devotion encompass the whole of life, not only a cultic aspect of it.[71] Tilling applies a "relational" approach to answering the criticisms of those involved in the "Jewish monotheism" and "divine-Christology" debates.[72] The same approach, he contends, serves to show that, in Paul, Jesus's relationships with believers mirror Yahweh's relationships with Israel/Israelite. In Tilling's words:

> [T]his pattern of Christ-relation language in Paul is only that which a Jew used to express the relation between Israel/the individual Jew and YHWH. No other figure of any kind, apart from YHWH, was related to in the same way, with the same pattern of language, not even the various exalted human and angelic intermediary figures in the literature of Second Temple Judaism that occasionally receive worship and are described in very exalted terms.[73]

70. On the textual variant and arguments for the longer reading of 8:3 see Tilling, *Paul's Divine Christology*, 77-81.

71. Tilling, *Paul's Divine Christology*, 71.

72. Scholars like Litwa, Fletcher-Louis, and McGrath insist that in light of a polytheistic Ancient Near Eastern background and intertestamental Jewish and Greco-Roman literature, where intermediate divine figures received worship, Paul's Jesus should be understood as one of these mediate deities. Fletcher-Louis, *All Glory of Adam*; McGrath, *Only True God*.

73. Tilling, *Paul's Divine Christology*, 73 (italics in original). Besides 8:4-6, Tilling adduces other texts in 1 Corinthians, where the same "pattern" occurs. 8:12 indicates that sin against brothers is sin against Christ, just as violation of God's commandments was a sin against God. In 10:4, 9 Paul compares the misbehavior of Israel's ancestors against God with the Corinthians's sinning against Christ. Tilling, *Paul's Divine*

Tilling succeeds in demonstrating that in Paul, as well as in a number of Second Temple texts (i.e., the Similitudes of Enoch, the *Life of Adam and Eve* and Sirach 44-50),[74] one can find the same pattern. The life of worship that constitutes "love-oriented" monotheistic relationships between the elect people and God also constitutes the attitude of believers to Christ.

At the same time, the identity of God and Jesus are distinct, so that God is named the "Father" of Jesus while Jesus is called the "Lord" and the mediator (δι' οὗ) in God's protology (ἐξ οὗ), soteriology and teleology (εἰς αὐτόν, 8:6).[75] By assigning to Jesus the mediating role at creation, Paul indicates his belief in the pre-existence of the one who is now known as Jesus the Messiah.[76] Taking into account the way Paul reinterprets the Shema in light of Christ's divine identity, Wright is correct when he writes, "God and the people of God are both redefined through Jesus the Messiah."[77]

Hill regrets that this element of the distinct identities of God and Jesus is lost in Bauckham's attempt to include Jesus in one divine identity of Jewish monotheism. It would lead to a modalistic undifferentiated divine identity. Therefore, the faithful interpretation of 1 Cor 8:4-5 would preserve both the equality and distinction of the divine identities of God and Jesus. Hill appropriately states that the mediatorial role of Jesus is individuated within

---

Christology, 93-96.

74. In contrast to Fletcher-Louis, Tilling extensively argues that it is the God-data and not honored figures-data in these apocryphal texts that corresponds to Christ-data in Paul. "The *God*-relation language in these texts is almost exactly the same complex of interrelated themes that one finds in Paul's Christ-relation language. Paul's Christ-devotion language is indeed Jewish in its shape and origin, but it is so as a reworking of Jewish God-relation themes." Tilling, *Paul's Divine Christology*, 206 (emphasis original). In respect to the Similitudes of Enoch, he concludes, "the Pauline Christ-relation far more closely corresponds with the Lord-of-Spirits-relation than the Son-of-Man-relation." Tilling, *Paul's Divine Christology*, 217. If it is correct, then even "the Son of Man" in 1 Enoch, which Bauckham distinguished as an exception to the rule (Bauckham, *Jesus and God of Israel*, 16), does not negate the divine-christology "pattern" in Paul, because this title corresponds more to believers in Christ, rather than to Christ.

75. Hill, *Paul and Trinity*, 116. Kammler summarized the importance of the prepositions for distinction in the God-talk, "Die unterschiedlichen präpositionalen Wendungen–ἐξ οὗ und εἰς αὐτόν beim Vater, δι' οὗ und δι' αὐτοῦ beim Sohn–heben dementsprechend nicht auf eine *ontologische* Differenz zwischen Vater und Sohn ab, sondern sie markieren–im Sinne einer *inner-göttlichen* Unterscheidung–die *Unumkehrbarkeit* der Beziehung von Vater und Sohn." Kammler, "Die Prädikation Jesu Christi," 174-75 (emphasis original). This mediatory role of Jesus leads Dunn to stress that early believers continued to worship one God but after the Christ-event *in* and *through* Jesus. Dunn, *Did the First Christians Worship Jesus?*, 146.

76. Wright, *Climax of Covenant*, 131. Contrary to Dunn's rejection of Jesus's pre-existence in 1 Cor 8:4. Dunn, *Christology in Making*, 182.

77. Wright, *Climax of Covenant*, 133.

the one God, "Rather, in a non-competitive and mutually complementary way, affirming God the Father and Jesus together *as* the 'one God' of Deut 6:4 and affirming their irreducible distinction from one another as unique agents or 'persons' is to do justice to both of those elements as present in 1 Cor 8:6."[78] Hill correctly utilizes the traditional trinitarian resources of redoublement, whereby the irreducible distinction of personal identities in Godhead is linked with the account of God's essential oneness.[79]

When Paul applies his redefined Christ-inclusive monotheistic theology to ethics in 1 Cor 10, the distinctive feature of Jewish monotheism becomes apparent. According to the apostle, the non-Jewish idol-worshipping is, in reality, demon-worshipping (κοινωνοὺς τῶν δαιμονίων), not God-worshipping (1 Cor 10:19–20). Idols are not icons of lower deities, but rather they are human-made religious objects that mask created spiritual beings, powerful enemies of God. While it is appropriate to partake in God's good creation with thanksgiving (10:26, 30), it is inappropriate to share in the cup (ποτήριον) and table of demons (τραπέζης δαιμονίων, 10:21). If Paul perceived Jesus to be one of a multitude of mediate divinities, as Litwa argues, his objection to sharing in the Lord's or Jesus's (cf., 1 Cor 8:6) table and the demonic one would be pointless. Correspondently, worshipping lower deities or idols does not increase God's glory as Litwa concludes in Phil 2:11.[80] On the contrary, the prohibition of participation in demonic idolatrous rituals makes a robust disparaging claim on their divine status.

Consequently, participation in Jesus's Eucharistic communion (10:16–17) is distinguished as a unique act of sharing the communion with the divine being. The identification of Jesus with God is evident in 10:20–21. There is a definite parallel between sacrificing and sharing in demons and sacrificing to God and sharing in the Lord's Table:

demons	God/Lord
v. 20 ἀλλ' ὅτι ἃ θύουσιν, δαιμονίοις καὶ οὐ θέλω δὲ ὑμᾶς κοινωνοὺς τῶν δαιμονίων γίνεσθαι	οὐ θεῷ
v. 21 ποτήριον δαιμονίων,	οὐ δύνασθε ποτήριον κυρίου πίνειν καὶ

78. Hill, *Paul and Trinity*, 120.

79. Hill, *Paul and Trinity*, 119.

80. "But the Father's deity was not threatened by Christ, who remained in subordination (1 Cor 15:28). The creator God Christ shows that sharing divine identity does not create a situation of conflict, but adds 'glory to God the Father' (Phil 2:11)." Litwa, *We Are Being Transformed*, 273.

demons	God/Lord
τραπέζης δαιμονίων.	οὐ δύνασθε τραπέζης κυρίου μετέχειν καὶ

The sacrifices that non-Jews offer to demons make them sharers in demons (κοινωνοὺς τῶν δαιμονίων, 10:20). To complete Paul's parallel, by "sacrificing" to God, believers become sharers in God, just as Israelites were the sharers of the altar (10:18). Perhaps, Paul does not complete this parallel because Jesus-followers do not offer animal sacrifices any longer and/or intentionally avoids an explicit language of participation in God, preferring a more moderate language of participation in the altar.[81] 10:21 contains a complete parallel, wherein the cup of demons is juxtaposed with the cup of the Lord, as well as the table of demons is juxtaposed with the table of the Lord. Particularly interesting in this context is the LXX translation of 2 Kgs 17:11–12 with its thematic connections to 1 Cor 10:20–21. Israelites, following surrounding nations, "made incense offerings" (ἐθυμίασαν) to other gods/idols, were "made partners" with nations/gods (ἐποίησαν κοινωνοὺς), and "provoked the Lord" (παροργίσαι τὸν κύριον). If Paul is alluding to this text, then the κύριος of 1 Cor 10:21 is the κύριος of 2 Kgs 17:11.

This line of thought is supported by a rhetorical question in 10:22, "Or do we provoke the Lord to jealousy?" (ἢ παραζηλοῦμεν τὸν κύριον;). That the κύριος of v. 22 is Jesus, is evident from a preceding verse, where the κύριος is linked with the eucharistic cup and table, which in their turn are connected to the cup and bread and, correspondingly, the blood and body of Christ (v. 16). Some OT passages include warnings against and statements about "provoking" the Lord in the context of idolatry (e.g., Deut 4:25; 9:18; 32:21; 1 Kgs 14:19; 16:13; Isa 65:3; Jer 11:17).[82] Again, in 10:22, Paul identifies the jealous Lord God of Israel, who was provoked and tested by Israelites through their idolatry (see Deut 6:4–16), with the Lord Jesus, who could be provoked by converts through their indiscriminate participation in idolatrous sacrifices.[83] Thus, Paul placed Jesus on the side of God in the

---

81. Nonetheless, there are good reasons to think that Paul envisioned a vertical covenantal dimension of κοινωνία as well as horizontal. Tilling, *Paul's Divine Christology*, 97–100.

82. The LXX translates the same Hebrew word כָּעַס differently παροργίζω (Deut 4:25; 2 Chr 34:25; Jer 11:17), παροξύνω (Deut 9:18; Isa 65:3), παραπικραίνω (Jer 39:29; 44:3 and cognate πικραίνω, Jer 32:32). Although Paul is using παραζηλόω instead of these Greek equivalents, Rom 10:19 seems to use παραζηλόω and παροργίζω as parallels if not interchangeably.

83. Tilling, *Paul's Divine Christology*, 101–3.

God-idols divide. Contrary to Litwa, the verse could be understood not as God's jealousy in relation to a threat represented by other gods, but God's jealousy for the undivided hearts of his worshippers.[84] The relational aspect of the monotheistic worship of God is also seen in 1 Thess 1:9, where the result of "turning" from idols is not the rejection of their existence or simply the right doctrine, but "serving the living and true God" (δουλεύειν θεῷ ζῶντι καὶ ἀληθινῷ).

1 Corinthians 15:24–28 is often cited to bolster a subordinate Christology in Paul. The close intertextual reading of this passage, however, leads Hill to undermine this conclusion. Paul's allusion to Pss 8:6[7] and 110:1b modifies the agent of submission in 1 Cor 15:24–25. Whereas in Psalms, the one who submits πάντα (including enemies) to a human or messianic figure is κύριος, Yahweh, in 1 Cor 15:24–25 it is Christ himself, who "hands over" (παραδιδόναι) the kingdom to God the Father, "destroys" (καταργεῖν) all dominion, authority, and power, and "puts" (τίθημι) all his enemies under his feet.[85] Hence, Christ assumes the role ascribed to God in the alluded Psalms. Also, the qualifiers of God as ὁ πατήρ and Christ as ὁ υἱός in a chiastic structure of vv. 24, 28 asymmetrically identify them together. The eschatological identity of God, who will be "all in all" (πάντα ἐν πᾶσιν, v. 28), is, nonetheless, determined by the fact that he is the Father of the Son who "will subject himself" (ὑποταγήσεται) to the Father (v. 24).[86] Consequently, the κύριος of Psalm 110:1, for Paul, is equally constituted by both the Father and Son, which at the same time exist in asymmetrical mutuality and differentiation, whereby the Father submits everything to the Son and the Son submits himself to the Father (vv. 27–28). Hill contends that the mutuality (sharing the identity of κύριος) and distinction (the eschatological subjection of the Son to the Father) should not be juxtaposed, "these two aspects of the text—his inclusion in the unique divine identity (vv. 24–25) and his irreducible difference from the one called 'Father'—are non-overlapping, non-competitive, complementary aspects. They neither infringe on one another nor detract from one another."[87]

84. Litwa, *We Are Being Transformed*, 248n51.

85. Hill, *Paul and Trinity*, 126; Kreitzer, *Jesus and God*, 150; Fee, *Pauline Christology*, 111.

86. Hill, *Paul and Trinity*, 129.

87. Hill, *Paul and Trinity*, 132. Moltmann infers that all Christ's soteriological functions and titles, except sonship, are provisional from an eschatological perspective. The transfer of the Son's lordship to the Father means "the consummation of his sonship." He writes, "According to Paul, the whole Christian eschatology ends in this inner-trinitarian process, through which the kingdom passes from the Son to the Father. Eschatology accordingly is not simply what takes place in the Last Days in heaven and on earth; it is what takes place in God's essential nature." Moltmann, *Trinity and Kingdom*, 92.

On the question whether Christ as the "last Adam" was the *human* representative, Litwa responds, "Christ as the 'last Adam' far outstrips the nature of a human being and is in fact assumed to be divine in Paul's churches. The resurrected Christ, in 1 Cor 15, has characteristics which would have been recognized in Paul's context as clearly divine characteristics."[88] This response indicates Litwa's assumption that Christ after resurrection assumed a pneumatic body, which is essentially different from the human body. Christ's metamorphosis reveals him no longer human, but divine, "Christ makes the transition, in other words, from an Adamic (psychic) human to a divine being by becoming a 'life-creating pneuma' (1 Cor 15:45)."[89]

The close attention to the text, however, indicates that Paul does not discuss the transition to a new level of being from human to divine. In 1 Cor 15:45, Paul quotes Gen 2:7, "So it is written: 'The first man Adam became a living being'; the last Adam, a life-giving spirit" (οὕτως καὶ γέγραπται · ἐγένετο ὁ πρῶτος ἄνθρωπος Ἀδὰμ εἰς ψυχὴν ζῶσαν, ὁ ἔσχατος Ἀδὰμ εἰς πνεῦμα ζῳοποιοῦν). If Paul had a change of nature in mind, what was the natural change that Adam experienced by becoming a "living soul"? It is more appropriate to view this text as a statement about the passive reception of life by the first human being in comparison to the active life-giving function of Christ. In light of this interpretation, Christ's divine prerogative to dispense life does not reduce or necessitate the shedding of the assumed human nature. The reason Litwa infers Christ's transition into a state of divine being is Paul's statement about a superhuman "celestial" quality acquired by Jesus after his resurrection (ἐπουράνιος, 1 Cor 15:48). In the preceding verse, however, the apostle compares Adam's and Christ's origination and calls them "human" (ἄνθρωπος, v. 47). An interpretation of 1 Cor 15 that disproves the continuity of human nature in Christ after resurrection cannot account for the language of identification of Christ with a human being in v. 47.

Similarly questionable is Litwa's treatment of 1 Cor 6:17, where he perceives Paul's indication of connaturality between Jesus and the deified. The parallel statement in v. 16, however, demonstrates that the union of a male convert with a prostitute cannot be connatural because they already share the same nature and no change to the nature of a participant happen (cf., 1 Cor 12:13). Perhaps, the meaning of ἓν πνεῦμά ἐστιν in 1 Cor 6:17 is an equivalent of ἕν εἰσιν in 1 Cor 3:8, where the one who plants and the one who waters are one in the sense of a common goal. Similarly, ἓν πνεῦμα in Eph 4:4 is best understood in the context of the preceding verse that calls

---

88. Litwa, *We Are Being Transformed*, 164.
89. Litwa, *We Are Being Transformed*, 164.

upon the Ephesians to maintain "the unity of the Spirit" (τὴν ἑνότητα τοῦ πνεύματος, 4:3) and has no connaturality in view. To be one spirit with the Lord then is not to share his pneumatic body, but to be in close personal union and communion. Such an intimate union of persons, in the language of Paul, can be characterized as "it is no longer I who live, but Christ lives in me; and the life which I now live in the flesh I live by faith in the Son of God, who loved me, and gave himself for me" (Gal 2:20). Obviously, there is no fusion of personal identities even in this psychological exchange, because it requires a self-conscious being to make such a statement. Personal spiritual union with Christ did not negate the fact that Paul still lives in the human flesh (ἐν σαρκί) and did not receive spiritual body (as the present tense of the verb εἶναι in 1 Cor 6:17 requires).

Ben C. Blackwell

In an attempt to provide a historical grounding of Paul's version of *theosis* lacking in Stephen Finlan[90] and Gorman, Ben C. Blackwell demonstrates how early interpreters of Paul, such as Irenaeus of Lyons and Cyril of Alexandria, understood Paul's teaching regarding deification. Participation in divine attributes such as life, immortality, and glory is the result of humans partaking directly in God himself or Christ through the Spirit. Creatures, however, remain distinct from the Creator. Blackwell identifies three main soteriological concepts in Irenaeus, "Adoption, vision, and union are three main ways Irenaeus speaks about the divine-human relationship, and we see that they are deeply interconnected."[91] Likewise, Cyril presented deification as an essentially trinitarian outworking of salvation through participation in the divine nature and attributes through the Spirit.[92] Here is how Blackwell summarizes the views on deification by the two fathers:

> Deification, for Irenaeus and Cyril, is the process of restoring likeness to God, primarily experienced as incorruption and sanctification, through a participatory relationship with God mediated by Christ and the Spirit. Through the Son and the Spirit believers become adopted sons of God, even gods, by grace and not by nature, because they participate in divine attributes.[93]

---

90. Finlan, "Can We Speak?"
91. Blackwell, *Christosis*, 52.
92. Blackwell, *Christosis*, 79–80.
93. Blackwell, *Christosis*, 244.

Blackwell, however, prefers the term *christosis* to more traditional *theosis* due to Paul's greater emphasis on conformation to the image of Christ in his life and resurrection. Besides, the term *theosis* in the period after Gregory Palamas acquired a distinct philosophical connotation that was foreign to the ancient world of Paul. Blackwell, however, recognizes the shortcomings of the notion *christosis*, "While the shape of Pauline soteriology is specifically christo-form, the clear emphasis on the roles of God (the Father) and the Holy Spirit stands as a possible limitation on using the term christosis."[94]

This book is in basic agreement with Blackwell's appeal to the patristic resources for expounding Paul's soteriology. Chapter 1 demonstrated the need for a theological reassessment of the apostle's ideas with the aid of the hermeneutical lens provided by church fathers such as Irenaeus, the Cappadocians, and Cyril. While endorsing Blackwell's patristic rereading of Paul, my main contention relates to his narrowing down Paul's soteriology to Christology that Blackwell encapsulates in the term *christosis*. To paraphrase Karl Rahner's famous statement, despite their orthodox confession of the Trinity, many Christians, including scholars, are in their theologizing almost mere "monotheists" or at best "binitarians."[95] Further, Rahner laments, "We must be willing to admit that, should the doctrine of the Trinity have to be dropped as false, the major part of religious literature could well remain virtually unchanged."[96] The doctrine of the incarnation in contemporary research often leads scholars not to the corollary that the second person of the Trinity, the Son, has become a man, but merely that (a) God has become a man.

Blackwell's Christocentric reading of Paul's texts allows him to acknowledge theological and pneumatological dimensions, albeit in a diminished fashion, "While God and the Spirit play a role in this process of salvation, Christ stands at the center because believers are conformed to his death and resurrection."[97] Again later, "The Spirit is central to Paul's portrayal of the believer's experience of the divine, but this experience is christo-telic in nature, such that believers embody the Christ-narrative in

---

94. Blackwell, *Christosis*, 247. This statement, in part, incited me to think about the issue in terms of *triadosis* to avoid the limitations of *christosis*.

95. Rahner, *Trinity*, 10. Alternatively, as Torrance prefers to name them, "unitarians." Torrance, "Doctrine of Trinity," 3.

96. Rahner, *Trinity*, 10–11. Rahner thinks that the doctrine of the Trinity is intrinsically connected to soteriology, because "no adequate distinction can be made between the doctrine of the Trinity and the doctrine of the economy of salvation." Rahner, *Trinity*, 24.

97. Blackwell, *Christosis*, 209.

death and life."[98] A deficiency of a strictly christological soteriology consists in diminishing the presentation of the New Testament God, Father, Son, and Holy Spirit. In Bruce D. Marshall's words, "As the logic of the New Testament's talk of God is incarnational, it is also pneumatological, and so trinitarian. Israel's God gives himself to the world not only in the sending of his Son (or Word) but in the sending of his Spirit, not only on Golgotha, but at Pentecost."[99] There are several problems with an exclusively christological form of *theosis*, i.e., *christosis*.

Christosis and the Father

Blackwell's christocentrism diminishes the role of the Father and downplays the mutuality of divine identities. As was shown above, most of the church fathers, and especially the Cappadocians, were keen to formulate their theologies with a distinctive trinitarian emphasis. Even Irenaeus and Cyril, whom Blackwell engages in his thesis, affirmed salvation as an act of the Father through the Son in the Holy Spirit. The importance of the Son's dispensation notwithstanding, a soteriology that does not originate in the Father and come to realization by the Spirit is incomplete, patristically speaking. A soteriology that is overshadowed by Christology will have difficulty explaining texts such as Gal 1:4; 4:4 where Christ's sacrificial death is a realization of the will of the Father, who presented the Son as a propitiation (Rom 3:25).

Close attention to Pauline depictions of the divine persons reveals not only their economic functions concerning the world and people but also their interrelations and mutual identification. Accordingly, Wesley Hill provides a helpful exegetical discussion of texts such as Gal 1:1; Rom 4:24; 8:11, 28–32, whereby the identity of God is closely connected with the resurrection of Jesus. There he points that these texts contain liturgical formulas that arguably predate Paul's epistles and serve as "identity descriptions," which associate God with resurrecting Jesus even before the Christ-event occurred.[100] Hill suggests that grasping the identity of the God of Abraham must involve reference to Jesus. For Paul, the God of Abraham, from the beginning, was the one who would raise Jesus from the dead. In respect

---

98. Blackwell, *Christosis*, 245, 265–67.

99. Marshall, "Christ and Cultures," 95.

100. Hill, *Paul and Trinity*, 53. Hill challenges Dunn's and Hurtado's model, whereby Paul in these texts articulates the traditional Jewish monotheism and only later shifts to its christological reworking. Instead, Hill suggests that already in these texts Paul identifies the God of Abraham as the one who will raise Jesus from the dead.

to Rom 4:24, Hill concludes, "The identity of the God of Abraham—who God was in the past, for Abraham—is bound up with the identity of God as the God of Jesus—who God is as the one who raised Jesus. God *was* for Abraham the God who would raise Jesus."[101] The act of Jesus's resurrection defines not only Christology but also theology proper even before the Christ-event. Hill convincingly argues that the identification of God with raising Jesus from the dead is not a Pauline modification or an extension of Jewish "monotheism," but rather intrinsic to God's self-definition (Rom 8:11).[102] Similarly, in Rom 8:29–30, the apostle expresses the view that God's foreknowledge and predestination of believers are Christ-oriented, even before the Son was sent.

> God is, from the time before the sending of the Son, the God whose identity is bound up with the Son. God's christological aim in God's foreknowledge enables Paul to discern a Christ-oriented identity of God prior to the Christ-event. God does not become what God was not, for Paul does not know a time when God was not already the God who would send his Son so that believers might be conformed to his image.[103]

Therefore, from eternity-past God's identity is defined as the one who has the Son, whom he will send to restore the fallen creation.[104] In this way, the identities of the persons of Godhead are interdependent and mutually determining.

Undoubtedly, the grammar of Paul's Christology requires postulating an asymmetry between the Father, who sends, raises, and exalts Jesus, and the Son, who is sent, obeys, and returns glory to the Father (Gal 4:4; Rom 4:24; Phil 2:6–11; 1 Cor 15:20–28).[105] This asymmetrical relationship, however, does not by necessity imply "subordination" or impinge on their unity. It is necessary to express the mutual co-determination of the divine persons and at the same time to preserve the economic diversity of Father, Son, and Spirit. In light of the Christ-event, the God of Israel is no longer known as simply one God, but as the Father of the Lord Jesus Christ. Hill argues that the application of the name κύριος to Jesus in Phil 2:10–11 indicates his oneness and equality with God Yahweh of Isa 45:23–25, as was shown in the previous section.[106] The ending of verse 11 ("to the glory of

101. Hill, *Paul and Trinity*, 61 (emphasis original).
102. Hill, *Paul and Trinity*, 74.
103. Hill, *Paul and Trinity*, 64.
104. Hill, *Paul and Trinity*.
105. Hill, *Paul and Trinity*, chap. 3.
106. Hill, *Paul and Trinity*, 96.

God the Father"), which is often used as an indication of the exalted Christ's subordination to God,[107] could be interpreted as a link to the familial relationship of the Son with the Father and their differentiation. Therefore, the identity of the God who is glorified is connected with and determined by Jesus's exaltation by the Father. Accordingly, God is glorified and identified as the "Father" as long as the "Son" is exalted as κύριος Ἰησοῦς Χριστὸς above all names. Marshall succinctly supports this corollary, "Not just the Son and the Spirit, but also the Father, can be identified by us only through this sequence of actions and events."[108] Hence, this asymmetry is, nonetheless, mutually definitive for Jesus and God. Equally, Rahner argues that a self-communication of one of the divine persons cannot occur in isolation from the other two:

> Should a divine person communicate himself otherwise than in and through his relations to the other persons, so as to have his own relation to the justified (and the other way around), this would presuppose that each single divine person, even as such, as mentally distinct from the one and same essence, would be something absolute and not merely relative. We would no longer be speaking of the Trinity. In other words: these three self-communications are the self-communication of the one God in the three relative ways in which God subsists.[109]

From a dogmatic viewpoint, as was noted by Zizioulas in chapter 4, Christian monotheism is grounded on the "relational oneness" of God, so that the term "Father" is a relational category.[110] Consequently, a christological soteriology, which lacks an appropriate emphasis on theology proper, is not entirely christological either, because the Christ-talk unconditioned by the God-talk is incomplete. The theology of the Father must not slip into the background because of the theology of the Son.

---

107. For instance, Hurtado concludes, "That is, while asserting an astonishing "binitarian" view, in which Jesus is linked with God and with divine purposes in an unprecedented way, the passage also reflects a concern to emphasize that Jesus's career and his subsequent exaltation as well do not really represent a threat to the one God of biblical tradition. Jesus's exaltation, in fact, has its basis and its ultimate meaning in the glory of the one God." Hurtado, "'Case Study,'" 106.

108. Marshall, "Christ and Cultures," 96.

109. Rahner, *Trinity*, 35.

110. Zizioulas, "Doctrine of God," 22.

Christosis and the Spirit

Christosis overshadows a no less significant role and identity of the Spirit so that Christology may become a "christo-monism."[111] In fact, the identification of believers with Christ in his death, resurrection, glorification, and transformation into the likeness of Christ, including immortalization is unthinkable without the mediatory activity of the Spirit. Litwa's pneumatification will not do either because for him it is not a personal transforming encounter with the Holy Spirit. Rather, it is a metamorphosis of human nature into the pneumatic nature of Christ. In this sense, Litwa's version of Paul's *theosis* is essentially *christosis*, because Paul's converts undergo assimilation not to God generally, but particularly to a God, Christ.[112] Thus, the work of the Spirit in a strictly Christocentric soteriology is superficial and even superfluous.[113] For Paul, however, the role of the Spirit is not a continuation of Christ's incarnation, but a fully-fledged mission with its—using the later theological language—kenotic indwelling of human hypostases.[114] The Spirit's soteriological activity is not an *instrumental* outworking of Christ's redemption. Instead, the Spirit is *personally* present within believers and makes personal the Father's and the Son's indwelling. Hence, the pneumatological dimension of the one soteriological mission of God should not be divorced from its christological dimension.

In some sense, the church is the Spirit's incarnation.[115] As Gunton notes, theologians often overemphasize Christ's role in establishing the church,

---

111. The term is from Jansen, "I Cor. 15. 24-28," 569. A prominent Christology at the expense of adequate pneumatology is a much-discussed trait in Karl Barth, which left its imprint on many subsequent theologians. For a succinct discussion see Rogers, *After the Spirit*, 19–23. Rogers summarizes the pneumatological deficiency of many trinitarian accounts in the last two centuries by the following statement, "Anything the Spirit can do, the Son can do better." Rogers, *After the Spirit*, 33.

112. Litwa, *We Are Being Transformed*, 217. Litwa espouses a version of *christosis*, when he argues, "Paul, when speaking of the pneumatic body, does not propound conformity to 'divinity' in general but to a specific divine being, namely Christ." But then regrettably adds that participants "share Christ's nature (pneuma)." Litwa, *We Are Being Transformed*, 169.

113. Even the stress on the fatherhood/sonship in God will not suffice, "When the Father/Son imagery is imposed upon the trinitarian structure, rather than seen as an alternative picture, the superfluousness of the Spirit is only one of the problems that arises." Williams, "Fatherhood of God," 100.

114. Del Colle, *Christ and Spirit*, 25.

115. Rabens comes to a similar observation in Rom 8:26, "The Spirit of God identifies and shows solidarity with creation in an almost incarnational way, because the Spirit articulates on behalf of the world the experience of incompleteness and fragility in a depth that the world itself cannot express ('sighs too deep for words')." Rabens, "Power from In Between," 154.

underlining the body-head metaphor (1 Cor 12; Eph 5:23; Col 1:18).[116] Such Christocentric ecclesiology reduced the Spirit's role to a mere instrumentality and charismatic fuel. However, the Holy Spirit accomplishes not only the maintaining work in the church but also the constitutional one alongside Christ. In Zizioulas's words, the church is essentially pneumatological.

> The Spirit is not something that "animates" a Church which already somehow exists. The Spirit makes the Church *be*. Pneumatology does not refer to the well-being but to the very being of the Church. It is not about a dynamism which is added to the essence of the Church. It is the very essence of the Church. The Church is *constituted* in and through eschatology and communion. Pneumatology is an ontological category for ecclesiology.[117]

The Spirit constitutes the ontology of church since he is the bond that unites believers with Christ, the Father, and each other in one body (1 Cor 12:13). The divine indwelling in the church is realized through the Spirit, thus making the community of believers a Spirit-filled and transformed entity. If christoforminity is the shape of ecclesiology, then pneumaformity is the content. Gunton also notes Lossky's distinction between Christ as a general principle and the Spirit as a particularising principle in relation to humanity. "Christ becomes the sole image appropriate to the common nature of humanity. The Holy Spirit grants to each person created in the image of God the possibility of fulfilling the likeness in the common nature."[118] The same observation applies to the Spirit's endowment of believers with particular *charismata* for the sake of the one body of Christ.

Hill's insights into mutually definitive and asymmetrical relations among the Father, Son, and Spirit are useful for balancing Blackwell's overly christological construal. The Christ-discourse, for Paul, always presupposes the Father- and the Spirit-discourses. The Spirit's personal identity is derivative from, but also constitutive of the identities of the Father and the Son. The mutual identification of God, Christ, and the Spirit are abundant (Rom 8:9, 11, 14; 15:19; 1 Cor 2:11; 6:11; 7:40; 12:3; 2 Cor 3:3; Phil 3:3). In this way, the God of Paul is the one who is identified with the Spirit, just as the Spirit is a divine person, who is identified with God and Christ. This mutuality is not without asymmetry: it is always "the Spirit of God" and "the Spirit of Christ/Son," never "the God of the Spirit" or "the Christ/Son of the Spirit." In

---

116. Gunton, "Spirit in Trinity," 127.
117. Zizioulas, *Being as Communion*, 132 (emphasis original).
118. Lossky, *Mystical Theology*, 166.

C. Kavin Rowe's words, "the relational determination of the Spirit's identity" cannot be abstracted from God and Christ.[119]

The dual relationality of God and Spirit is equally constitutive for the identity of Christ and the Spirit. Paul's clarification in 1 Cor 12:3, in response to some confusion in the Corinthian public worship practices, presents an example of the closely related and mutually determining identities of Jesus and the Spirit. The true Spirit-ignited utterance is recognizable by the way it acknowledges the lordship of Jesus. A worshipper does not need to speak in tongues to be able to acknowledge that God conferred on Jesus the same name that identifies him as Lord, κύριος. This confession is made exclusively through the testimony of the Holy Spirit (ἐν πνεύματι ἁγίῳ). Equally, the identity of Spirit is recognized when one confesses Jesus as Lord.[120]

Another example of the mutual co-identification of the Son and the Spirit with the Father is Gal 4:4–7. Here the Father sends both the Son and the Spirit. Precisely, God as the subject of the verb sends out not merely his Spirit but the Spirit of his Son (τὸ πνεῦμα τοῦ υἱοῦ αὐτοῦ, Gal 4:6; cf., πνεῦμα Χριστοῦ, Rom 8:9 and τοῦ πνεύματος Ἰησοῦ Χριστοῦ, Phil 1:19). Hence, the adoption of the Galatians is dependent on a three-fold involvement: God, who sends the Son and the Spirit. The relationship of the divine agents is mutual and circular. The Father sends the Son, who appropriates human "sons" and heirs to the Father (v. 7). The Father also sends the Spirit of his Son into the hearts of new sons and daughters, who, in turn, receive internal testimony and boldness to address God as "Abba! Father!" (v. 6). The Son makes the adoption of human sons possible, while the Spirit of God's Son continues the work of the Son, culminating it in focusing on God. Thus, the Son constitutes God's fatherhood just as the Father constitutes the Son's sonship; both the Son and the Father constitute the identity of the Spirit. The identities of God, Jesus, and the Spirit, for Paul, are intertwined and mutually constitutive from eternity (cf., τὸ πλήρωμα τοῦ χρόνου, Gal 4:4). A certain chronological sequence of sending shows some temporal asymmetry between the persons, whereby God is the one who sends the Son first and then the Spirit of his Son. On the personal level of the Galatians, no clear chronological order would implicate the experience of adoption before the reception of the Spirit (cf., Gal 3:1–5). Rather, the internal witness of the Spirit manifests the fact of their adoption.

---

119. Rowe, "Trinity in Letters," 50. Similarly, Marshall, "the persons of the Trinity have their personal uniqueness only in their relations to and interactions with one another..." Marshall, "Christ and Cultures," 96.

120. Hill, *Paul and Trinity*, 140.

Further evidence for the mutual identification of Christ and the Spirit could be seen in the Spirit's agency in resurrecting Jesus from the dead (Rom 1:4; 8:11). Fee strangely claims that the Spirit in Rom 8:11 does not play the role of agency in Christ's resurrection but assures future resurrection of believers:

> Finally, despite much that is asserted or argued to the contrary, Paul neither says nor does the logic of the sentence demand that God raised Christ by means of the Spirit. In fact, despite the prevalence of this idea in Christian circles, Paul nowhere explicitly suggests as much; it is doubtful whether it is implicit in the few texts—including this one—that are often read this way. . . . His reason for identifying the Spirit as "the Spirit of him who raised Christ from the dead" is not to say something about the role of the Spirit in Christ's having been raised, but to make the closest possible connection between Christ's resurrection and ours.[121]

Despite Fee's claim against the Spirit's agency in God's act of resurrection, Hill correctly connects the two resurrections with the Spirit: the indwelling of the Spirit in believers is the foundation for their confidence in the final resurrection because the Spirit is God's instrumental power that will raise them, just as he raised Jesus from the dead.[122] Hence, God's identification with Jesus through the act of resurrection is intrinsically connected with the Spirit's agency. Hill concludes, "God and Jesus are who they are only in relation to this action of the Spirit, just as the Spirit is who the Spirit is only as the Spirit of God and of Jesus."[123] When Paul applies the same life-giving function (ζωοποιέω) to Christ (1 Cor 15:22, 45) and the Spirit (2 Cor 3:6), he identifies them as the divine agents of life. To determine the Spirit in Paul one needs to invoke the identities of God and Christ and vice versa. Blackwell himself most likely would not espouse a binitarian theology, and there is no reason to doubt his trinitarian convictions. Like much modern theology, his approach is not incorrect, but rather disproportioned regarding the emphasis on Christology and fragmented: the ontology of Father and Spirit is not adequately represented in his reading. Therefore, *christosis*,

---

121. Fee, *God's Empowering Presence*, 553.

122. Hill, *Paul and Trinity*, 160–62.

123. Hill, *Paul and Trinity*, 163. See also Marshall's statement, "Thus in order to pick out the Father as a particular person—to grasp his unsubstitutable personal uniqueness—we have to be able to pick out the Son and the Spirit as particular persons; the same goes, *mutatis mutandis*, for identifying the Son and the Spirit as well." Marshall, "Christ and Cultures," 96.

as essentially a christological soteriology, would benefit greatly from taking on board an incipient trinitarian account of Paul's soteriology.[124]

Together with Fee and Tilling, I disagree with Hays, Blackwell, Hill, and others in their interpretation of κύριος in 2 Cor 3:17 as the Spirit.[125] This position would fit well Hill's identification of all three persons with the name κύριος, but the argument is not completely sustainable.[126] Nowhere in the Pauline corpus is κύριος applied to the Spirit, which makes this passage the only exception if the Spirit is indeed κύριος. Further, v. 14 clearly states that the divine agent of unveiling is Christ. Therefore, it is natural to understand "the Lord" in v. 16 as Christ, who is also associated with the Spirit and his liberating activity in v. 17. The divinity of the Spirit, however, does not depend on this text's interpretation. Rather, the close relationality and personal interconnections of God, Christ, and the Spirit are fruitful ground for such inference.

Christosis and Eschatology

Blackwell's christo-telic reading of Pauline soteriological anthropology, arguably, mistreats Paul's eschatological view of the God-human relations.[127] The apostle's eschatological perspective, I contend, does not perpetuate redemptive mediation between believers and God, even christological mediation. Arguably, some church fathers, Calvin, and his disciples assumed that the redemptive mediation of Christ has a temporary role.[128] For instance,

124. Ironically, binitarianism and the Christocentric reading of Pauline soteriology is so embedded in contemporary scholarship that even when a scholar's primary focus is on a pneumatological aspect of deification (e.g., Rabens), he concludes with *christosis* as a "particularly fitting" designation, leaving merely an instrumental role to the Spirit. Rabens, "Holy Spirit and Deification," 219.

125. Fee, *Pauline Christology*, 178–80, 190; Tilling, *Paul's Divine Christology*, 119–20; Hays, *Echoes of Scripture*, 143; Blackwell, *Christosis*, 182; Hill, *Paul and Trinity*, 147–50.

126. See the problematic nature of such interpretation in Fatehi, *Spirit's Relation*, 289–301.

127. As Finlan states in relation to post-resurrection bodies, "we must let Paul be eschatological. Not everything is reducible to *this*-worldly realities." Finlan, "Can We Speak?," 70 (emphasis original).

128. See the discussion on the cessation of Christ's mediation in relation to the *eschaton* in Marcellus of Ancyra and Eusebius in Robertson, *Christ as Mediator*, 215n225. Also, on Calvin's and Arnold A. Van Ruler's view see Jansen, "I Cor. 15. 24–28." Jansen comments on Van Ruler's trinitarian emphasis, "He disavowed the tendency to interpret the first and third articles of the creed by the second. Too often, he says, theologians have sought in the 'solus Christus' a hermeneutical attempt to read all of scripture as though it were simply a witness to Christ." Jansen, "I Cor. 15. 24–28," 563. Van Ruler

Basil of Caesarea made a distinction between the immanent doxology of the Son, "Glory be to the Father *with* the Son, *with* the Holy Spirit" and the economic doxology, "Glory be to the Father, *through* the Son, *in* the Holy Spirit" (*De Sp. S.* 7.16). On the danger of oversimplification, one can assume that the equality of divine persons can facilitate equal access to each without mediation at least from a perspective of the immanent Trinity.

Even though Calvin's view on the future of Christ's humanity in eternity is disputed, it seems that certain texts in Calvin can imply that Christ's redemptive mediation will be completed when he submits his rule to the Father. In light of 1 Cor 15:24-28, where God the Father receives all authority after the Son's subjugation of all enemies, including death,[129] there is, arguably, no need for the diversification of power and mediation. Calvin's exposition of this text demonstrates his view on the cessation of Christ's earthly mediatorial vocation:

> Until he comes forth as judge of the world Christ will therefore reign, joining us to the Father as the measure of our weakness permits. But when as partakers in heavenly glory we shall see God as he is, Christ, having then discharged the office of Mediator, will cease to be the ambassador of his Father, and will be satisfied with that glory which he enjoyed before the creation of the world (*Inst.* 2.14.3; McNeill, 1:485).[130]

Christ's earthly lordship entrusted by the Father also has a temporal function with its eschatological consummation.

> That is, to him was lordship committed by the Father, until such time as we should see his divine majesty face to face. Then he returns the lordship to his Father so that—far from diminishing his own majesty—it may shine all the more brightly. Then, also, God shall cease to be the Head of Christ, for Christ's own deity will shine of itself, although as yet it is covered by a veil (*Inst.* 2.14.3; McNeill, 1:486).

Commenting on Phil 2:9-11, Calvin wrote, "Thus Paul rightly infers: God will then of himself become the sole Head of the church, since the duties of Christ in defending the church will have been accomplished" (*Inst.* 2.15.5; McNeill, 1:501). In the previous paragraph of the *Institutes*,

---

openly developed the idea of unmediated eschatological relations of restored creation with the triune Creator.

129. For the discussion of the subject of the verb in 1 Cor 15:27, whether it is God or Christ, see Fee, *First Epistle to the Corinthians*, 757-59.

130. Calvin, *Calvin*.

Calvin states that besides redemption, Christ's mediatory role in the present life is "to lead us little by little to a firm union with God." It seems reasonable to conclude that the Reformer expounds his fully trinitarian theology, wherein its economic asymmetry gives way to immanent equality. If Christ as the divine agent fulfills his prophetic, kingly, and priestly functions as the head of the church, then the will of the Father to be all in all is finally achieved in the equal reign of the divine persons over the whole creation. Berkhof rightly stressed that dissolution of Christ's redemptive mediation does not mean the abrogation of Christ's eternal coordination, "We shall not come to God without Christ, nor via Christ, but rather together with Christ as 'the first born of many brethren' and therefore around him as the center."[131]

The eternal mediation of the Son is linked with a conceptual overlap between the immanent and economic Trinity. John Zizioulas rightly indicated some problems with the Rahnerian formula: the immanent Trinity is the economic Trinity and vice versa.[132] If God is outside and transcends the created world and economy (as Irenaeus and Athanasius affirmed), then our understanding of the Trinity should not be limited only to the economy.[133] Zizioulas insists that the divine epistemology should not restrict the divine ontology, i.e., "although the Economic Trinity is the Immanent Trinity, the Immanent Trinity is not exhausted in the Economic Trinity."[134] Thus, our understanding of the second person of the Trinity should not be bound to his economic mediation between the Father and the redeemed world. Such a position helps to avoid a subordinationist reading of 1 Cor 15:24-28 since the Son completes his economic role and resumes his relationship with the world as one of the immanent Trinity alongside with the Father and the Spirit. The economic, functional distinctions of the Trinity yield to the immanent equality of persons so that adopted children will have equal, direct access to all three persons of the Trinity. Accordingly, if *christosis* has a role to play, it is only in the pre-*eschaton* reality. Gorman insightfully writes, "Paul's famous phrase 'in Christ' is his shorthand for 'in God/in Christ/in the Spirit.' That is, his Christocentricity is really an implicit Trinitarianism."[135] It is to Gorman that we now turn.

131. Berkhof, *Christian Faith*, 536. Jansen further comments, "The 'via Christ' applies to the present mediation of redemption—and that will be completed. But the 'with Christ' will apply to the realm of glory as much as it applies to the present realm of grace." Jansen, "I Cor. 15. 24-28," 569.

132. Rahner, *Trinity*, 22.

133. Zizioulas, "Doctrine of God," 23.

134. Zizioulas, "Doctrine of God," 24.

135. Gorman, *Inhabiting Cruciform God*, 4.

Michael J. Gorman

In contrast to Russell, Michael J. Gorman, a well-known Protestant defender of *theosis* in the theology of Paul, employs a definition of *theosis* that is not formulated based on Greco-Roman studies or patristic research, but primarily on the exegesis of Paul's epistles. His fresh reading of Paul through the lens of *theosis* is welcomed. In his *Inhabiting the Crucified God*, Gorman claims that participation in Christ through co-crucifixion is an essential element in understanding justification and likeness to God.[136] His exegetical treatments of key christological and soteriological texts, such as Phil 2 and Rom 5–7, propose a peculiar reading of the traditional justification-sanctification passages in the context of the patristic doctrine of *theosis*.[137]

Gorman recognizes that Paul's experience of the Christ-event is an experience of God the Trinity.[138] The real essence of God's existence manifested in the self-giving character of Christ on the cross. In other words, Christ is the true manifestation of the kenotic self-giving nature of God. To participate in Christ means to participate in the cruciform identity of the Trinity.[139] In Gorman's words, "to be in Christ is to be in God. At the very least, this means that for Paul cruciformity—conformity to the crucified Christ—is really theoformity, or theosis."[140] For Gorman, *theosis* is becoming like God through "transformative participation in the kenotic, cruciform character of God through Spirit-enabled conformity to the incarnate, crucified, and resurrected/glorified Christ."[141] Thus, he affirms full affinity of *theosis* in Paul, stating that justification and even participation are not comprehensive enough terms to express Paul's "central concern."

In this highly commendable book, however, Gorman makes bold but biblically and historically unwarranted claims about *ontological*

---

136. Gorman, *Inhabiting Cruciform God*, 90. Gorman states, "What justification by co-crucifixion will imply, however, and not surprisingly, is that a theological rift between justification and sanctification is impossible, because the same Spirit effects both initial and ongoing cocrucifixion with Christ among believers, a lifelong experience of cruciformity or, in light of chapter one, theoformity—theosis." Gorman, *Inhabiting Cruciform God*, 40.

137. Gorman develops his view in a number of other publications. Gorman, *Cruciformity*; Gorman, "Paul and Cruciform Way"; Gorman, *Death of Messiah*.

138. Gorman, *Cruciformity*, 64–74; Gorman, "Paul and Cruciform Way," 70.

139. Gorman, *Apostle of Crucified Lord*, 117–18.

140. Gorman, *Inhabiting Cruciform God*, 4; Gorman, "Paul and Cruciform Way," 83.

141. Gorman, *Inhabiting Cruciform God*, 7.

participation in God's being.[142] Macaskill criticizes Gorman for indiscriminate use of *theosis* and *kenosis* as if these were uncontested and inflexible terms.[143] It seemed, at times, that Gorman loses the theological balance of the essential distinction between human and divine, compromising the uniqueness of God by the language of human incorporation into the divine identity.[144] One of the objections to Gorman's development of this theme is his insistence that Christ's crucifixion and resurrection demonstrate the essence of God. This account becomes problematic when one introduces the idea of a believer's participation in the narrative of Christ. The corollary to such an understanding would be the participation of creation in God's essence through identification with the Christ-narrative. These claims are implausible for the following reasons.

First, do divine acts and attributes constitute the essence of God? In his comment on 1 Cor 1:30, Gorman states, "But this differentiation between divine activity and divine attribute is a false one. God's actions are self-revelatory, the expression of God's essence or character."[145] In his later publication, *The Death of the Messiah and the Birth of the New Covenant*, where Gorman develops a covenantal understanding of redemption, he continues to use ontological language in relation to Christ's acts, "Thus, discipleship is not merely following the Son of God who accidentally or arbitrarily died, but following the one who has died because that is the fullest manifestation of the self-giving and reconciling nature of the Son of God, and thus of God himself."[146] The author concludes that since divine acts and characteristics expose the essence of God, participation in these divine acts and qualities substantiates Christian deification, i.e., believers share in the divine essence. The identification of God's act with his being is a particularly Barthian "actualistic ontology."[147] For Barth, "God is who He is in His works . . . He is not, therefore, who He is only in His works. Yet in Himself He is not another than He is in His works,"[148] and in God's self-revelation one finds "not only His reality for us—certainly that—but at the same time His own, inner, proper reality, behind which and above which there is no other."[149] Thus,

---

142. Gorman, *Inhabiting Cruciform God*, 85.

143. Macaskill, *Union with Christ*, 27.

144. Gorman, *Inhabiting Cruciform God*, 93; Macaskill, *Union with Christ*, 28.

145. Gorman, *Inhabiting Cruciform God*, 111.

146. Gorman, *Death of Messiah*, 36.

147. Nimmo, *Being in Action*, 7. "The true identity of God, in other words, is revealed in the works of God."

148. Barth, *Church Dogmatics*, 2/1:260.

149. Barth, *Church Dogmatics*, 2/1:262.

Barth's statement could be read *mutatis mutandis*, according to Gorman's logic, as follows "the kenotic action of Christ is the *being* of God in Christ, but it is this kenotic *action* that is the being."[150] It appears that Gorman operates with the same type of ontology but in his theological claims, he neglects the animated theological discussion that surrounds this question.

In this regard, Litwa agrees with Gorman contra Blackwell that the revelatory attributes of God constitute God's nature and, therefore, ought to be considered as essential attributes. Litwa asks, "[D]oes not Christ's divine humility *define* the nature of Paul's God?"[151] Litwa concludes from 2 Cor 5:21 that those who "become the righteousness of God" really are "participating in God's just nature" and "partially become what God is (Justice itself)."[152] He claims that this way of thinking is characteristic of ancient people. However, even if it is for Plato, whose impersonal God is Justice, what is the reason to think that a Jewish thinker like Paul would contemplate his initiation into the divine essence of Yahweh?

Litwa, likewise, asks, "If, for Paul, Christ's virtue of self-subordinating love defines the identity of God, can one with the *same virtue* as Christ participate in Christ's divine identity?"[153] What is the basis for thinking that sharing in one of the personal qualities means participation in the identity or nature of that person? Paul calls his churches to imitate him and his co-workers, as well as God (μιμηταί, συμμιμηταί, 1 Cor 4:16; Phil 3:17; Eph 5:1). He also confirms that Philemon is his sharer (literally, κοινωνός, Phlm 1:17). Does this mean that these believers, who are identified with the apostle and share his attributes, become sharers of his identity? What would that mean in any case? What would sharing in God's identity mean for humans? It seems that Gorman would not side with Litwa in claiming that people become lesser deities in the hierarchy of gods by sharing the divine nature of Christ. Nonetheless, his unspecified use of God's nature makes him open to such association.

Further, Paul's statement that "God made Christ sin for us" (ὑπὲρ ἡμῶν ἁμαρτίαν ἐποίησεν, 2 Cor 5:21) could not mean that Christ's divine essence changed into something sinful. Correspondently, the result that believers "become the righteousness of God in him" (γενώμεθα δικαιοσύνη θεοῦ ἐν αὐτῷ) could not mean that their human nature is changed into the divine righteousness, whatever that means ontologically. It is more natural to interpret this statement as participation in the attribute of the divine person,

---

150. Barth, *Church Dogmatics*, 1/1:323.
151. Litwa, *We Are Being Transformed*, 223 (emphasis original).
152. Litwa, *We Are Being Transformed*, 223.
153. Litwa, *We Are Being Transformed*, 223 (emphasis original).

who exhibits righteousness. It would be difficult to define what "righteous essence" means and how it manifests apart from the righteous person. If Gorman and Litwa are ready to say that Christ is the justice of God in 1 Cor 1:30 and so are those who are identified with him, then they must be ready to conclude that believers are also wisdom, holiness, and redemption like Christ is, which is pointless to think that the Corinthians become the redemption of God. Hence, it is unwarranted to state that some acts or qualities fully reveal the essence of God's being. God's acts do reveal to us something about who the three divine persons are in relation to creation, but these acts do not necessarily constitute or exhaust the eternal nature of God *in se*. In John Webster's words, "The outer works of God are *his* works, not some remote operation which is not proper to him, and this continuity of acting subject means that God's economic acts elucidate his inner being, even though they do not exhaust it."[154] Attributes or acts do not equal essence, as, for instance, God's wrath reveals God's holiness and reaction to sin, but not that God essentially is wrathful. Likewise, the fact that God condemns sinners demonstrates his uncompromising justice and righteousness, but that does not mean that he essentially is judgmental.

Second, this leads to an objection to Gorman's argument in the first chapter of *Inhabiting the Cruciform God* that God's essence is cruciformity, "Kenosis is thus the *sine qua non* of both divinity and humanity, as revealed in the incarnation and cross of Christ, the one who was truly God and became truly human."[155] Without an appropriate distinction between economic roles of the Father and the Son, Gorman states that "God is like Christ crucified,"[156] which is not far from the ancient error of *patripassionism*. What would the death of God mean beyond showing God's compassion with sufferings of human beings? The language of suffering God goes against the testimony of the New Testament, which consistently ascribes suffering and death to Jesus, not to the Father or God in general.[157] It seems that Gorman advocates for a version of ontological kenoticism. Oliver Crisp, however, persuasively argues that an ontological kenoticism is a diversion from a Chalcedonian Christology.[158] The biblical narrative allows only

---

154. Webster, "Place of Christology," 615.

155. Gorman, *Inhabiting Cruciform God*, 36.

156. Gorman, *Inhabiting Cruciform God*, 113. See Moltmann, *Crucified God*. Against this conflation of divine and human realities in Christ Habets employs the discussion of *extra Calvinisticum*, claiming that in the incarnation the humanity of Christ did not exhaust his divine identity. Habets, "Putting 'Extra' Back."

157. For a similar criticism of Bauckham see McCartney, "Review of *God Crucified*."

158. Crisp, *Divinity and Humanity*, chap. 5. Instead, he argues for a "krypsis christology," i.e., human limitations were assumed by the incarnate Logos, without

speaking of the Son's kenosis, not God's kenosis. The economic account of the Trinity assumes only the incarnation of the second person, who forever retains his humanity.[159] Although it is correct to state that God became a man due to the Son's full divinity, it is incorrect to say that the Father or the Spirit became man also. Since such a narrative is peculiar exclusively to the Son, it is inappropriate to think that kenosis also characterizes the Father or the Spirit.[160] What might apply to the Father and the Spirit, in this regard, is a humble predisposition and sacrificial selflessness. But kenosis, strictly speaking, is a historical notion, not an ontological. The simplicity of God *ad intra* does not allow for a kenotic change of the God *ad extra*.

Zizioulas appropriately objects to the talk about the *kenotic* nature of relationships in the immanent Trinity, "Suffering, like death, remains an 'enemy' of love; the Resurrection rules out a 'metaphysics of suffering.'"[161] Kenoticism and cruciformity reveal some aspects of the Trinity's selfless love in relationships, thus, personal predispositions, rather than disclose the fullness or, at least, the core of God's historically transcended essence. If one introduces sufferings in the essence of God, how then does God transcend history? In fact, God would become locked up in the history of suffering in order to be what he is.[162] God unveiled himself in history, but he is also beyond history. To this extent, the opponents of the Rahner's axiom are correct, maintaining that God's essence remains transcendent and unknown,

---

relinquishing any of his divine attributes. In this sense, Crisp claims that there is no kenosis of the Word as such, because "the Word actually [does not] restrict the exercise of his divine attributes *per se*." Crisp, *Divinity and Humanity*, 151.

159. John of Damascus in *An Exact Exposition of the Orthodox Faith* 3.6, commenting on Pseudo-Dionysius's statement of communion between the Divinity and humanity, writes, "But, certainly, let us not be constrained to say that all the Persons of the sacred Godhead, the Three, that is, were hypostatically united to all the persons of humanity. For in no wise did the Father and the Holy Ghost participate in the incarnation of the Word of God except by Their good pleasure and will. We do say that the entire substance of the Divinity was united to the entire human nature." John of Damascus, *Writings*, 279–80.

160. Habets points that theologies of the cross undermine incarnation and salvation, "the Son of God became man so that as man, and not as God, he could freely offer his human life to the Father as a loving sacrifice for our sin. It is what the Son of God does as man that is salvific. Otherwise, the humanity of Jesus would merely be an instrumental shell in which God chose to suffer as God." Habets, "Putting 'Extra' Back," 454.

161. "It is for this reason that I find it difficult to endorse the introduction of any form of 'kenoticism' into the immanent Trinity, as is done, e.g., by S. Boulgakov (see his *The Lamb of God*, 1933), or in J. Moltmann's *The Crucified God* (1974)." Zizioulas, *Communion and Otherness*, 2006, 63n145. Just as self-giving without appropriate modifying context can be unholy sexual relations, as Gorman himself acknowledges. Gorman, *Inhabiting Cruciform God*, 119.

162. Zizioulas, "Doctrine of God Trinity," 24.

while the divine hypostases reveal God's being to the created world through their economic relations.[163]

Finally, Gorman, while using patristic categories of essence and attributes, departs from the consistent traditional views. One needs to define clearly, what one means by "identity" before using this term in an interpretation of Paul. If the Son shares in the identity of the Father, they are equally divine. The corollary of believers sharing in Christ's and God's identity would mean that they should be equally divine, which is a *non sequitur*, according to the orthodox thought. Hence, a personal "identity" in a patristic account is an essence-person entity, wherein the essence of an entity is unknown and encountered only through the person, and not the other way around. Therefore, the divine essence as an abstract entity, which is recognized exclusively through its personal manifestations, ever remains unshareable to those who do not constitute the essence-person entity of the Trinity. The church fathers maintained that God's essence remains unknown and imparticipable to humans, while the divine attributes reveal personal qualities of the Trinity. In like vein, Luther and Calvin opposed the idea of essential participation in God, arguing for personal union with Christ. When one ignores this sound patristic distinction, she is in danger of minimizing the transcendent nature of God or overstating the human potential for assimilation to God.

Conclusion

In summary, both negative and positive points could be made. On the negative side, the analysis of the three proponents of *theosis* in relation to Paul's theology has shown that merely historical, patristic or exegetical location of the theme's origin cannot provide an adequate account of both *theosis* and Paul's thought without prioritizing one aspect and diminishing another. Litwa's attempt to locate Paul in his Jewish and Greco-Roman background to the exclusion of all subsequent theological developments tends to overemphasize similarity and neglect crucial distinctions between the apostle and his contemporaries that later were acknowledged by generations of theologians. Blackwell helpfully mends this problem by addressing the patristic interpretation of *theosis*. A strong leaning toward Christocentricity, however, diminishes a trinitarian framework and the role of the Father and the Spirit in Paul's theology. Finally, Gorman's close attention to Paul's

---

163. Del Colle, *Christ and Spirit*, 15. The Orthodox tradition preserved this distinction between two trinities. Although, according to Palamas, the hypostatic uncreated energies communicate divinity, he retained the view of God's essential inaccessibility.

narrative of Christ's death and resurrection yields a new reading through christoformity. However, his incautious use of ontological categories places his account on the verge of a theological mistake, against which the church fathers and Reformers warned long ago.

On the positive side, an adequate account of *theosis* in relation to Paul should include both the antecedent historical and subsequent doctrinal developments of the doctrine. In recovering these diverse strands of thought, one must not minimize or exaggerate diversity, but try to understand and preserve the complexity of the idea. A scholar will be on the much safer ground when she works with a precise definition of key terms and appropriates exegetical, historical and theological resources. A Pauline soteriology can be expressed using such a category as *theosis* when a balanced presentation of Father, Son, and Holy Spirit is preserved.

Chapter 6

Conclusion

Summary of Argument

THIS RESEARCH HAS DEMONSTRATED that the concepts of *"theosis"* and "Trinity" in conjunction can inform our reading of Paul's soteriology. Recently a number of studies were dedicated to retrieving the patristic doctrine of *theosis* as a fresh approach to Paul's soteriology through the prism of participation in God through Christ. These studies, however, have manifested that Pauline scholars have an inadequate or misguided understanding of *theosis*. The deficiencies vary from a lack of historical background (Gorman), minimizing the role of the Father and the Spirit (Blackwell) to minimizing distinctions between Paul and his religious context on the verge of parallelomania (Litwa). A lack of adequate account for the complexity of *theosis* and precision in definition has invited the examination of the patristic traditions.

By taking into account the long history of soteriological interpretation, this book has outlined four different approaches to *theosis* in the patristic era. I have argued that the diversity and complexity of *theosis* in the church fathers manifest in concrete trajectories:

1. the transformation of Christian gnostics into bodiless spiritual beings through *apotheosis*;

2. the transformation of saints into Christlikeness through *christosis*;

3. the transformation of believers into the image of the tripersonal God through *triadosis*, which is realized in the church; and

4. the transformation of Christian contemplators into Godlikeness through *energeosis*.

It then was suggested that *triadosis* provides a useful lens for reading Luther and Calvin in a fresh way. With the incentives of the Finnish

Lutheran School and J. Todd Billings, a new reading of Luther and Calvin in light of *theosis* has demonstrated that the Reformers were much in line with the fathers's participationist accounts of salvation. It was noted that Luther's account of deification does not read Paul in isolation from other parts of the New Testament (e.g., 2 Pet 1:4), but it still draws its principal set of concepts (particularly those of presence and gift) from Paul. More precisely, I have argued that *triadosis* is a useful concept to convey the trinitarian dimension of soteriologies espoused by Luther and Calvin. The argument then moved to exploring Zizioulas's relational model of personhood, which originated, according to the Metropolitan, from the Cappadocian understanding of the Trinity. This chapter has concluded that for Zizioulas, the salvation of a person is constituted by the restoration of an isolated individual sinner into relationships with the tripersonal God and other believers through participation in the person of Christ.

The next chapter has concentrated on the three most influential advocates for reading Paul's soteriology in light of *theosis*. Despite the historically well-informed study, Litwa's account of Paul's version of deification distorts some fundamental distinctions between the apostle and his contemporaries. Litwa is inconsistent in his taxonomy and operates with some problematic premises, such as the superiority of antecedent historical reconstruction over subsequent traditional interpretations and a questionable understanding of Jewish monotheism. Blackwell incorporates patristic material in his reading of Paul in light of traditional *theosis*, which yields a more balanced account. Nonetheless, a Christocentric reconstruction of the apostle's soteriology can lead to misrepresentation of Paul's theology proper and pneumatology. Finally, Gorman's exegetical analysis of the main soteriological texts further substantiates the appropriateness of *theosis* as a category in Pauline studies. Gorman's account, however, lacks precision in theological terminology, which may lead to unorthodox conclusions.

Original Contribution

The original contribution of this dissertation consists in a more nuanced presentation of *theosis* in the interpretation of Paul, which has been inadequate or imprecise in some of its treatments. One should not lose the diversity of patristic accounts in sweeping generalizations. Although this study does not claim to present all facets of the idea, it has sought to reflect faithfully on the multifaceted nature of *theosis*. Hence, in any application of *theosis* to biblical and theological studies, the student has to clarify what type of *theosis* she implies.

Another contribution pertains to the area of Paul's soteriology. It has been argued in this monograph that the traditional presentations of Paul's teaching, which are commonly anthropocentric or Christocentric, should be reoriented toward a thoroughly trinitarian presentation. The God of the apostle Paul was not an individual Creator with two divine agents, Jesus Christ and the Spirit. Rather, the God of Paul was Father, Son, and Holy Spirit, who are one in will and act, whose personal identity depends on the others being and communion. Therefore, the redemptive work of Christ is not merely his alone, but always in conjunction with the Father and the Spirit. The justifying role of the Father is always in Christ and through the Spirit. Similarly, the Spirit does not accomplish the sanctifying activity in isolation from the other two persons of the Trinity. If human beings were created in the image of the triune God, then the realization of this image means people are saved and transformed in communion with other persons divine and human. Believers experience transfiguration not in the likeness of God as an abstract divine being, but in the likeness of a personal God, who is the Trinity. To rephrase a patristic dictum: a human being was created in the image of the divine community to achieve by grace likeness to the divine persons in the community of equal human persons, the church. This is the nature of *triadosis*, which is not an infringement on divine status or identity, but a true communion of persons.

Further Implications

This monograph is an attempt to read Paul and the Reformers afresh in light of the theological developments of *theosis* and Trinity. It was argued that a concept of *triadosis* could allow bringing more coherence to theologies of the apostle, Luther, and Calvin. Hence, the initial probing of the trinitarian soteriological idea requires substantial reflection in respective theological figures. Further research could concentrate on a question how these theologians understood the Trinity and its role in soteriology. Particularly, what is the character of human participation in the Trinity—the imitation of divine attributes, acquiring superhuman characteristics, communion on the level of persons or a combination of such changes?

The sheer complexity of deification continues to motivate scholars to reflect on its different aspects in different patristic authors. As was indicated in the introduction, a number of patristic and modern thinkers was intrigued by the concept of *theosis*, whose ideas are worth studying in light of trinitarian soteriology. Inquiry into similarities and diversities of deification views among Roman Catholic, Eastern Orthodox, and Protestant traditions could do a great service to the Christian church.

This book has purported that patristic studies or historical theology in general can be a stimulating tool for new insights in biblical studies. Thus, the bridging of fragmented areas of biblical and theological studies is possible and promising. The cross-disciplinary research such as the present one can contribute to the theological interpretation of Scripture by bringing expertize from different fields of theology.

Finally, the limitations of this study do not allow for the constructive development of a new concept of *triadosis*, but, perhaps, it will become a stimulus for further reflection and analysis of the Trinity's role in the process of deification. *Theosis* has proven to be a fruitful ground for ecumenical dialogue. Thus, clarity in understanding and definition of the key concept should elucidate further theological discussions among Christian communities. Further research can focus on such Pauline images as adoption, baptism, the body of Christ, temple, and marriage to elucidate the external and corporate effect of *triadosis*. Similarly, the notions of conformation to the image of Christ, immortalization of the resurrected glorious body, new closing in Christ can explicate the internal personal effect of *triadosis*. Arguably, all these concepts are not limited to the christological framework but operate in the trinitarian context.

Bibliography

Ables, Travis E. "Being Church: A Critique of Zizioulas' Communion Ecclesiology." In *Ecumenical Ecclesiology: Unity, Diversity and Otherness in a Fragmented World*, edited by Gesa Elsbeth Thiessen, 115–27. Ecclesiological Investigations 5. London: T. & T. Clark, 2009.

———. "On the Very Idea of an Ontology of Communion: Being, Relation and Freedom in Zizioulas and Levinas." *Heythrop Journal* 52 (2011) 672–83.

Aden, Ross. "Justification and Sanctification: A Conversation between Lutheranism and Orthodoxy." *St. Vladimir's Theological Quarterly* 38 (1994) 87–109.

Althaus, Paul. *The Theology of Martin Luther*. Translated by Robert C. Schultz. Philadelphia: Fortress, 1966.

Anastos, Thomas L. "Gregory Palamas' Radicalization of the Essence, Energies, and Hypostasis Model of God." *Greek Orthodox Theological Review* 38 (1993) 335–49.

Ashwin-Siejkowski, Piotr. *Clement of Alexandria: A Project of Christian Perfection*. London: T. & T. Clark, 2008.

———. *Clement of Alexandria on Trial: The Evidence of "Heresy" from Photius' Bibliotheca*. VCSup 101. Leiden: Brill, 2010.

Awad, Najeeb G. "Between Subordination and Koinonia: Toward a New Reading of the Cappadocian Theology." *Modern Theology* 23 (2007) 181–204.

———. "Personhood as Particularity: John Zizioulas, Colin Gunton, and the Trinitarian Theology of Personhood." *Journal of Reformed Theology* 4 (2010) 1–22.

Ayres, Lewis. "On Not Three People: The Fundamental Themes of Gregory of Nyssa's Trinitarian Theology as Seen in To Ablabius: On Not Three Gods." In *Re-Thinking Gregory of Nyssa*, edited by Sarah Coakley, 15–44. Oxford: Blackwell, 2003.

Bakhtin, Mikhail M. "Response to a Question from the Novy Mir Editorial Staff." In *Speech Genres and Other Late Essays*, edited by Caryl Emerson and Michael Holquist, translated by Vern McGee, 1–9. Austin: University of Texas Press, 1986.

Bakken, Kenneth L. "Holy Spirit and Theosis: Toward a Lutheran Theology of Healing." *St Vladimir's Theological Quarterly* 38 (1994) 409–23.

Balás, David L. *Μετουσία Θεοῦ: Man's Participation in God's Perfections According to Saint Gregory of Nyssa*. SA 55. Romae: Libreria Herder, 1966.

Barnes, Michel Rene. "Divine Unity and the Divided Self: Gregory of Nyssa's Trinitarian Theology in Its Psychological Context." In *Re-Thinking Gregory of Nyssa*, edited by Sarah Coakley, 45–66. Oxford: Blackwell, 2003.

BIBLIOGRAPHY

Barth, Karl. *Church Dogmatics*. Edited by Geoffrey W. Bromiley and Thomas F. Torrance, vol. 1. Edinburgh: T. & T. Clark, 1957.

———. *Church Dogmatics*. Edited by Geoffrey W. Bromiley and Thomas F. Torrance. 2nd ed. Vol. 2. Edinburgh: T. & T. Clark, 1975.

Barton, John. "Historical-Critical Approaches." In *The Cambridge Companion to Biblical Interpretation*, edited by John Barton, 9–20. CCR. Cambridge: Cambridge University Press, 1998.

Basil of Caesarea. *Basil: The Letters*. Translated by Roy Joseph Deferrari. 4 vols. LCL. Cambridge: Harvard University Press, 1926.

———. *Letters 1–185*. Translated by Agnes Clare Way. FC 13. Washington, DC: Catholic University of America Press, 1951.

Bathrellos, Demetrios. "Church, Eucharist, Bishop: The Early Church in the Ecclesiology of John Zizioulas." In *The Theology of John Zizioulas: Personhood and the Church*, edited by Douglas H. Knight, 133–45. Burlington, VT: Ashgate, 2007.

Bauckham, Richard. *Jesus and the God of Israel: God Crucified and Other Studies on the New Testament's Christology of Divine Identity*. Grand Rapids: Eerdmans, 2009.

———. "The Worship of Jesus in Apocalyptic Christianity." *New Testament Studies* 27 (1981) 322–41.

Bayer, Oswald. *Martin Luther's Theology: A Contemporary Interpretation*. Translated by Thomas H. Trapp. Grand Rapids: Eerdmans, 2008.

Beeley, Christopher A. *Gregory of Nazianzus on the Trinity and the Knowledge of God: In Your Light We Shall See Light*. Oxford: Oxford University Press, 2008.

Beilby, James. "Lecture on the Doctrine of God." Bethel Theological Seminary, October 9, 2000.

Bente, F., and W. H. T. Dau. *Concordia Triglotta*. St. Louis: Concordia, 1921.

Berkhof, H. *Christian Faith: An Introduction to the Study of the Faith*. Grand Rapids: Eerdmans, 1979.

Bielfeldt, Dennis. "Response to Sammeli Juntunen, 'Luther and Metaphysics.'" In *Union with Christ: The New Finnish Interpretation of Luther*, edited by Carl E. Braaten and Robert W. Jenson, 161–66. Grand Rapids: Eerdmans, 1998.

Billings, J. Todd. *Calvin, Participation, and the Gift: The Activity of Believers in Union with Christ*. Oxford: Oxford University Press, 2007.

———. "John Calvin's Soteriology: On the Multifaceted 'Sum' of the Gospel." *International Journal of Systematic Theology* 11 (2009) 428–47.

———. "United to God through Christ: Assessing Calvin on the Question of Deification." *Harvard Theological Review* 98 (2005) 315–34.

Blackwell, Ben C. *Christosis: Pauline Soteriology in Light of Deification in Irenaeus and Cyril of Alexandria*. WUNT 314. Tübingen: Mohr Siebeck, 2011.

Blosser, Benjamin P. *Become Like the Angels: Origen's Doctrine of the Soul*. Washington, DC: Catholic University of America Press, 2012.

Bockmuehl, Markus. *Seeing the Word: Refocusing New Testament Study*. STI. Grand Rapids: Baker Academic, 2006.

Borysov, Eduard. "The Doctrine of Deification in the Works of Pavel Florensky and John Meyendorff: A Critical Examination." *Greek Orthodox Theological Review* 57 (2012) 115–34.

Bouteneff, Peter. "Soteriological Imagery in Gregory of Nyssa's Antirrheticus." In *Athanasius and His Opponents, Cappadocian Fathers, Other Greek Writers after*

Nicaea, edited by Elizabeth A. Livingstone, 81–86. StPatr 32. Leuven: Peeters, 1997.
Braaten, Carl E., and Robert W. Jenson, eds. *Union with Christ: The New Finnish Interpretation of Luther*. Grand Rapids: Eerdmans, 1998.
Bradshaw, David. *Aristotle East and West: Metaphysics and the Division of Christendom*. Cambridge: Cambridge University Press, 2004.
Briskina, Anna. "An Orthodox View of Finnish Luther Research." Translated by Dennis Bielfeldt. *Lutheran Quarterly* 22 (2008) 16–39.
Brown, Alan. "On the Criticism of Being as Communion in Anglophone Orthodox Theology." In *The Theology of John Zizioulas: Personhood and the Church*, edited by Douglas H. Knight, 35–78. Burlington, VT: Ashgate, 2007.
Bucur, Bogdan Gabriel. *Angelomorphic Pneumatology: Clement of Alexandria and Other Early Christian Witnesses*. VCSup 95. Leiden: Brill, 2009.
Butin, Philip Walker. *Revelation, Redemption, and Response: Calvin's Trinitarian Understanding of the Divine-Human Relationship*. Oxford: Oxford University Press, 1995.
Calvin, John. *The Bondage and Liberation of the Will: A Defence of the Orthodox Doctrine of Human Choice against Pighius*. Edited by A. N. S. Lane and Graham I. Davies. Grand Rapids: Paternoster, 1996.
———. *Calvin: Institutes of the Christian Religion*. Edited by John T. McNeill. Translated by Ford Lewis Battles. 2 vols. LCC. Louisville: Westminster John Knox, 2006.
Campbell, Constantine R. *Paul and Union with Christ: An Exegetical and Theological Study*. Grand Rapids: Zondervan, 2012.
Canlis, Julie. "Being Made Human: The Significance of Creation for Irenaeus' Doctrine of Participation." *Scottish Journal of Theology* 58 (2005) 434–54.
———. "Calvin, Osiander and Participation in God." *International Journal of Systematic Theology* 6 (2004) 169–84.
———. *Calvin's Ladder: A Spiritual Theology of Ascent and Ascension*. Grand Rapids: Eerdmans, 2010.
Carpenter, Craig B. "A Question of Union with Christ? Calvin and Trent on Justification." *Westminster Theological Journal* 64 (2002) 363–86.
Casiday, Augustine. *Evagrius Ponticus*. London: Routledge, 2006.
———. "On Heresy in Modern Patristic Scholarship: The Case of Evagrius Ponticus." *Heythrop Journal* 53 (2012) 241–52.
Cavanaugh, William T. "A Joint Declaration?: Justification as Theosis in Aquinas and Luther." *Heythrop Journal* 41 (2000) 265–80.
Chadwick, Henry, and J. E. L. Oulton, eds. *Alexandrian Christianity: Selected Translations of Clement and Origen*. LCC. London: SCM, 1954.
Childs, Brevard S. *Introduction to Old Testament as Scripture*. Philadelphia: Fortress, 1979.
Christensen, Michael J., and Jeffery A. Wittung, eds. *Partakers of the Divine Nature: The History and Development of Deification in the Christian Traditions*. Grand Rapids: Baker Academic, 2008.
Ciraulo, Jonathan Martin. "Sacraments and Personhood: John Zizioulas' Impasse and a Way Forward." *Heythrop Journal* 53 (2012) 993–1004.
Clark, R. Scott. "Iustitia Imputata Christi: Alien or Proper to Luther's Doctrine of Justification?" *Concordia Theological Quarterly* 70 (2006) 269–310.

Clement of Alexandria. *Clement of Alexandria: Stromata*. Edited by Alexander Roberts and James Donaldson. ANF 2. Edinburgh: T. & T. Clark, 1994.
Clendenin, Daniel B. *Eastern Orthodox Christianity: A Western Perspective*. 2nd ed. Grand Rapids: Baker Academic, 2003.
———. "Partakers of Divinity: The Orthodox Doctrine of Theosis." *Journal of the Evangelical Theological Society* 37 (1994) 365–79.
Coates, Thomas. "Calvin's Doctrine of Justification." In *An Elaboration of the Theology of Calvin*, edited by Richard C. Gamble, 193–203. Articles on Calvin and Calvinism 8. New York: Garland, 1992.
Collins, Paul M. *Partaking in Divine Nature: Deification and Communion*. London: T. & T. Clark, 2010.
Contos, Leonidas C. "Essence-Energies Structure of Saint Gregory Palamas with a Brief Examination of Its Patristic Foundation." *Greek Orthodox Theological Review* 12 (1967) 283–94.
Corrigan, Kevin. *Evagrius and Gregory: Mind, Soul and Body in the 4th Century*. Farnham: Ashgate, 2009.
Crisp, Oliver D. *Divinity and Humanity: The Incarnation Reconsidered*. Current Issues in Theology. Cambridge: Cambridge University Press, 2007.
Cyril of Alexandria. *Commentary on the Gospel according to St. John IX–XXI*. Translated by T. Randell. LFHCC 48. London: Walter Smith, 1885.
———. *Commentary upon the Gospel according to St. Luke*. Translated by R. Payne Smith. New York: Studion, 1983.
———. *Cyril of Alexandria: Select Letters*. Edited by Lionel R. Wickham. Oxford: Clarendon, 1983.
———. *Dialogues sur la Trinité*. Translated by Georges-Matthieu de Durand. 3 vols. SC 231, 237, 246. Paris: Cerf, 1976.
———. *Lukas-Kommentare aus der griechischen Kirche*. Edited by Joseph Reuss. Berlin: Akademie, 1984.
———. *Sancti Patris Nostri Cyrilli Archiepiscopi Alexandrini in D. Ioannis Evangelium*. Edited by Philip Edward Pusey. 7 vols. Oxford: Clarendon, 1868.
Cyril of Jerusalem, and Gregory Nazianzen. *Cyril of Jerusalem, Gregory Nazianzen*. Translated by Charles Gordon Browne and James Edward Swallow. Vol. 7. NPNF 2. Edinburgh: T. & T. Clark, 1890.
Daley, Brian E. "Divine Transcendence and Human Transformation: Gregory of Nyssa's Anti-Apollinarian Christology." In *Re-Thinking Gregory of Nyssa*, edited by Sarah Coakley, 67–76. Oxford: Blackwell, 2003.
———. "Is Patristic Exegesis Still Usable? Some Reflections on Early Christian Interpretation of the Psalms." In *The Art of Reading Scripture*, edited by Ellen F. Davis and Richard B. Hays, 69–88. Grand Rapids: Eerdmans, 2003.
Dalferth, Ingolf U. *Crucified and Resurrected: Restructuring the Grammar of Christology*. Translated by Jo Bennett. Grand Rapids: Baker Academic, 2015.
Davidson, Ivor. "Theologizing the Human Jesus: An Ancient (and Modern) Approach to Christology Reassessed." *International Journal of Systematic Theology* 3 (2001) 129–53.
Davies, Philip R. *Whose Bible Is It Anyway?* JSOTSup 204. Sheffield: Sheffield Academic, 1995.
Davis, Ellen F., and Richard B. Hays, eds. *The Art of Reading Scripture*. Grand Rapids: Eerdmans, 2003.

Del Colle, Ralph. *Christ and the Spirit: Spirit-Christology in Trinitarian Perspective*. New York: Oxford University Press, 1994.
Dunn, James D. G. *Christology in the Making: A New Testament Inquiry into the Origins of the Doctrine of the Incarnation*. Philadelphia: Westminster, 1980.
———. *Did the First Christians Worship Jesus?: The New Testament Evidence*. London: SPCK, 2010.
Edmondson, Stephen. *Calvin's Christology*. Cambridge: Cambridge University Press, 2004.
Edwards, Mark Julian. *Origen against Plato*. Burlington, VT: Ashgate, 2002.
Egan, John P. "ἄτιος/'Author,' αἰτία/'Cause' and ἀρχή/'Origin': Synonyms in Selected Texts of Gregory Nazianzen." In *Athanasius and His Opponents, Cappadocian Fathers, Other Greek Writers after Nicaea*, edited by Elizabeth A. Livingstone, 102–7. StPatr 32. Leuven: Peeters, 1997.
Fairbairn, Donald. "Patristic Soteriology: Three Trajectories." *Journal of the Evangelical Theological Society* 50 (2007) 289–310.
Farrow, Douglas. "Person and Nature: The Necessity—Freedom Dialectic in John Zizioulas." In *The Theology of John Zizioulas: Personhood and the Church*, edited by Douglas H. Knight, 109–23. Burlington, VT: Ashgate, 2007.
Fatehi, Mehrdad. *The Spirit's Relation to the Risen Lord in Paul: An Examination of Its Christological Implications*. WUNT 128. Tübingen: Mohr Siebeck, 2000.
Fee, Gordon D. *The First Epistle to the Corinthians*. NICNT. Grand Rapids: Eerdmans, 1987.
———. *God's Empowering Presence: The Holy Spirit in the Letters of Paul*. Peabody, MA: Hendrickson, 1994.
———. *Pauline Christology: An Exegetical-Theological Study*. Peabody, MA: Hendrickson, 2007.
Ferguson, Everett. "Exhortations to Baptism in the Cappadocians." In *Athanasius and His Opponents, Cappadocian Fathers, Other Greek Writers after Nicaea*, edited by Elizabeth A. Livingstone, 121–29. StPatr 32. Leuven: Peeters, 1997.
Finlan, Stephen. "Can We Speak of Theosis in Paul?" In *Partakers of the Divine Nature: The History and Development of Deification in the Christian Traditions*, edited by Michael J. Christensen and Jeffery A. Wittung, 68–80. Grand Rapids: Baker Academic, 2008.
Fletcher-Louis, Crispin H. T. *All the Glory of Adam: Liturgical Anthropology in the Dead Sea Scrolls*. STDJ 42. Leiden: Brill, 2002.
Flogaus, Reinhard. *Theosis bei Palamas und Luther: Ein Beitrag zum okumenischen Gesprach*. Göttingen: Vandenhoeck & Ruprecht, 1997.
Fowl, Stephen E. *Engaging Scripture: A Model for Theological Interpretation*. Oxford: Blackwell, 1998.
Fox, Michael V. "Bible Scholarship and Faith-Based Study: My View." *SBL Forum*, 2006. https://www.sbl-site.org/publications/article.aspx?ArticleId=490.
Gadamer, Hans-Georg. *Truth and Method*. Translated by Joel C. Weinsheimer and Donald G. Marshall. 2nd ed. London: Sheed & Ward, 1989.
Gavrilyuk, Paul L. "The Retrieval of Deification: How a Once-Despised Archaism Became an Ecumenical Desideratum." *Modern Theology* 25 (2009) 647–59.
Gebremedhin, Ezra. *Life-Giving Blessing: Inquiry into the Eucharistic Doctrine of Cyril of Alexandria*. Studia Doctrinae Christianae Upsaliensia 17. Uppsala: Uppsala Universitet, 1977.

Gorman, Michael J. *Apostle of the Crucified Lord: A Theological Introduction to Paul and His Letters*. Grand Rapids: Eerdmans, 2004.
———. *Cruciformity: Paul's Narrative Spirituality of the Cross*. Grand Rapids: Eerdmans, 2001.
———. *The Death of the Messiah and the Birth of the New Covenant: A (Not So) New Model of the Atonement*. Eugene, OR: Wipf & Stock, 2014.
———. *Inhabiting the Cruciform God: Kenosis, Justification, and Theosis in Paul's Narrative Soteriology*. Grand Rapids: Eerdmans, 2009.
———. "Paul and the Cruciform Way of God in Christ." *Journal of Moral Theology* 2 (2013) 64–83.
———. "A 'Seamless Garment' Approach to Biblical Interpretation?" *Journal of Theological Interpretation* 1 (2007) 117–28.
Green, Lowell C. "The Question of Theosis in the Perspective of Lutheran Christology." In *All Theology Is Christology: Essays in Honor of David P. Scaer*, edited by Dean O. Wenthe, William C. Weinrich, Arthur A. Just Jr., Daniel L. Gard, and Thomas L. Olson, 163–80. Fort Wayne, IN: Concordia Theological Seminary Press, 2000.
Greggs, Tom. *Barth, Origen, and Universal Salvation: Restoring Particularity*. Oxford: Oxford University Press, 2009.
Gregory Akindynos. *Letters of Gregory Akindynos*. Edited by Angela Constantinides Hero. Corpus Fontium Historiae Byzantinae 21. Washington, DC: Dumbarton Oaks, 1983.
Gregory of Nazianzus. *Select Orations*. Translated by Martha Pollard Vinson. FC 107. Washington, DC: Catholic University of America Press, 2003.
Gregory of Nyssa. *The Catechetical Oration of Gregory of Nyssa*. Edited by James Herbert Srawley. Cambridge: Cambridge University Press, 1903.
———. *Gregorii Nysseni Opera*. Edited by Werner Jaeger, Hermann Langerbeck, Heinrich Dörrie, and Hadwig Hoerner. Leiden: Brill, 1958.
Gregory of Nyssa, and Anna M. Silvas. *Gregory of Nyssa: The Letters: Introduction, Translation and Commentary*. VCSup 83. Leiden: Brill, 2007.
Gregory Palamas. *Gregory Palamas: The One Hundred and Fifty Chapters—A Critical Edition, Translation and Study*. Edited by Robert E. Sinkewicz. Studies and Texts 83. Toronto: Pontifical Institute of Medieval Studies, 1988.
———. *Grigoriou tou Palama Syngrammata*. Edited by P. K. Christou. 3 vols. Thessalonike: n. p., 1962.
———. *The Triads*. Edited by John Meyendorff. Translated by Nicholas Gendle. New York: Paulist, 1983.
———. *Tu en hagios patros hemōn Gregoriu archiepiskopu Thessalonikēs, tu Palama, Homiliai 22*. Edited by Sophoklēs Oikonomos. Athens: Karampinē, 1861.
Grenz, Stanley J. *Rediscovering the Triune God: The Trinity in Contemporary Theology*. Minneapolis: Fortress, 2004.
Gross, Jules. *The Divinization of the Christian according to the Greek Fathers*. Translated by Paul A. Onica. Anaheim: A & C, 2002.
Gunnarsson, Håkan. *Mystical Realism in the Early Theology of Gregory Palamas: Context and Analysis*. Göteborg: Göteborg University, 2002.
Gunton, Colin E. "Persons and Particularity." In *The Theology of John Zizioulas: Personhood and the Church*, edited by Douglas H. Knight, 97–107. Burlington, VT: Ashgate, 2007.
———. *The Promise of Trinitarian Theology*. London: T. & T. Clark, 2003.

———. "The Spirit in the Trinity." In *The Forgotten Trinity: A Selection of Papers Presented to the B.C.C. Study Commission on Trinitarian Doctrine Today*, edited by Alasdair I. C. Heron, 3:123–35. London: British Council of Churches, 1991.
Habets, Myk. "Putting the 'Extra' Back into Calvinism." *Scottish Journal of Theology* 62 (2009) 441–56.
Hägg, Henny Fiskå. *Clement of Alexandria and the Beginnings of Christian Apophaticism*. OECS. Oxford: Oxford University Press, 2006.
Hallonsten, Gösta. "Theosis in Recent Research: A Renewal of Interest and a Need for Clarity." In *Partakers of the Divine Nature: The History and Development of Deification in the Christian Traditions*, edited by Michael J. Christensen and Jeffery A. Wittung, 281–93. Grand Rapids: Baker Academic, 2008.
Harmless, William. *Mystics*. Oxford: Oxford University Press, 2008.
Harrison, Nonna Verna. "Zizioulas on Communion and Otherness." *St Vladimir's Theological Quarterly* 42 (1998) 273–300.
Hays, Richard B. *Echoes of Scripture in the Letters of Paul*. New Haven: Yale University Press, 1989.
———. "Knowing Jesus: Story, History and the Question of Truth." In *Jesus, Paul and the People of God: A Theological Dialogue with N. T. Wright*, edited by Nicholas Perrin and Richard B. Hays, 41–61. Downers Grove, IL: InterVarsity, 2011.
———. "Reading the Bible with Eyes of Faith: The Practice of Theological Exegesis." *Journal of Theological Interpretation* 1 (2007) 5–21.
Helmer, Christine. *The Trinity and Martin Luther: A Study on the Relationship between Genre, Language and the Trinity in Luther's Works (1523–1546)*. Veröffentlichungen Des Instituts Für Europäische Geschichte Mainz 174. Mainz: von Zabern, 1999.
Hildebrand, Stephen M. *The Trinitarian Theology of Basil of Caesarea: A Synthesis of Greek Thought and Biblical Interpretation*. Washington, DC: Catholic University of America Press, 2007.
Hill, Wesley. *Paul and the Trinity: Persons, Relations, and the Pauline Letters*. Grand Rapids: Eerdmans, 2015.
Hinlicky, Paul R. "Theological Anthropology: Toward Integrating Theosis and Justification by Faith." *Journal of Ecumenical Studies* 34 (1997) 38–73.
Hurtado, Larry W. *At the Origins of Christian Worship: The Context and Character of Earliest Christian Devotion*. Grand Rapids: Eerdmans, 2000.
———. "A 'Case Study' in Early Christian Devotion to Jesus: Philippians 2:6–11." In *How on Earth Did Jesus Become a God?: Historical Questions about Earliest Devotion to Jesus*, 83–107. Grand Rapids: Eerdmans, 2005.
———. *Lord Jesus Christ: Devotion to Jesus in Earliest Christianity*. Grand Rapids: Eerdmans, 2003.
———. *One God, One Lord: Early Christian Devotion and Ancient Jewish Monotheism*. 2nd ed. Edinburgh: T. & T. Clark, 1998.
Hussey, M. Edmund. "The Persons-Energy Structure in the Theology of St. Gregory Palamas." *St Vladimir's Theological Quarterly* 18 (1974) 22–43.
Irenaeus of Lyons. *Irenaeus: Against Heresies*. Edited by Alexander Roberts and James Donaldson. ANF 1. Edinburgh: T. & T. Clark, 1996.
———. *Proof of the Apostolic Preaching*. Translated by Joseph P. Smith. ACW 16. London: Newman, 1952.
Itter, Andrew C. *Esoteric Teaching in the Stromateis of Clement of Alexandria*. VCSup 97. Leiden: Brill, 2009.

Jansen, J. F. "I Cor. 15. 24-28 and the Future of Jesus Christ." *Scottish Journal of Theology* 40 (1987) 543-70.
Jauss, Hans Robert. "Literary History as a Challenge to Literary Theory." In *Toward an Aesthetic of Reception*, translated by Timothy Bahti, 3-45. Minneapolis: University of Minnesota Press, 1982.
Jensen, Richard A. "Theosis and Preaching: Implications for Preaching in the Finnish Luther Research." *Currents in Theology and Mission* 31 (2004) 432-37.
Jenson, Robert W. "Response to Mark Seifrid, Paul Metzger, and Carl Trueman on Finnish Luther Research." *Westminster Theological Journal* 65 (2003) 245-50.
John of Damascus. *Writings*. Translated by Frederic H. Chase. FC 37. Washington, DC: Catholic University of America Press, 1999.
Johnson, Marcus P. "Luther and Calvin on Union with Christ." *Fides et Historia* 39 (2007) 59-77.
———. "New or Nuanced Perspective on Calvin? A Reply to Thomas Wenger." *Journal of the Evangelical Theological Society* 51 (2008) 543-58.
Juntunen, Sammeli. "Luther and Metaphysics: What Is the Structure of Being according to Luther?" In *Union with Christ: The New Finnish Interpretation of Luther*, edited by Carl E. Braaten and Robert W. Jenson, 129-60. Grand Rapids: Eerdmans, 1998.
Kammler, Hans-Christian. "Die Prädikation Jesu Christi Als 'Gott' Und Die Paulinische Christologie: Erwägungen Zur Exegese von Röm 9,5b." *Zeitschrift Für Die Neutestamentliche Wissenschaft Und Die Kunde Der Älteren Kirche* 94 (2003) 164-80.
Kärkkäinen, Pekka. *Luthers Trinitarische Theologie Des Heiligen Geistes*. Mainz: von Zabern, 2005.
Kärkkäinen, Veli-Matti. *One with God: Salvation as Deification and Justification*. Collegeville, MN: Liturgical Press, 2004.
———. "Salvation as Justification and Theosis: The Contribution of the New Finnish Luther Interpretation to Our Ecumenical Future." *Dialog* 45 (2006) 74-82.
Karmiris, John N. *A Synopsis of the Dogmatic Theology of the Orthodox Catholic Church*. Translated by George Dimopoulos. n. c.: Christian Orthodox Edition, 1973.
Keating, Daniel A. *The Appropriation of Divine Life in Cyril of Alexandria*. Oxford: Oxford University Press, 2004.
Keck, Leander E. "Toward the Renewal of New Testament Christology." *New Testament Studies* 32 (1986) 362-77.
Kelly, J. N. D. *Early Christian Doctrines*. 4th ed. London: A & C, 1968.
Kilby, Karen. "Perichoresis and Projection: Problems with Social Doctrines of the Trinity." *New Blackfriars* 81 (2000) 432-45.
Knight, Douglas H. "The Spirit and Persons in the Liturgy." In *The Theology of John Zizioulas: Personhood and the Church*, edited by Douglas H. Knight, 183-96. Burlington, VT: Ashgate, 2007.
Kolb, Robert. *Martin Luther: Confessor of the Faith*. New York: Oxford University Press, 2009.
Kolb, Robert, and Charles P. Arand. *The Genius of Luther's Theology: A Wittenberg Way of Thinking for the Contemporary Church*. Grand Rapids: Baker Academic, 2008.
Kreitzer, Larry J. *Jesus and God in Paul's Eschatology*. JSNTSup 19. Sheffield: Sheffield Academic, 1987.
Laato, Timo. "Justification: The Stumbling Block of the Finnish Luther School." *Concordia Theological Quarterly* 72 (2008) 327-46.

LaCugna, Catherine Mowry. *God for Us: The Trinity and Christian Life*. San Francisco: HarperSanFrancisco, 1991.
Laird, Martin. *Gregory of Nyssa and the Grasp of Faith: Union, Knowledge, and Divine Presence*. OECS. Oxford: Oxford University Press, 2004.
———. "Under Solomon's Tutelage: The Education of Desire in the Homilies on the Song of Songs." In *Re-Thinking Gregory of Nyssa*, edited by Sarah Coakley, 77–96. Oxford: Blackwell, 2003.
Lee, Yang-Ho. "Calvin on Deification: A Reply to Carl Mosser and Jonathan Slater." *Scottish Journal of Theology* 63 (2010) 272–84.
Leithart, Peter J. "Justification as Verdict and Deliverance: A Biblical Perspective." *Pro Ecclesia* 16 (2007) 56–72.
Lilla, Salvatore R. C. *Clement of Alexandria: A Study in Christian Platonism and Gnosticism*. London: Oxford University Press, 1971.
Litwa, M. David. *Becoming Divine: An Introduction to Deification in Western Culture*. Eugene, OR: Wipf & Stock, 2013.
———. *We Are Being Transformed: Deification in Paul's Soteriology*. Berlin: de Gruyter, 2012.
Loon, Hans van. *The Dyophysite Christology of Cyril of Alexandria*. VCSup 96. Leiden: Brill, 2009.
Lossky, Vladimir. *The Mystical Theology of the Eastern Church*. Crestwood: St. Vladimir's Seminary Press, 1976.
———. *The Vision of God*. Leighton Buzzard: Faith Press, 1963.
Loudovikos, Nicholas. "Christian Life and Institutional Church." In *The Theology of John Zizioulas: Personhood and the Church*, edited by Douglas H. Knight, 125–32. Burlington, VT: Ashgate, 2007.
———. "Person Instead of Grace and Dictated Otherness: John Zizioulas' Final Theological Position." *Heythrop Journal* 52 (2011) 684–99.
Luther, Martin. *The Book of Concord: The Confessions of the Evangelical Lutheran Church*. Edited by Robert Kolb and Timothy J. Wengert. Translated by Charles Arand. Minneapolis: Fortress, 2000.
———. *Luther: Early Theological Works*. Translated by James Atkinson. LCC 16. Philadelphia: Westminster, 1962.
———. *Luther's Works*. Edited by Jaroslav Pelikan and Helmut T. Lehmann. 55 vols. Philadelphia: Fortress, 1955.
Macaskill, Grant. *Union with Christ in the New Testament*. Oxford: Oxford University Press, 2013.
MacDonald, Nathan. *Deuteronomy and the Meaning of "Monotheism."* FAT 1. Tübingen: Mohr Siebeck, 2003.
Mannermaa, Tuomo. *Christ Present in Faith: Luther's View of Justification*. Edited by Kirsi Stjerna. Minneapolis: Fortress, 2005.
———. "Justification and Theosis in Lutheran-Orthodox Perspective." In *Union with Christ: The New Finnish Interpretation of Luther*, edited by Carl E. Braaten and Robert W. Jenson, 25–41. Grand Rapids: Eerdmans, 1998.
———. "Theosis as a Subject of Finnish Luther Research." Translated by Norman M. Watt. *Pro Ecclesia* 4 (1995) 37–47.
———. "Why Is Luther So Fascinating? Modern Finnish Luther Research." In *Union with Christ: The New Finnish Interpretation of Luther*, edited by Carl E. Braaten and Robert W. Jenson, 1–20. Grand Rapids: Eerdmans, 1998.

Mantzaridis, Georgios I. *The Deification of Man: St Gregory Palamas and the Orthodox Tradition*. Translated by Liadain Sherrard. Crestwood: St. Vladimir's Seminary Press, 1984.

Marquart, Kurt E. "Luther and Theosis." *Concordia Theological Quarterly* 64 (2000) 182–205.

Marshall, Bruce D. "Christ and the Cultures: The Jewish People and Christian Theology." In *The Cambridge Companion to Christian Doctrine*, edited by Colin E. Gunton, 81–100. CCR. Cambridge: Cambridge University Press, 1997.

———. "Justification as Declaration and Deification." *International Journal of Systematic Theology* 4 (2002) 3–28.

Maspero, Giulio. "Ad Ablabium, Quod Non Sint Tres Dei." Edited by Lucas F. Mateo-Seco. *The Brill Dictionary of Gregory of Nyssa*. VCSup 99. Leiden: Brill, 2010.

Mattes, Mark C. "Luther on Justification as Forensic and Effective." In *The Oxford Handbook of Martin Luther's Theology*, edited by Robert Kolb, Irene Dingel, and L'ubomir Batka, 264–73. Oxford: Oxford University Press, 2014.

McCall, Tom. "Holy Love and Divine Aseity in the Theology of John Zizioulas." *Scottish Journal of Theology* 61 (2008) 191–205.

McCartney, Dan G. "Review of *God Crucified: Monotheism and Christology in the New Testament*, by Richard Bauckham." *The Westminster Theological Journal* 61 (1999) 283–86.

McClean, John. "Perichoresis, Theosis and Union with Christ in the Thought of John Calvin." *Reformed Theological Review* 68 (2009) 130–41.

McCormack, Bruce L. "Union with Christ in Calvin's Theology: Grounds for a Divinisation Theory?" In *Tributes to John Calvin: A Celebration of His Quincentenary*, edited by David W. Hall, 504–29. Phillipsburg: P & R, 2010.

McGrath, Alister E. "Forerunners of the Reformation: A Critical Examination of the Evidence for Precursors of the Reformation Doctrines of Justification." *Harvard Theological Review* 75 (1982) 219–42.

McGrath, James F. *Only True God: Early Christian Monotheism in Its Jewish Context*. Chicago: University of Illinois Press, 2009.

McGuckin, John A. *St. Cyril of Alexandria: The Christological Controversy: Its History, Theology, and Texts*. VCSup 23. Leiden: Brill, 1994.

———. *The Transfiguration of Christ in Scripture and Tradition*. Lewiston, NY: Mellen, 1986.

———. "The Vision of God in St. Gregory Nazianzen." In *Athanasius and His Opponents, Cappadocian Fathers, Other Greek Writers after Nicaea*, edited by Elizabeth A. Livingstone, 145–52. StPatr 32. Leuven: Peeters, 1997.

McLelland, Joseph C. "Sailing to Byzantium: Orthodox-Reformed Dialogue: A Personal Perspective." In *The New Man: An Orthodox and Reformed Dialogue*, edited by John Meyendorff and Joseph C. McLelland, 10–25. New Brunswick: Agora, 1973.

Meredith, Anthony. *Gregory of Nyssa*. London: Routledge, 1999.

Metzger, Paul Louis. "Luther and the Finnish School: Mystical Union with Christ: An Alternative to Blood Transfusions and Legal Fictions." *Westminster Theological Journal* 65 (2003) 201–13.

Milbank, John. "Alternative Protestantism." In *Radical Orthodoxy and the Reformed Tradition: Creation, Covenant, and Participation*, edited by James K. A. Smith and James H. Olthuis, 25–41. Grand Rapids: Baker Academic, 2005.

Minns, Denis. *Irenaeus: An Introduction*. London: T. & T. Clark, 2010.

Moberly, R. W. L. "Toward an Interpretation of the Shema." In *Theological Exegesis: Essays in Honor of Brevard S. Childs*, edited by Christopher R. Seitz and Kathryn Greene-McCreight, 124–44. Grand Rapids: Eerdmans, 1999.

Moltmann, Jürgen. *The Crucified God: The Cross of Christ as the Foundation and Criticism of Christian Theology*. Minneapolis: Fortress, 1993.

———. *The Trinity and the Kingdom: The Doctrine of God*. Translated by Margaret Kohl. Minneapolis: Fortress, 1993.

Mosser, Carl. "The Earliest Patristic Interpretations of Psalm 82, Jewish Antecedents, and the Origin of Christian Deification." *Journal of Theological Studies* 56 (2005) 30–74.

———. "The Greatest Possible Blessing: Calvin and Deification." *Scottish Journal of Theology* 55 (2002) 36–57.

Muller, Richard A. *Post-Reformation Reformed Dogmatics: The Rise and Development of Reformed Orthodoxy, Ca. 1520 to Ca. 1725: The Triunity of God*. vol. 4. Grand Rapids: Baker Academic, 2003.

Murphy, Gannon. "Reformed Theosis?" *Theology Today* 65 (2008) 191–212.

Ngien, Dennis. *The Suffering of God according to Martin Luther's "Theologia Crucis."* 2nd ed. Vancouver: Regent College, 2005.

Niesel, Wilhelm. *The Theology of Calvin*. Translated by Harold Knight. Philadelphia: Westminster, 1956.

Nimmo, Paul T. *Being in Action: The Theological Shape of Barth's Ethical Vision*. London: T. & T. Clark, 2007.

Nispel, Mark D. "Christian Deification and the Early Testimonia." *Vigiliae Christianae* 53 (1999) 289–304.

Norris, F. W. "Deification: Consensual and Cogent." *Scottish Journal of Theology* 49 (1996) 411–28.

O'Keefe, John J. "Incorruption, Anti-Origenism, and Incarnation: Eschatology in the Thought of Cyril of Alexandria." In *The Theology of St. Cyril of Alexandria: A Critical Appreciation*, edited by Thomas G. Weinandy and Daniel A. Keating, 187–204. London: T. & T. Clark, 2003.

O'Kelley, Aaron T. "Luther and Melanchthon on Justification: Continuity or Discontinuity?" In *Since We Are Justified by Faith: Justification in the Theologies of the Protestant Reformations*, edited by Michael Parsons, 30–43. Studies in Christian History and Thought. Milton Keynes: Paternoster, 2012.

Olson, Roger E. "Deification in Contemporary Theology." *Theology Today* 64 (2007) 186–200.

Origen of Alexandria. *Commentary on the Epistle to the Romans: Books 6–10*. Translated by Thomas P. Scheck. FC 104. Washington, DC: Catholic University of America Press, 2002.

———. *Origenes Werke*. Translated by Paul Koetschau, Erich Klostermann, Erwin Preuschen, and W. A. Baehrens. 12 vols. GCS. Leipzig; Berlin: Hinrichs; Akademie, 1899.

Osborn, Eric. *Clement of Alexandria*. Cambridge: Cambridge University Press, 2005.

———. *Irenaeus of Lyons*. Cambridge: Cambridge University Press, 2001.

Paddison, Angus. *Scripture: A Very Theological Proposal*. London: T. & T. Clark, 2009.

Pannenberg, Wolfhart. "Divine Economy and Eternal Trinity." In *The Theology of John Zizioulas: Personhood and the Church*, edited by Douglas H. Knight, 79–86. Burlington, VT: Ashgate, 2007.

Papanikolaou, Aristotle. "Divine Energies or Divine Personhood: Vladimir Lossky and John Zizioulas on Conceiving the Transcendent and Immanent God." *Modern Theology* 19 (2003) 357–85.

———. "Is John Zizioulas an Existentialist in Disguise?: Response to Lucian Turcescu." *Modern Theology* 20 (2004) 601–07.

Peura, Simo. "Christ as Favor and Gift (Donum): The Challenge of Luther's Understanding of Justification." In *Union with Christ: The New Finnish Interpretation of Luther*, edited by Carl E. Braaten and Robert W. Jenson, 42–69. Grand Rapids: Eerdmans, 1998.

———. "What God Gives Man Receives: Luther on Salvation." In *Union with Christ: The New Finnish Interpretation of Luther*, edited by Carl E. Braaten and Robert W. Jenson, 76–95. Grand Rapids: Eerdmans, 1998.

Polkinghorne, J. C. *Science and the Trinity: The Christian Encounter with Reality*. New Haven: Yale University Press, 2004.

Pomazansky, Michael. *Orthodox Dogmatic Theology: A Concise Exposition*. Translated by Seraphim Rose. Platina: Saint Herman of Alaska Brotherhood, 1984.

Powell, Samuel M. "Rethinking Trinitarian Theology: Theology since the Reformation." In *Rethinking Trinitarian Theology: Disputed Questions and Contemporary Issues in Trinitarian Theology*, edited by Giulio Maspero and Robert J. Wozniak, 44–68. London: T. & T. Clark, 2012.

———. *The Trinity in German Thought*. Cambridge: Cambridge University Press, 2001.

Prestige, G. L. *God in Patristic Thought*. London: SPCK, 1952.

Rabens, Volker. "The Holy Spirit and Deification in Paul: A 'Western' Perspective." In *The Holy Spirit and the Church according to the New Testament: Sixth International East-West Symposium of New Testament Scholars, Belgrade, August 25 to 31, 2013*, edited by Predrag Dragutinović et al., 187–220. WUNT 354. Tübingen: Mohr Siebeck, 2016.

———. "Power from In Between: The Relational Experience of the Holy Spirit and Spiritual Gifts in Paul's Churches." In *The Spirit and Christ in the New Testament and Christian Theology: Essays in Honor of Max Turner*, edited by I. Howard Marshall, Volker Rabens, and Cornelis Bennema, 138–55. Grand Rapids: Eerdmans, 2012.

Radde-Gallwitz, Andrew. *Basil of Caesarea, Gregory of Nyssa, and the Transformation of Divine Simplicity*. OECS. Oxford: Oxford University Press, 2009.

Rae, Murray A. "Texts in Context: Scripture and the Divine Economy." *Journal of Theological Interpretation* 1 (2007) 23–45.

Rahner, Karl. *The Trinity*. Translated by Joseph Donceel. London: Burns & Oates, 2001.

Räisänen, Heikki. *Beyond New Testament Theology: A Story and a Programme*. 2nd ed. London: SCM, 2000.

Raith, Charles, II. *Aquinas and Calvin on Romans: God's Justification and Our Participation*. Oxford: Oxford University Press, 2014.

Rakestraw, Robert V. "Becoming Like God: An Evangelical Doctrine of Theosis." *Journal of the Evangelical Theological Society* 40 (1997) 257–69.

Ramelli, Ilaria L. E. "Origen, Greek Philosophy, and the Birth of the Trinitarian Meaning of Hypostasis." *Harvard Theological Review* 105 (2012) 302–50.

———. "Origen's Anti-Subordinationism and Its Heritage in the Nicene and Cappadocian Line." *Vigiliae Christianae* 65 (2011) 21–49.

Rasmussen, Mette Sophia Bøcher. "Like a Rock or Like God? The Concept of Apatheia in the Monastic Theology of Evagrius of Pontus." *Studia Theologica* 59 (2005) 147–62.
Reasoner, Mark. *Romans in Full Circle: A History of Interpretation*. Louisville: Westminster John Knox, 2005.
Roberts, Alexander, and James Donaldson, eds. *The Ante-Nicene Fathers*. 10 vols. Peabody, MA: Hendrickson, 1994.
Robertson, Jon M. *Christ as Mediator: A Study of the Theologies of Eusebius of Caesarea, Marcellus of Ancyra, and Athanasius of Alexandria*. Oxford Theological Monographs. Oxford: Oxford University Press, 2007.
Rogers, Eugene F. *After the Spirit: A Constructive Pneumatology from Resources Outside the Modern West*. Grand Rapids: Eerdmans, 2005.
Rossum, Joost van. "Deification in Palamas and Aquinas." *St Vladimir's Theological Quarterly* 47 (2003) 365–82.
Rostock, Nigel. "Two Different Gods or Two Types of Unity?: A Critical Response to Zizioulas' Presentation of 'The Father as Cause' with Reference to the Cappadocian Fathers and Augustine." *New Blackfriars* 91 (2008) 321–34.
Rousseau, Philip. *Basil of Caesarea*. Transformation of the Classical Heritage 20. Berkeley: University of California Press, 1994.
Rowe, C. Kavin. *Early Narrative Christology: The Lord in the Gospel of Luke*. Grand Rapids: Baker, 2009.
———. "The Trinity in the Letters of St. Paul and Hebrews." In *The Oxford Handbook of the Trinity*, edited by Gilles Emery and Matthew Levering, 41–54. Oxford Handbooks in Religion and Theology. New York: Oxford University Press, 2011.
Russell, Edward. "Reconsidering Relational Anthropology: A Critical Assessment of John Zizioulas's Theological Anthropology." *International Journal of Systematic Theology* 5 (2003) 168–86.
Russell, Norman. *Cyril of Alexandria*. London: Routledge, 2000.
———. *The Doctrine of Deification in the Greek Patristic Tradition*. Oxford: Oxford University Press, 2004.
———. "Theosis and Gregory Palamas: Continuity or Doctrinal Change?" *St Vladimir's Theological Quarterly* 50 (2006) 357–79.
Saarinen, Risto. "Justification by Faith: The View of the Mannermaa School." In *The Oxford Handbook of Martin Luther's Theology*, edited by Robert Kolb, Irene Dingel, and L'ubomir Batka, 254–63. Oxford: Oxford University Press, 2014.
Sandys-Wunsch, John, and Laurence Eldredge. "J. P. Gabler and the Distinction between Biblical and Dogmatic Theology: Translation, Commentary, and Discussion of His Originality." *Scottish Journal of Theology* 33 (1980) 133–58.
Schaff, Philip, ed. *Nicene and Post-Nicene Fathers*. Edinburgh: T. & T. Clark, 1880.
Scheck, Thomas P. *Origen and the History of Justification: The Legacy of Origen's Commentary on Romans*. Notre Dame: University of Notre Dame Press, 2008.
Schmid, Konrad. "Sind Die Historisch-Kritischen Kritischer Geworden?: Überlegungen Zu Stellung Und Potential Der Bibelwissenschaften." Translated by Peter Altmann. *Jahrbuch Biblische Theologie* 25 (2011) 63–78.
Schroeder, C. Paul. "Suffering towards Personhood: John Zizioulas and Fyodor Dostoevsky in Conversation on Freedom and the Human Person." *St Vladimir's Theological Quarterly* 45 (2001) 243–64.

Schwarzwäller, Klaus. "Verantwortung des Glaubens. Freiheit und Liebe nach der Dekalogauslegung Martin Luthers." In *Freiheit als Liebe bei Martin Luther/Freedom as love in Martin Luther*, edited by Dennis D. Bielfeldt and Klaus Schwarzwäller, 133-58. Frankfurt am Main: Lang, 1995.

Schweitzer, Albert. *The Mysticism of Paul the Apostle*. Translated by W. Montgomery. New York: Seabury, 1968.

Scott, Alan. *Origen and the Life of the Stars: A History of an Idea*. OECS. Oxford; New York: Oxford University Press; Clarendon Press, 1991.

Scully, Jason. "Angelic Pneumatology in the Egyptian Desert: The Role of the Angels and the Holy Spirit in Evagrian Asceticism." *Journal of Early Christian Studies* 19 (2011) 287-305.

Seifrid, Mark A. "Paul, Luther, and Justification in Gal 2:15-21." *Westminster Theological Journal* 65 (2003) 215-30.

Sinkewicz, Robert E. *Evagrius of Pontus: The Greek Ascetic Corpus*. OECS. Oxford: Oxford University Press, 2006.

Slater, Jonathan. "Salvation as Participation in the Humanity of the Mediator in Calvin's Institutes of the Christian Religion: A Reply to Carl Mosser." *Scottish Journal of Theology* 58 (2005) 39-58.

Steenberg, M. C. *Irenaeus on Creation: The Cosmic Christ and the Saga of Redemption*. VCSup 91. Leiden: Brill, 2008.

———. *Of God and Man: Theology as Anthropology from Irenaeus to Athanasius*. London: T. & T. Clark, 2009.

Stefaniw, Blossom. "Evagrius Ponticus on Image and Material." *Cistercian Studies Quarterly* 42 (2007) 125-35.

———. *Mind, Text, and Commentary: Noetic Exegesis in Origen of Alexandria, Didymus the Blind, and Evagrius Ponticus*. Early Christianity in the Context of Antiquity 6. Frankfurt am Main: Lang, 2010.

Steinmetz, David C. "Uncovering a Second Narrative: Detective Fiction and the Construction of Historical Method." In *The Art of Reading Scripture*, edited by Ellen F. Davis and Richard B. Hays, 54-65. Grand Rapids: Eerdmans, 2003.

Stewart, Columba. "Imageless Prayer and the Theological Vision of Evagrius Ponticus." *Journal of Early Christian Studies* 9 (2001) 173-204.

Stewart, James S. *A Man in Christ: The Vital Elements of St. Paul's Religion*. Vancouver: Regent College, 2002.

Strehle, Stephen. "Imputatio Iustitiae: Its Origin in Melanchthon, Its Opposition in Osiander." *Theologische Zeitschrift* 50 (1994) 201-19.

Stroumsa, Gedaliahu. "The Incorporeality of God: Context and Implications of Origen's Position." *Religion* 13 (1983) 345-58.

Tamburello, Dennis E. *Union with Christ: John Calvin and the Mysticism of St. Bernard*. Louisville: Westminster John Knox, 1994.

Tanner, Kathryn. *Christ the Key*. Current Issues in Theology. Cambridge: Cambridge University Press, 2010.

———. *Jesus, Humanity and the Trinity: A Brief Systematic Theology*. Edinburgh: T. & T. Clark, 2001.

"Theosis/Deification: Christian Doctrines of Divinization East and West." *KU Leuven*, January 29, 2015. https://theo.kuleuven.be/en/research/centres/institute_spirituality/theosis-conference.

Thunberg, Lars. *Man and the Cosmos: The Vision of St. Maximus the Confessor.* Crestwood: St. Vladimir's Seminary Press, 1985.
Tilling, Chris. *Paul's Divine Christology.* Grand Rapids: Eerdmans, 2015.
Tollefsen, Torstein Theodor. *Activity and Participation in Late Antique and Early Christian Thought.* OECS. Oxford: Oxford University Press, 2012.
Torrance, Alan J. *Persons in Communion: An Essay on Trinitarian Description and Human Participation, with Special Reference to Volume One of Karl Barth's Church Dogmatics.* Edinburgh: T. & T. Clark, 1996.
Torrance, Alexis. "Precedents for Palamas' Essence-Energies Theology in the Cappadocian Fathers." *Vigiliae Christianae* 63 (2009) 47–70.
Torrance, James B. "The Doctrine of the Trinity in Our Contemporary Situation." In *The Forgotten Trinity: A Selection of Papers Presented to the B.C.C. Study Commission on Trinitarian Doctrine Today*, edited by Alasdair I. C. Heron, 3:3–17. London: British Council of Churches, 1991.
Torrance, Thomas F. "Calvin's Doctrine of the Trinity." *Calvin Theological Journal* 25 (1990) 165–93.
———. *The Trinitarian Faith: The Evangelical Theology of the Ancient Catholic Church.* Edinburgh: T. & T. Clark, 1988.
Treier, Daniel J. "Biblical Theology and/or Theological Interpretation of Scripture?" *Scottish Journal of Theology* 61 (2008) 16–31.
Turcescu, Lucian. "'Person' versus 'Individual,' and Other Modern Misreadings of Gregory of Nyssa." *Modern Theology* 18 (2002) 527–39.
———. "Prosōpon and Hypostasis in Basil of Caesarea's Against Eunomius and the Epistles." *Vigiliae Christianae* 51 (1997) 374–95.
Turner, Robert. "Eschatology and Truth." In *The Theology of John Zizioulas: Personhood and the Church*, edited by Douglas H. Knight, 15–34. Burlington, VT: Ashgate, 2007.
Tylenda, Joseph. "Calvin's Understanding of the Communication of Properties." In *An Elaboration of the Theology of Calvin*, edited by Richard C. Gamble, 148–59. Articles on Calvin and Calvinism 8. New York: Garland, 1992.
———. "Christ the Mediator: Calvin versus Stancaro." In *Calvin's Opponents*, edited by Richard C. Gamble. Articles on Calvin and Calvinism 5. New York: Garland, 1992.
Tzamalikos, P. *Origen: Philosophy of History & Eschatology.* VCSup 85. Leiden: Brill, 2007.
Vainio, Olli-Pekka. *Justification and Participation in Christ: The Development of the Lutheran Doctrine of Justification from Luther to the Formula of Concord (1580).* Studies in Medieval and Reformation Traditions 130. Leiden: Brill, 2008.
Vanhoozer, Kevin J. *First Theology: God, Scripture and Hermeneutics.* Downers Grove, IL: InterVarsity, 2002.
———. "From 'Blessed in Christ' to 'Being in Christ': The State of Union and the Place of Participation in Paul's Discourse, New Testament Exegesis, and Systematic Theology Today." In *"In Christ" in Paul: Explorations in Paul's Theology of Union and Participation*, edited by Michael J. Thate, Kevin J. Vanhoozer, and Constantine R. Campbell, 3–33. WUNT 384. Tübingen: Mohr Siebeck, 2014.
———. "Introduction: What Is Theological Interpretation of the Bible?" In *Dictionary for Theological Interpretation of the Bible*, edited by Kevin J. Vanhoozer, Craig G. Bartholomew, Daniel J. Treier, and N. T. Wright, 19–26. Grand Rapids: Baker Academic, 2005.

Voegelin, Eric. *Israel and Revelation*. Edited by Maurice P. Hogan. Vol. 1. Order and History 14. Columbia: University of Missouri Press, 2001.

Volf, Miroslav. *After Our Likeness: The Church as the Image of the Trinity*. Grand Rapids: Eerdmans, 1998.

Watson, Francis. *Text, Church, and World: Biblical Interpretation in Theological Perspective*. Grand Rapids: Eerdmans, 1994.

Webster, John. "The Place of Christology in Systematic Theology." In *The Oxford Handbook of Christology*, edited by Francesca Aran Murphy, 611-27. Oxford Handbooks in Religion and Theology. Oxford: Oxford University Press, 2015.

———. *Word and Church: Essays in Christian Dogmatics*. Edinburgh: T. & T. Clark, 2001.

Weinandy, Thomas G. *The Father's Spirit of Sonship: Reconceiving the Trinity*. Edinburgh: T. & T. Clark, 1995.

Weis, James. "Calvin versus Osiander on Justification." In *Calvin's Opponents*, edited by Richard C. Gamble. Articles on Calvin and Calvinism 5. New York: Garland, 1992.

Wendel, François. *Calvin: Origins and Development of His Religious Thought*. Translated by Philip Mairet. London: Collins, 1963.

Wenger, Thomas L. "The New Perspective on Calvin: Responding to Recent Calvin Interpretations." *Journal of the Evangelical Theological Society* 50 (2007) 311-28.

Wenz, Gunther. "Unio. Zur Differenzierung einer Leitkategorie finnischer Lutherforschung im Anschluß an CA I-VI." In *Unio: Gott und Mensch in der nachreformatorischen Theologie: Referate des Symposiums der Finnischen Theologischen Literaturgesellschaft in Helsinki 15.-16. November 1994*, edited by Matti Repo and Rainer Vinke, 333-80. SLAG 35. Helsinki: Suomalainen Tiedeakatemia, 1996.

Wesche, Kenneth Paul. "Eastern Orthodox Spirituality: Union with God in Theosis." *Theology Today* 56 (1999) 29-43.

———. "The Doctrine of Deification: A Call to Worship." *Theology Today* 65 (2008) 169-79.

Westerholm, Stephen. *Perspectives Old and New on Paul: The "Lutheran" Paul and His Critics*. Grand Rapids: Eerdmans, 2004.

Whapham, Theodore James. *The Term "Person" in the Trinitarian Theology of Wolfhart Pannenberg*. AUS 7. New York: Lang, 2012.

Widdicombe, Peter. *The Fatherhood of God from Origen to Athanasius*. Oxford Theological Monographs. Oxford: Oxford University Press, 2000.

Wikenhauser, Alfred. *Die Christusmystik des hl. Paulus*. BZ 12. Münster: Aschendorff, 1928.

Wilks, John G. F. "The Trinitarian Ontology of John Zizioulas." *Vox Evangelica* 25 (1995) 63-88.

Williams, A. N. *The Ground of Union: Deification in Aquinas and Palamas*. Oxford: Oxford University Press, 1999.

Williams, Jane. "The Fatherhood of God." In *The Forgotten Trinity: A Selection of Papers Presented to the B.C.C. Study Commission on Trinitarian Doctrine Today*, edited by Alasdair I. C. Heron, 3:91-101. London: British Council of Churches, 1991.

Williams, Rowan. "Philosophical Structures of Palamism." *Eastern Churches Review* 9 (1977) 27-44.

Willis, E. David. *Calvin's Catholic Christology: The Function of the So-Called Extra Calvinisticum in Calvin's Theology*. Studies in Medieval and Reformation Thought 2. Leiden: Brill, 1966.

BIBLIOGRAPHY

Wisse, Maarten. *Trinitarian Theology beyond Participation: Augustine's De Trinitate and Contemporary Theology*. London: T. & T. Clark, 2011.
Wrede, William. "The Task and Methods of 'New Testament Theology.'" In *The Nature of New Testament Theology: The Contribution of William Wrede and Adolf Schlatter*, edited by Robert Morgan, 68–116. SBT 25. Naperville, IL: Allenson, 1973.
Wright, N. T. *The Climax of the Covenant: Christ and the Law in Pauline Theology*. Edinburgh: T. & T. Clark, 1991.
———. *Paul and the Faithfulness of God*. Minneapolis: Fortress, 2013.
Yeago, David S. "The New Testament and the Nicene Dogma: A Contribution to the Recovery of Theological Exegesis." *Pro Ecclesia* 3 (1994) 152–64.
Young, Frances. *The Art of Performance: Towards a Theology of Holy Scripture*. London: Darton Longman & Todd, 1990.
Zinkovskiy, Methody. *Patristic Categories and the Theology of Person [Святоотеческие категории и богословие личности]*. Saint Petersburg: Olega Abyshko, 2014.
———. *Theology of Person in XIX-XX Centuries [Богословие Личности В XIX-XX Вв.]*. Saint Petersburg: Olega Abyshko, 2014.
Zizioulas, John D. *Being as Communion: Studies in Personhood and the Church*. Crestwood: St. Vladimir's Seminary Press, 1997.
———. "The Church as Communion." *St Vladimir's Theological Quarterly* 38 (1994) 3–16.
———. "Communion and Otherness." *St Vladimir's Theological Quarterly* 38 (1994) 347–61.
———. *Communion and Otherness: Further Studies in Personhood and the Church*. Edited by Paul McPartlan. London: T. & T. Clark, 2006.
———. "The Doctrine of the Holy Trinity: The Significance of the Cappadocian Contribution." In *Trinitarian Theology Today: Essays on Divine Being and Act*, edited by Christoph Schwöbel, 44–60. Edinburgh: T. & T. Clark, 1995.
———. "The Doctrine of God the Trinity Today: Suggestions for an Ecumenical Study." In *The Forgotten Trinity: A Selection of Papers Presented to the B.C.C. Study Commission on Trinitarian Doctrine Today*, edited by Alasdair I. C. Heron, 3:19–32. London: British Council of Churches, 1991.
———. "Human Capacity and Human Incapacity: A Theological Exploration of Personhood." *Scottish Journal of Theology* 28 (1975) 401–47.
———. *Lectures in Christian Dogmatics*. Edited by Douglas H. Knight. London: T. & T. Clark, 2008.
———. "The Local Church in a Eucharistic Perspective: An Orthodox Contribution." *Mid-Stream* 33 (1994) 421–34.
———. "On Being a Person: Towards an Ontology of Personhood." In *Persons, Divine and Human: King's College Essays in Theological Anthropology*, edited by Christoph Schwöbel and Colin E. Gunton, 33–46. Edinburgh: T. & T. Clark, 1991.

Subject and Author Index

Abraham, 16, 93, 178, 179
abrogation, 49, 54, 80, 86
absconditus, 99
absorption, 14, 26, 38, 60, 65, 107n68, 115n93, 142, 145
accommodation, 20, 24, 41, 42, 45, 61, 107, 148, 151
accustomization, 42, 44
acedia, 36, 38
actualization, 20, 30, 41, 42, 44, 68, 100
Adam, 19, 21, 28, 40-42, 45, 46, 52, 61, 66, 78, 85, 87, 103, 112, 133, 147, 175
adaptation, 158, 159
adoption, 17, 31, 39, 42-46, 49, 54, 58, 66, 72n198, 82, 90, 103, 104, 106, 111, 113-15n92, 141, 153, 176, 183
adoptionism, 41n86, 165
adoration, 22, 24
afterlife, 26, 33, 34n57, 54, 79
agency, 7n14, 90, 103, 106, 108, 184
agent, 27n35, 29, 47, 48n107, 49, 51, 60, 68, 115, 145, 168, 169, 172, 174, 183-85
ahistorical, 150
Akindynos, 72, 77, 78
Althaus, Paul, 86, 89n13
anachronistic, 1, 8, 9, 11, 14, 34n58, 39, 87, 102n58, 149, 150, 157, 158, 163
analogy, 47, 70, 73, 78n223, 132, 144, 159, 163

analysis, 3, 5, 6, 13, 83, 132, 158
Anastos, Thomas L., 73, 79, 80
angels, 24, 25, 34, 35, 37, 38, 44, 61, 69, 72, 124, 165, 170
anhypostasis, 124, 167n62
antecedent, 1, 149, 158, 162, 165n49
anthropology, 2, 6, 21, 31, 45, 52, 103, 115, 123, 132-34, 137, 146, 157, 185
anti-Arian, 49, 60, 66
anti-subordinationism, 60, 154n16, 156
apatheia, 24, 36, 63, 79
apokatastasis, 34, 38, 157
apophaticism, 20, 22, 64, 68, 69, 72, 73, 78, 82, 125n6, 132, 135
apotheosis, 26, 34, 39, 81, 118n100, 123, 150, 157
archetype, 21, 31, 41, 45, 68, 125
Arianism, 47, 56, 60, 107, 155, 156, 164, 165n49
ascension, ascent, 22, 23, 26, 32, 34-36, 39, 44, 45, 54, 63-65, 69, 70, 72, 73, 81, 112, 114, 115, 123, 124
asceticism, 24, 35-39, 45, 56, 58, 63, 69, 70, 79, 81, 82, 123
assimilation, 14, 23, 24, 28, 31, 38-40, 45, 50n116, 69, 151, 152, 159, 163, 181
assumption, 20, 21, 35, 39, 41, 45, 48, 62, 66, 78, 90, 167, 174, 175
asymmetry, 15, 16, 129, 131n35, 132n38, 133, 167, 174, 179, 180, 182, 183

217

Athanasius of Alexandria, 45, 46, 48, 58, 98, 118, 121, 122, 129, 156, 157
atonement, 88, 90n17, 91, 115n92
attribute, 14, 18, 26, 28, 32, 42, 43, 45, 46, 48, 49, 54, 56, 59, 61, 62, 66, 73–75, 77, 78n223, 91, 94, 102, 103, 108, 114, 120, 121, 141, 150, 176
axis, vertical, 16, 151, 162

Bakhtin, Mikhail, 10
baptism, 14, 21, 23, 29, 33, 39, 41n86, 44–46, 49, 51, 58, 63, 67, 70, 78, 82, 112, 113, 116, 122, 136, 139, 142n74, 144n79
Barlaam the Calabrian, 72, 76, 77
Basilides, 19, 29, 153
Basil of Caesarea, 18, 55–59, 65, 67, 126, 128, 130, 186
Bauckham, Richard, 166–168, 171
beatific vision, 39, 113
begottenness, 31, 57, 67, 68, 131
Billings, J. Todd, 3, 84, 102, 103, 105, 109, 111–14, 117, 118, 121
binitarianism, 2, 8, 163, 177, 180n107, 184, 185n124
biological existence, hypostasis, 134, 136, 139n63, 143, 144n79, 148
Blackwell, Ben C., 1, 4–6, 9, 11, 13, 43, 45, 53–55, 83, 149, 150, 152, 163, 176–78, 182, 184, 185
Blosser, Benjamin, 27, 32, 33
bond, 92, 107, 109, 110, 117, 182

Calvin, John, 3, 5, 83–87, 102–22, 147, 185, 186
Campbell, Constantine R., 15–17
capacity, 1n1, 28, 40, 45, 58, 61, 64, 66, 72n198, 75n213, 82, 107, 108, 114, 137n55, 140
Cappadocian fathers, 16, 19, 55, 59, 71, 82, 97, 123–27, 129, 130, 140, 147, 155–57, 177, 178
Casiday, Augustine, 34, 39
christocentrism, 15, 45, 46, 97, 114, 160, 177, 181, 182, 185n124

christoforminity, 177, 182
christo-monism, 8, 181
christosis, 4, 45, 54, 55, 82, 83, 99, 102, 119, 141, 147, 177, 178, 181, 184, 185n124
christo-telic, 177, 185
Clement of Alexandria, 18–29, 31, 32, 34, 124, 152–154, 156, 157
communicatio idiomatum, 47, 96, 98n45
communion, community, 4n7, 7n15, 12, 16, 18, 23, 30, 37, 39, 42, 43, 45, 47, 52, 55, 60, 71, 79, 88, 92, 94, 106–8, 115–17, 120, 121, 124–44, 146–48, 150, 161, 172, 176, 182
connaturality, 153, 154, 164, 175, 176
consubstantiality, 20, 48, 53, 58, 67, 68, 115, 133, 153, 154
consummation, 24, 28, 41, 44n93, 45, 100, 174n87, 186
contemplation, 18, 22–27, 29, 31, 32, 34–39, 45, 46, 55, 58, 60, 63–65, 69, 70, 72–74, 79, 81, 106, 123, 124, 153
corporeality, 3, 22, 32, 33, 35, 38, 39, 51n119, 124, 151
corruption, 42, 44, 45, 51, 54, 61, 85, 103, 104, 143
cross, 29, 41, 42, 89, 92, 98, 105, 107, 109, 114, 134, 139, 141
Cyril of Alexandria, 5, 18, 26, 45–55, 82, 83, 113, 152, 176–78

darkness, 22, 63–65
death, 13, 14, 41, 42, 45, 50, 66, 67, 72, 78, 82, 85, 86, 91, 95, 99, 104, 108, 109, 114, 135–38, 140, 163, 164, 177, 178, 181, 186
deification, 1, 3–6, 8, 12–14, 18, 19, 21, 23–27, 29, 30, 32–34, 38, 39, 44–46, 48, 50, 53–55, 57, 58, 61–63, 65–73, 78, 79, 81–84, 89, 94, 95, 100–3, 113, 114, 118–25, 138n57, 141, 143, 144, 146, 149–52, 158, 159, 161–64, 166, 176, 185n124

deified, 18, 21-23, 25, 30-32, 35, 37, 39, 43, 46, 47, 49, 50-54, 57, 58, 62n164, 63, 65, 67, 69, 70, 73, 76, 77, 79-82, 95, 96, 107, 123, 125, 149, 152, 162, 165, 166, 175
deifier, 43, 67
deities, 68, 163-165, 169, 170n72, 172
demons, 33, 35, 37, 38, 164, 169, 172, 173
destiny, 14, 19, 25, 26, 37, 38, 69, 137n53, 140, 143
dictum, 13, 69, 95, 112
Dionysius the Areopagite, 66, 72
dissolution, 37, 38, 60, 65, 69, 107, 132
divinity, 14, 20n10, 23, 45, 49, 50, 52, 53, 57-60, 62, 63, 65-69, 77, 78, 97-99, 102n58, 105-8, 121, 150, 151, 153, 154, 158, 162-66, 170, 172, 181n112, 185
divinization, 23, 69, 103, 118n100, 119, 138, 140, 165
divinized, 14, 38, 62

Eastern Orthodox, 2, 5, 12, 13, 19, 20, 68, 71, 81-83, 119, 123, 125, 127, 130, 139, 147, 148, 152
ecclesiology, 8, 123, 144, 147, 182
eclecticism, 13, 157
economy, divine, 39, 40, 45, 71, 108, 167
ecstasy, 23, 37, 64, 65, 72, 73
ek-stasis, 131, 132, 134, 135, 139, 147
energeosis, 81, 82, 119, 123, 125, 138
energies, 3, 19, 62, 71, 74-82, 94, 102, 124, 125, 133, 137, 138, 141, 146, 163
enhypostasization, 48, 74, 130, 134
eschatology, 4, 15, 24, 37, 39, 66, 70, 123, 142, 143, 147, 174, 182, 185, 186
eschaton, 28, 145
essence, 18, 20, 26, 30, 37, 56, 57, 60, 62, 64, 68, 69, 71-78, 80, 81, 94, 96, 98, 99, 102, 106, 115, 116, 124, 125, 127, 130, 135-37, 142, 146, 148, 150-53, 155, 156, 163, 164, 180, 182

essence-energies, 20, 81, 103, 118, 138
essentialism, 4, 121, 127, 163, 164
eternity, 24, 33, 40, 45, 65, 82, 98, 114, 124, 156, 179, 183, 186
eucharist, 23, 44, 45, 47, 51-53, 58, 63, 78, 79, 82, 112, 113, 143, 145, 172, 173
Eunomius, 56, 60, 69
Evagrius Ponticus, 18, 34-39, 45, 54, 81, 123, 124
ex nihilo, 150, 157

faith, 2, 23, 24, 28, 29, 32, 36, 45, 49, 50, 53, 54, 62, 64, 65, 70, 82, 84-93, 96, 97, 100-102, 104-6, 109-11, 113, 119, 120, 140n66, 147, 176
fall, 19, 27, 28, 35, 40, 46, 58, 61, 66, 78, 85, 101n54, 103, 134, 136
Farrow, Douglas, 143-45
fiction, legal, 84, 101
filiation, 14, 31, 33, 82
Filioque, 98, 130
Finlan, Stephen, 1, 185n127
Finnish Lutheran School, 1, 3, 12, 84, 89, 90, 92, 94, 97, 100, 101n54, 119
forgiveness, 88, 90, 92, 93, 101, 113
fröhlicher Wechsel, 90
fusion, 33, 65, 107, 121, 122, 150, 164, 176

generation, eternal, 20, 30, 31, 68, 71n196, 80n234, 97n42, 155
giver, Christ, 3, 45n95, 84, 90, 91, 98
glorification, 80, 102n58, 106n67, 150, 181
glory, 29, 32, 39, 43, 44, 48n108, 65, 70, 73, 77, 78, 81, 86n4, 106, 107, 112-14, 116, 165, 172, 176, 179, 186
gnosis, 22, 23, 29, 34, 36, 54
gnostic, Christian, 22, 24-26, 152n10
godlikeness, 21, 26, 28, 67
God-man, 67, 144
Gorman, Michael J., 1, 4, 6, 7n14, 83, 149, 176

grace, 1n1, 21, 23, 26, 28, 31–35, 37, 39, 42, 46, 49–51, 54, 57, 67, 70, 73–75, 77–79, 81, 84, 86, 87, 89, 91–95, 99, 101, 102, 104, 105, 107–11, 113–16, 118, 121, 139, 152, 163, 176
Gregory of Nazianzus, 55, 58, 65–71, 116, 130, 157
Gregory of Nyssa, 46, 55, 58, 59, 61–63, 65, 67, 72, 118, 130
Gregory Palamas, 16, 19, 71–82, 94, 102, 103, 118, 119, 121, 123–25, 138, 177
Gross, Jules, 13, 14, 33, 62
Gunton, Colin E., 127, 131, 137, 181, 182

Hägg, Henny Fiskå, 20, 153, 154
Hays, Richard B., 6, 10, 185
healing, 42, 45, 51, 64, 66
heart, 25, 63, 79, 85, 87, 93, 99, 105, 106, 174, 183
heaven, 54, 58, 89, 92, 93, 105, 111–14
heresy, heretics, 27n34, 43, 57n142, 76, 87, 98, 153, 155, 156
hesychast, hesychia, 35, 36, 71–74, 76, 79
Hill, Wesley, 4, 11, 16, 159, 161–63, 167, 168, 171, 172, 174, 178, 179, 182, 184, 185
historical-critical approach, 4, 6, 8, 9, 161
holiness, 3, 45, 49, 50, 58, 87, 91, 106n65
Hurtado, Larry W., 2, 150, 167, 170, 178n100, 180n107
hypostasis, hypostatic, 52, 55n132, 57, 59, 68, 74–76, 80, 108, 116, 124–30, 134–44, 146, 156, 158, 181

identification, 2, 13, 45, 56, 96, 107n68, 120, 129, 144–47, 164, 172, 175, 178, 179, 181, 182, 184, 185
identity, 4, 5, 10, 16, 33, 65–67, 69, 88, 92, 96, 101, 107, 108, 120, 126, 128–130, 132, 133, 135, 138, 139, 141, 142, 145–148, 150, 155, 159n24, 162–64, 166–69, 171, 172n80, 174, 176, 178–84

idol, idolatry, 97, 112, 136, 140, 168, 169, 172–174
illumination, 21, 23, 35, 37, 50, 53, 58, 65, 70, 71, 73, 78, 87, 110, 114, 158, 159
image, imago Dei, 3, 14, 17–21, 28, 31, 32, 34, 37, 38, 40, 41, 44–46, 50, 52, 57, 61, 63, 64, 71, 72, 78, 82, 87, 88, 95, 101, 103, 104, 106, 117, 127, 134, 135, 137n53, 139–42, 145, 147, 151, 166, 177, 179, 182
imago Trinitatis, 140
imitation, imitator, 3, 18, 21, 22, 28, 32, 34, 45, 46, 49, 50, 58, 62, 70, 79, 81, 82, 111, 112, 115, 141, 153, 157, 163
immaturity, 19, 40–42
immortality, 14, 21–23, 25n27, 30, 40–45, 51, 52, 61, 63, 69, 107, 112, 114, 115, 121, 136, 150, 151, 153, 154, 164, 165, 176, 181
impassibility, 24, 36, 61, 67
imputation, 84, 86, 88–93, 100, 101n55, 102n57, 103, 105, 106n65, 109n79, 110, 113, 118
incarnation, 18–21, 26–28, 30, 34, 35, 39–47, 49–51, 54, 61–63, 66, 67, 76, 81–83, 93, 98, 106, 114, 122–24, 129, 137n57, 141, 146, 153, 154, 157, 160, 167, 177, 178, 181
incorporation, incorporeality, 30, 31, 33, 37, 38n73, 45n95, 52, 66, 82, 97n42, 102, 110, 115, 117, 121, 122, 141, 147
incorruptibility, incorruption, 14, 21, 23, 26, 41–47, 51, 52, 53n125, 54, 55, 61, 63, 78, 150, 151, 164, 176
individual, individuality, individualism, 24, 28, 33, 34, 38, 39, 43, 44, 50, 60, 62, 76, 78, 100, 126, 127, 133–39, 141, 142, 144, 145, 147, 150, 154, 171
indwelling, 17, 22, 23, 43, 51, 53, 64, 67, 88, 92, 95, 101, 105, 106, 112, 120, 132, 133, 148, 181, 182, 184
infusion, 57, 92, 105, 106, 112

ingrafting, 103–5, 111, 112
intellect, intelligence, 21–23, 26, 30,
    34–40, 46, 61, 64–66, 69, 72–74,
    79, 81, 97, 105, 124, 156
intermingling, 67, 69, 79
interpenetration, 47, 103, 113, 121, 132
interrelation, 11, 55, 68, 128, 132, 178
intratrinitarian, 68, 108, 129, 142
Irenaeus of Lyons, 5, 18–21, 39–45, 50,
    54, 82, 83, 95, 117, 121, 122,
    152, 156, 157, 176–78
isolation, 37, 126, 127, 130, 133, 135–38,
    140, 142, 144, 147, 148, 180

justification, 2, 28, 29, 50, 53, 84, 86–93,
    96, 100–102, 104–6, 108–11,
    114–16, 119, 121, 122, 147, 180

kataphatic, 22, 82
kenosis, 141, 143, 181
kinship, 28, 49, 55
Knight, Douglas H., 136, 143, 146
knowledge, 20–25, 29–32, 35–40, 56,
    64–66, 69–73, 95, 114, 116, 140,
    153, 155, 161, 170

LaCugna, Catherine Mowry, 130, 134
Laird, Martin, 63, 64
light, divine, Taboric, 25, 37, 49, 54, 56,
    63–65, 69–71, 73–75, 77–81
likeness, divine, 1, 3, 12, 16, 18, 19, 21,
    23–25, 28, 31, 32, 34, 39–41,
    44–46, 48–52, 57, 58, 61, 64, 66,
    71, 79, 82, 95, 96, 102, 120, 121,
    124, 139, 141, 148, 150, 153,
    162, 176, 181, 182
Litwa, M. David, 1, 4–6, 13, 83, 121,
    149–54, 157–68, 172, 174, 175,
    181
logoi, 18, 20, 28, 30, 36, 123
Logos, 20–23, 26, 28, 30, 31, 34, 35, 37,
    39, 40, 42–44, 46, 47, 50, 51, 61,
    62, 66, 67, 91, 95, 123, 124, 146,
    153, 154, 157, 167
Lossky, Vladimir, 125, 137, 146, 182
love, 4, 23, 24, 27, 29, 30, 35, 36, 42, 58,
    64, 65, 69, 89, 94–97, 114, 118,
    121, 126, 132, 133, 135, 138,
    140, 142, 146, 154, 168, 170,
    171, 176
Luther, Martin, 3, 5, 83–102, 116,
    119–22, 147

Macaskill, Grant, 5, 16, 83, 122
Mannermaa, Tuommo, 12, 90, 91, 94,
    96, 101, 102, 119
Marshall, Bruce D., 100, 178, 180
maturity, 21, 29, 30, 40–42, 66, 111
Maximus the Confessor, 66, 72, 75, 124,
    141
mediation, mediator, medium, 14, 15,
    20, 22, 30, 31, 37, 41, 47, 48, 59,
    74, 82, 86, 98, 107, 108, 113–15,
    117, 121, 141, 163–65, 168, 171,
    172, 176, 181, 185, 186
merit, 29, 33, 34, 85, 91, 92, 97, 101
metamorphosis, 175, 181
metaphysics, 14, 37, 42, 95, 107, 122,
    150–53, 160
mind, 20, 22, 28, 32, 34, 35, 37, 38, 40,
    49, 60, 61, 63, 64, 66, 72, 79, 87,
    114, 123, 170
mingling, 33, 39, 48, 51, 58, 60, 61, 63,
    65, 95, 135
mixture, mixing, 49, 52, 61, 75, 115, 150
monarchia, monarchy of the Father,
    55, 57, 59, 68, 71, 98, 99, 116,
    129–32, 144, 155
monk, 35–38, 58, 69, 71, 73, 77, 81
monotheism, 4, 149, 160–62, 165, 168–
    172, 174, 177–80
mortality, 17, 40–42, 44, 46, 51, 61, 69,
    112, 136, 139
Moses, 22, 32, 63–65
mutuality, 4, 16, 47, 67, 92, 98, 114, 121,
    129, 132, 148, 160, 167, 170,
    172, 174, 178–80, 182–84
mystery, mystic, mysticism, 3, 13–16,
    22, 24, 25, 32, 34, 38, 47, 63,
    64, 70, 73, 74, 79, 106–8, 110,
    118–20, 150

Neoplatonist, 19, 27, 33
Nestorius, 45, 47, 48, 113, 121
Nicaea, 26, 82, 151, 152, 166
nourishment, 44, 51, 53, 104

obedience, 29, 40, 41, 44, 45, 50, 52, 79, 86, 88, 106-8, 130, 167, 179
oneness, 22, 117, 129, 130, 167-69, 172, 179, 180
ontology, 59, 83, 95, 121, 126, 133, 141, 142, 144, 146, 151, 152, 157, 169, 170, 182, 184
Origen of Alexandria, 18, 26-35, 38, 39, 46, 55, 60, 70, 81, 123, 124, 152, 154-57, 164
Osiander, 101, 105-7, 112, 122
otherness, 124, 126, 128, 130, 133-36, 138, 141-43, 146, 157

pantheism, 60, 76, 125, 135
Papanikolaou, Aristotle, 125, 130, 135, 137
partaker, 18, 23, 26, 30, 39, 40, 43-48, 50-54, 58, 63, 71, 76, 93, 96, 97, 102, 104, 107, 109-14, 116, 119, 121, 172, 176, 186
participant, 18, 22, 23, 30, 31, 39, 40, 42, 43, 46, 49, 51, 52, 58, 60, 63, 73-75, 77, 79, 80, 83, 85, 91, 94, 95, 98, 104-6, 112, 119-22, 124, 133, 136, 139, 148, 151, 163, 165, 175, 176
participation, 1, 3, 14, 16-19, 21, 23, 30, 32-34, 39, 42-46, 48-54, 58, 62, 63, 66, 67, 70-74, 77, 78, 80-82, 84, 89, 90, 92-96, 100-105, 107, 109, 111-15, 118-25, 133, 138-40, 146, 147, 149, 150, 152, 153, 157, 164-66, 172, 173, 176
particularity, 10, 116, 124, 134, 138, 141, 142, 144, 145, 147, 182
passion, 21, 23, 24, 29, 34-36, 39, 46, 50, 63, 65, 69, 79, 123
Paul, the apostle, 1-6, 8-17, 23, 32, 42, 54, 83, 86, 92, 95, 117, 119, 149-54, 157-59, 161-65, 167-79, 181-86
perfection, 21, 23-25, 28-30, 34-36, 38-42, 45, 58, 61, 65, 87, 124, 143
perichoresis, 98, 103, 117, 121, 129, 131, 132, 143, 145, 148

person, personality, personalization, 3, 8, 14, 16, 20, 22, 23, 25, 28, 29, 32-35, 40, 44, 45, 47, 53, 55-57, 59, 60, 64, 67-69, 71, 73-78, 80-82, 84-86, 90-92, 94-101, 103-6, 108, 110, 112, 113, 116-21, 123-48, 152, 154-56, 158, 160, 163, 169, 172, 176-83, 185, 186
personhood, 3, 59, 60, 68, 71, 123, 125-29, 133-35, 137-41, 143, 144, 147
Peura, Simo, 12, 92, 94, 95, 97
Philo of Alexandria, 19, 26, 27
Plato, Platonism, 27-29, 33, 62, 93, 123, 151, 152, 157, 166
Plotinus, 58, 59, 65
pneuma, pneumaformity, pneumatification, 124, 164, 165, 175, 176, 181, 182
pneumatology, 4, 8, 55, 66, 115, 117, 177, 178, 181, 182
polytheism, 59, 77, 170
prayer, 29, 37, 59, 72, 79, 121, 145, 155
pre-existence, 27, 28, 34, 38, 151, 157
pre-incarnate, 27, 35, 46
progress, spiritual, 21, 23, 25, 26, 29, 31, 33, 34, 44, 53, 65, 70, 79, 125
propitiation, 178
Protestant, 2, 3, 12, 84, 147, 148, 160
protology, 153, 171
Pseudo-Dionysius, 27, 31
purity, purification, 23, 25, 27, 29, 30, 32, 51, 63, 65, 70, 78, 79, 100, 111, 123, 160

race, human, 18, 21, 41, 42, 45, 46, 48, 52, 66, 104
radiance, 54, 69, 91, 146
Rahner, Karl, 177, 180
Ramelli, Ilaria, 60, 154, 156
recapitulation, 41, 42, 45, 82, 138
reciprocity, 26, 42, 45, 48, 130-33
reconciliation, 8, 42, 50, 86, 99, 108, 110, 111, 143
redemption, redeemer, 15, 21, 26, 27, 32, 41, 42, 46-48, 50, 57, 66, 67, 82, 86, 89, 98, 99, 101, 103, 107,

SUBJECT AND AUTHOR INDEX 223

109, 110, 114, 115, 121, 137,
  181, 185, 186
Reformer, 3, 5, 83, 84, 87–89, 91, 93–99,
  102–4, 108, 110, 112–14, 116,
  118, 119, 121, 122, 147
regeneration, 23, 67, 78, 88, 103, 105,
  109, 111, 115
relation, relatedness, 15, 16, 52, 68, 77,
  88, 116, 126, 128–34, 138, 139,
  142, 145, 147, 150, 152, 156,
  165, 167, 170, 174, 180, 182,
  184–86
relationality, 166, 167, 183, 185
relationship, 4, 10, 13–16, 19, 26, 31,
  33, 42, 43, 48, 49, 51, 59, 61, 62,
  65, 68, 71, 75, 77, 80, 82, 94, 96,
  97, 99, 100, 110, 114, 117, 118,
  120, 125, 126, 128, 129, 131–36,
  138–40, 142, 146, 148, 153, 162,
  166, 167, 170, 171, 176, 179,
  180, 183
repentance, 41, 62, 109
representative, human, 46–48, 133, 138,
  175
restoration, 24–28, 33–35, 38, 41, 42,
  44–46, 48, 50, 51, 53, 57, 61, 87,
  91, 96, 117, 138, 139, 141, 147,
  168, 176, 179, 186
resurrection, 2, 13, 14, 25, 33, 34, 38,
  41, 44, 54, 58, 65–67, 78, 82,
  104, 122, 138, 150, 163, 175,
  177–179, 181, 184
revelation, 20–22, 30, 35, 64, 67, 68, 73,
  76, 79, 82, 85, 97–99, 116, 125,
  127, 131, 135, 169, 175, 178
reward, 29, 70, 87, 97, 168
righteousness, 3, 45, 50, 52, 84–94, 96,
  97, 100–111, 113, 116, 119
righteousness alien, 86, 89, 92, 93n25
Russell, Norman, 14, 19, 21, 24–27, 32,
  33, 38, 42, 49, 50, 58, 62, 70, 72,
  74, 75, 77, 80, 137, 149, 150, 163

Sabellianism, 56, 57, 156
sacrament, 23, 33, 39, 50, 62, 78, 82, 89,
  96, 111, 112, 118, 122

saint, 21, 22, 28, 33, 34, 44, 51, 53, 62,
  65, 74, 76–79, 86, 87, 93, 114,
  125, 141, 152
salvation, 1, 3, 5, 8, 15, 22, 25, 28, 29, 34,
  35, 39, 42, 45, 53, 54, 59, 67, 70,
  82, 86, 87, 91, 92, 97–100, 104,
  106, 107, 110, 115, 116, 119,
  121, 123, 124, 137, 139–42, 144,
  145, 147, 167, 176–78
sameness, 10, 128, 135, 141, 142
sanctification, 28, 29, 47, 51, 68, 76, 79,
  84, 87, 88, 92, 97, 100, 102, 105,
  106, 108–11, 114, 116, 119, 121,
  127, 176
Savior, 25, 26, 29, 31, 32, 46, 47, 86, 96,
  99, 106, 147, 148
Schweitzer, Albert, 14, 15
self-divinization, 94, 95
Shema, 167, 169–171
simplicity, divine, 33, 56, 59, 61, 80
simul iustus et peccator, 86, 88
sinner, 24, 70, 86, 88, 90, 91, 94, 99, 101,
  111, 120, 134, 136, 147
sonship, 15, 30, 31, 33, 40, 42, 49, 54, 82,
  130, 153, 183
soteriology, 1–4, 6, 8, 11, 13, 17, 21, 31,
  34, 39, 45, 54, 55, 62, 66, 71, 82,
  83, 88–90, 97, 100, 102, 104,
  110, 114, 115, 119, 121, 123,
  125, 137, 139, 146, 147, 154,
  158, 171, 177, 178, 180, 181, 185
soul, 21, 22, 25–30, 32–36, 38, 44, 46,
  47, 51–53, 55, 57, 58, 61, 63–66,
  70, 77, 79, 105, 112, 157, 175
spiration, 130, 131
Spirit, Holy, 2, 4, 5, 8, 13–16, 23, 28–30,
  33, 35, 37, 40, 43–46, 48, 49,
  51–55, 57–60, 64, 65, 67, 68, 70,
  71, 73–78, 80, 87, 88, 93, 96–
  101, 104–9, 112–18, 120, 122,
  127–33, 141, 142, 144, 145, 147,
  148, 154–56, 161, 162, 176–86
Steenberg, M. C., 40, 41
stillness, 35, 36, 79
subordination, subordinationism, 25,
  34, 56, 71, 87, 130, 152–54,
  156–57 162, 165, 167, 168, 174,
  179, 180

substance, 33, 57, 80, 81, 112–15, 120, 122, 126–30, 132, 140, 146, 153, 154, 156, 164, 166
summodeism, 165
superessential, 69, 73, 79, 80
symbol, 73–77, 81, 112, 122
synergism, synergy, 87, 91, 101, 103, 118

taxonomy, 152, 157, 162, 168
teleology, 153, 171
telos, 104, 121
theandric, 108, 168
theology, 1–4, 6, 8–14, 16, 19, 20, 27, 34, 37, 56, 69, 73, 78, 81, 83, 84, 90, 92, 101, 103, 104, 111, 112, 118, 121–23, 127, 132, 146–49, 152–54, 157, 159–61, 168, 172, 178–80, 184
theosis, 1–6, 11–18, 21, 32, 33, 54, 57, 62, 67, 69, 71, 77, 78, 80–84, 89, 94–97, 99, 102, 116, 118, 119, 124, 125, 137, 139–41, 146, 148–50, 176–78, 181
Tilling, Chris, 4, 161, 167, 170, 171, 185
transcendence, 20, 22, 26, 30, 32, 49, 52, 54, 62, 65, 69, 72–75, 77, 80, 113, 135, 151, 152, 156, 157, 165
transfiguration, 33, 64, 65, 96
transformation, 1–3, 12, 14–17, 22, 25, 31–34, 40, 44–46, 50, 52, 53, 55, 61, 63, 67, 68, 70, 71, 73, 77, 79, 81, 82, 84, 87, 90, 92–94, 96, 97, 101, 102, 104, 105, 120–22, 124, 139, 141–43, 145, 147, 148, 151, 153, 157, 158, 164, 166, 181, 182
triadosis, 2, 4, 13, 16, 17, 55, 71, 82, 102, 118, 119, 141, 147–48, 177
trinification, 118
trinitarianism, 15, 82, 116, 127, 132, 133, 154
Trinity, 2, 3, 6, 10–12, 15, 27, 28, 33, 34, 37–41, 43, 45, 51–53, 55, 57–60, 65–71, 75, 76, 80, 82, 97–99, 106, 115–18, 121, 122, 124, 126–33, 138, 140–42, 147, 148, 152, 155, 156, 160, 177, 180, 186

unbegottenness, 57, 67–69, 131
uncreated, 28, 30, 41, 43, 54, 55, 71–75, 77–81, 102, 125, 138, 146
uniformity, 61, 65, 142
union, 1–3, 13–16, 18, 20, 22, 24, 30, 31, 33–35, 38, 39, 42–47, 49, 52, 54, 58, 61–67, 70, 76, 77, 79, 82, 84, 86, 90, 92–96, 101–3, 105–15, 117–21, 123–25, 137–39, 141, 142, 146–48, 158, 164, 175, 176
unity, 2, 16, 20, 21, 38, 43, 55, 57, 60, 68, 90, 98, 116–18, 121, 124, 126, 128, 130, 131, 137, 142, 143, 147, 154–56, 160, 167, 176, 179
unknowability, unknowing, 20, 62, 64, 72, 73, 164

Valentinians, 19, 29, 39, 40n80, 153
Vanhoozer, Kevin J., 4n7, 7, 10n28, 106n67, 107n67
virtue, 21–24, 26, 29, 31, 35, 36, 39, 47, 50, 51, 54, 57, 58, 61, 64, 65, 70, 71, 79, 81, 82, 112, 151
vision, 32, 36–39, 43, 44, 46, 58, 63, 65, 70, 72–77, 79, 113, 122, 151, 176
vocation, 40, 136, 143, 144, 186

weakness, 41, 45, 95, 96, 186
Webster, John, 160, 161, 169
wisdom, 20, 22, 29, 30, 36, 40, 91, 95, 110, 153, 155
Wright, N. T., 8, 10, 169, 171

Yahweh 163, 168–70, 174, 179

Zinkovskiy, Methody, 128, 130, 131, 136, 137, 141, 144
Zizioulas, John, 3, 5, 8, 12, 83, 123–47, 180, 182

Scripture Index

Genesis

1:26	20
2:7	175

Exodus

24:10–11	37n70

Deuteronomy

4:25	173
6:4–5	168, 170
6:4–16	173
6:4	168, 172
6:5	170
9:18	173
32:21	173

1 Kings

14:19	173
16:13	173

2 Kings

17:11–12	173
17:11	173

2 Chronicles

34:25	173n82

Psalms

8:6	174
82:6	18, 21, 24, 39, 43
100:3	155
110:1	174
130:1	99n48

Song of Songs

6	63

Isaiah

6:1	37n70
45	167
45:23–25	179
53	8n19
65:3	173

Jeremiah

11:17	172

Ezekiel

1:26	37n70
10:1	37n70

Daniel

7:11–12	165n54

Matthew

28:19	59

Luke

22:19–20	51

John

1:1	150
1:13	136n50
5:26	131
6:56	133
10:34–35	57
10:38	117
13:8	59
14:20	133
14:28	57, 68
17:21	133

Romans

1:4	184
1:8	145
3:25	178
4:17	158
4:24	178, 179
5–7	188
6	104
8	104
8:9	133, 182, 183
8:11	178, 179, 182, 184
8:14–15	54
8:14	182
8:15	145
8:24	24
8:26	145, 181n115
8:28–32	178
8:29–30	179
8:29–32	150
9:8	54
9:1–5	154
10:19	173n82
11	104
11:36	169
15:19	182
16:20	150, 165
16:27	145

1 Corinthians

1:13	110
1:30	110, 189, 191
2:11	182
3:8	175
3:21–23	150
4:15	136n50
4:16	190
6:2–3	150, 165
6:3	165
6:11	182
6:16	175
6:17	164, 175, 176
7:40	182
8:3	170
8:4	171n76
8:4–5	171
8:4–6	168–170
8:6	154, 165, 168, 169, 171, 172
8:12	170n73
9:16–19	14
10	172
10–12	122
10:4	170n73
10:9	170n73
10:14–22	169
10:16–17	172

10:16	173	\multicolumn{2}{c}{**Galatians**}
10:18	173		
10:19–20	172	1:1	178
10:20–21	173	1:4	178
10:20	172, 173	2:19–20	163
10:21	172, 173	2:20	14, 89n14, 92, 120, 176
10:22	173		
10:26	172	3:1–5	183
10:30	172	4:4–7	183
11	122	4:4	178, 179, 183
11:1	163	4:6	145, 183
12	182	4:7	183
12:3	182, 183	6:16	59
12:13	175, 182		
13	23		
13:12	71	\multicolumn{2}{c}{**Ephesians**}
14:15	145		
15	175	3:10	164
15:20–28	179	4:3	176
15:22	184	4:4	175
15:24	59	5:1	190
15:24–25	174	5:23	182
15:24–28	168, 174, 186, 187	5:30–31	112
15:24	174	5:30	120
15:27–28	174	6:12	164
15:27	186n129		
15:28	60n158, 165, 172n80, 174	\multicolumn{2}{c}{**Philippians**}
15:35–53	150		
15:45	175, 184	1:19	183
15:47	175	2	151, 169n66, 188
15:48	175	2:6–11	179
		2:9–11	186
		2:10–11	165, 179
\multicolumn{2}{c}{**2 Corinthians**}	2:11	167, 172
		3:3	182
3:3	182	3:6	85
3:6	184	3:12	14
3:14	185	3:16	59
3:16	185	3:17	190
3:17	185	3:21	150
3:18	32, 150		
5:14	14		
5:21	190		
8:9	42		

Colossians

1	169
1:16	164
1:15–17	170
1:18	182
2:15	164

1 Thessalonians

1:9	174
4:16	165
5:8	59

Philemon

1:17	190

2 Peter

1:4	18, 48–50, 53n125, 66, 93, 94, 107, 121, 123, 148, 196

You may also be interested in:

Imitation, Knowledge, and the Task of Christology in Maximus the Confessor
By Luke Steven

Maximus the Confessor (580-662) was a monk and theologian whose combustive historical era, committed doctrinal reflection, and loud and influential voice took him on a turbulent career of traveling and writing around the Mediterranean. Maximus was a spiritual teacher, an ascetic and a contemplative, but he was also a polemicist, a crafter of dogma, an embattled Christologian, a premeditating rhetorician.

In this study, Luke Steven binds together these two disparate sides of the man and his writings by showing that throughout his oeuvre the Confessor positions imitation as the key to knowledge. This lasting epistemology characterizes his earlier ascetic and spiritual works, and in his later works it prominently defines his dogmatic Christological method - that is, the means by which he communicates and persuades and brings people to understand and encounter Jesus Christ, the one with two natures, divine and human. This multifaceted study offers a deep assessment of Maximus's forebears, new insight on the animating assumptions of his thought, and an unprecedented focus on the rhetoric and method of his christological writings.

LUKE STEVEN is an ordinand in the Church of England at St Mellitus College, London. He previously gained his PhD in the Faculty of Divinity at the University of Cambridge. He is the author of a number of articles on topics relating to early Christianity and patristics.

Paperback ISBN: 9780227177525
PDF ISBN: 9780227907511
Published November 2021